THE END OF EUROPE

JAMES KIRCHICK

The End of Europe

DICTATORS, DEMAGOGUES,
AND THE COMING DARK AGE

Yale

UNIVERSITY PRESS

NEW HAVEN & LONDON

Published with assistance from the foundation established in memory
of Amasa Stone Mather of the Class of 1907, Yale College,
and from the Kingsley Trust Association Publication Fund established
by the Scroll and Key Society of Yale College.

Yale University Press books may be purchased in quantity for educational, business, or promotional use. For information, please e-mail
sales.press@yale.edu (U.S. office) or sales@yaleup.co.uk (U.K. office).

Set in Scala type by Westchester Publishing Services.
Printed in the United States of America.

Library of Congress Control Number: 2016957565
ISBN 978-0-300-21831-2 (hardcover : alk. paper)

A catalogue record for this book is available from the British Library.

This paper meets the requirements of ANSI/NISO Z39.48-1992
(Permanence of Paper).

10 9 8 7 6 5 4 3 2 1

For Josef

The war is over, beware of the peace!
Bertolt Brecht, *The Caucasian Chalk Circle*, 1948

CONTENTS

ACKNOWLEDGMENTS

SINCE I BEGAN REPORTING AROUND EUROPE and the former Soviet Union in 2010, I have come into contact with hundreds of people from all walks of life. From presidents and foreign ministers to economists, military officers, artists, and fellow journalists, each has helped shape my understanding of the continent and its manifold challenges in his or her own unique way. A full list of the individuals who influenced the writing of this book would be impossible to compile, but I mention the most significant ones here.

Jeff Gedmin and Jim Denton convened the Transatlantic Renewal Project in the summer of 2014, at a time when the world was still reeling from the annexation of Crimea and the fate of the international liberal order was beginning to fall into serious doubt. They were generous enough to include me as one of its regular participants. During a series of seminars in European capitals, I was able to develop the ideas for this book in diverse settings where the crises discussed herein were playing out in real time. I owe a particular debt to Jeff, who had earlier taken a chance on a 26-year-old American political journalist with little overseas experience by offering him a job at Radio Free Europe/Radio Liberty, a rare treasure of an institution whose top-notch journalists I feel enormously lucky to have worked alongside.

Paul Berman has been one of my intellectual heroes since I began reading his magisterial essays in *The New Republic* as an undergraduate at Yale, and I am grateful that he took the time to read the manuscript and offer his wisdom. I must also thank Chris Griffin, Mark Moyar, David Adesnik, and the rest of my colleagues at the Foreign Policy Initiative who provided such a supportive professional environment in which to write this book.

The following friends and colleagues either discussed the topics explored in this book with me, offered sage advice on the manuscript, or assisted in other ways: Eva Balogh, Adam Bellow, Marcus Bennsmann, Debra Cagan, Omri Ceren, Mark Falcoff, David Frum, Judy Goldstein, Jeffrey Herf, Donald Jensen, Robert Kagan, Craig Kennedy, Eli Lake, Walter Laqueur, Davis Lewin, Molly McKew, David Samuels, David Satter, Andras Simonyi, Constanze Stelzenmüller, Stephen Rodriguez, Dalibor Rohac, Jan Surotchak, Christopher Walker, and Nathalie Vogel. I owe particular thanks to Benjamin Haddad and Hannah Thoburn, who offered detailed comments throughout the text.

William Frucht was a careful and judicious editor whose considered suggestions restrained my more polemical impulses. Karen Olson, Ann-Marie Imbornoni, and Brian Ostrander saw to it that the entire publishing process moved along swimmingly and on time. Gail Naron Chalew diligently edited the manuscript. I would also like to thank the staff of the Wildacres Retreat, who provided me with a hospitable cabin in the deep woods of the Blue Ridge Mountains of North Carolina, where I could contemplate and write far away from the bubble of Washington, D.C.

Finally, my family. None of my life's achievements would have been possible without their unconditional love and support.

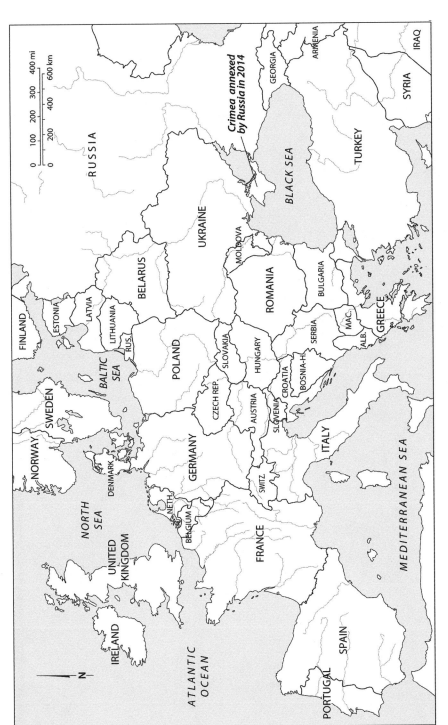

Political map of Europe. Map by Bill Nelson.

Introduction: The European Nightmare

THE END OF EUROPE IS UPON US.

For twenty-five years, the attainment of a Europe "whole, free and at peace" has been the mantra of American and European statesmen. It remains a noble and important vision. Yet this goal is becoming a vanishing reverie. Great Britain's decision to leave the European Union, an unprecedented move by a member state, has begun the bloc's slow unraveling, emboldening nationalist forces across the continent. In Greece, the far-left Syriza plunges that country further into economic distress. Meanwhile in Hungary, right-wing nationalist prime minister Viktor Orbán busily constructs an "illiberal democracy" while a neo-Nazi party pushes his government further and further to the extreme. A vast migratory wave from the Middle East exacerbates preexisting tensions with Muslim communities, and nearly a decade after the 2008 economic crash, the Eurozone continues to experience near-zero growth. Russia, fresh from perpetrating the first violent annexation of territory on the European continent since World War II, forges on with a dizzying military buildup and casually talks about the use of battlefield nuclear weapons against NATO members.

This book's title does not prophesize the literal dissolution of a continent or the demise of a supranational institution like the EU, though the latter is a real possibility. Rather, we are on the cusp of witnessing the end of Europe as we have known it for the past seven decades: a place of peace, stability, prosperity, cooperation, democracy, and social harmony. Europe today is breaking apart; it is increasingly undemocratic, economically stagnant, threatened by extremists of all stripes from the illiberal left to the authoritarian right, and slowly heading down the once unfathomable path to war. In some ways, the region's geopolitical turmoil evokes the perilous 1930s.

Hardly anyone predicted that, in 2014, Russia would perpetrate the first European land grab since World War II. Those who did warn of it, citing Moscow's 2008 invasion of Georgia as a portent, were written off as paranoid Cold Warriors or provincial Russophobes. Even fewer would have thought conceivable an actual shooting war that has claimed some 10,000 lives, including nearly 300 holidaymakers on a passenger jet passing through the skies of eastern Ukraine. But then, few could have conceived in 1904—the golden age of Einstein and Klimt, Mahler and Freud, Gropius and Debussy—that within ten years the European continent would be plunged into an abattoir of mechanized destruction and endure an even more horrific catastrophe less than three decades later.

That Europe is once again a global hotspot defies the conventional wisdom peddled for years by Western policy makers and most foreign affairs pundits. It was not so long ago that they extolled Europe as a pinnacle of human achievement, a social democratic, pacifist superpower to rival the United States. In 2002, Charles Kupchan, director of European affairs on the National Security Councils of both Bill Clinton and Barack Obama, published *The End of the American Era: U.S. Foreign Policy and the Geopolitics of the Twenty-First Century*. America's chief rival for global influence, Kupchan prophesied, would not be China, but "an integrating Europe that is rising as a counterweight to the United States." Two years later, in *The European Dream*, Jeremy Rifkin praised Europe's "rich multicultural diversity" over the American "melting pot," European-style "cooperation and consensus" over America's "go it alone approaches to foreign policy," and continental "leisure and even idleness" over American go-getting work habits. Just a year after Rifkin registered his prediction of Europe "eclipsing" America, Mark Leonard boasted that "Europe, quietly, has rediscovered within its foundations a revolutionary model for the future and an alternative to American hard power" in the unfortunately titled *Why Europe Will Run the 21st Century*.

Though recent events have proven these predictions wrong, to say the least, the signs of trouble have been visible for quite some time. Europe's financial crisis, nearly a decade old, reveals the unsustainability of the old social welfare state model. Thousands of young men journeying to the Islamic State show that European notions of multiculturalism are largely a delusion. Russia's war on a European country upends the once prevalent conviction that Moscow could play a constructive, rather than destructive, role in world affairs. A continent widely regarded as a "security exporter," blessed with an enviable *Pax Europa*, is itself becoming a zone of volatility where episodes of terrorist violence and political disorder are fast becoming regular occurrences.

As you read this, Europe is undergoing convulsions greater than anything it has experienced in decades. Just five years after winning the Nobel Peace Prize, the European Union, one of the most ambitious political projects in history, is crumbling. Threatening its very existence is the convergence of several crises: almost ten years of zero economic growth, a resurgent Russia, rising Islamic extremism, and the greatest mass movement of humanity since the late 1940s. These centrifugal forces expose an array of fissures within Europe. Imagine the continent on an x-y axis. The vertical dividing line, running roughly "from Stettin to Trieste" as Winston Churchill described the Iron Curtain, divides an Eastern Europe demanding a harder line against Russia from a Western Europe desiring accommodation. The eastern half also strenuously objects to Germany's insistence that Europe absorb well over a million African and Middle Eastern migrants. The horizontal dividing line pits the budget-conscious nations of Europe's north against the more prodigal economies of its south. Britain, more detached from continental affairs than at any time since it joined the European Economic Community (the EU's precursor) in 1973, scarcely fit into the diagram, even before voting to leave the EU in June 2016.

What once appeared irreversible—ever-greater political and economic integration on a continent where armed conflict had been banished to the dustbin of history along with totalitarian ideologies like communism and fascism—today seems a transient historical phase. Border controls have been reestablished where they had been absent for decades. A sequence of violently transformative events ranging from Russia's invasion of Ukraine to spectacular Islamist terrorist attacks, along with more transformative phenomena such as Britain's exit from the EU and the rise of "illiberal democracy" in places like Hungary and Poland, has put the continent's future stability in serious doubt. Thriving on disorder and uncertainty, populist political parties across the continent make steady electoral gains, a signal of growing exhaustion with the technocratic incrementalism of liberal democracy. Nationalist, anti-American, often racist and anti-Semitic, these forces evoke Europe's foulest traditions. Movements both left and right—to which, in light of their popularity, the qualifier "far" can no longer accurately be appended—promise a return to an idealized past through the efforts of strong men (and women). Discouraged by their governments' inability to handle a slew of problems, Europeans are questioning the very legitimacy and effectiveness of liberal democracy and turning to the siren calls of firebrands, who, whatever their ostensible political differences, all vow the restoration of a prelapsarian era that supposedly existed before European integration, when life was easier, cheaper, and safe. The echoes may be in different languages, but the rallying cry is the same. Agnes Heller, a liberal Hungarian philosopher, bemoans Europeans' low "frustration tolerance," how they "inevitably turn to dictators in times of crisis."[1] Europe's democratic backsliding mirrors a global trend: 2015 was the ninth straight year of decline in global freedom as measured by the human rights watchdog, Freedom House.

The problems described in this book have in common a loss of faith in the universal, humanistic values of what might be called the European idea. "The European idea is not a primary emotion like patriotism or ethnicity," the Viennese writer Stefan Zweig observed in 1934, "it is not born of a primitive instinct, but rather of perception; it is not the product of spontaneous fervor, but the slow-ripened fruit of a more elevated way of thinking."[2] Once, this idea was quite strong. In the wake of World War II, when Europe was divided, both the political left and right valued very highly what the West had and the East coveted: an environment of political and economic freedom, religious openness (even if it often shaded into religious indifference), and peace. The vision was never fulfilled as strongly, or as honestly, as Europeans liked to pretend: Their security was bought with a military force they did not have to pay for, and people of other races and religions were tolerated provided they kept to their place. Still, there existed a broad, if rough, consensus on a shared set of agreements and values.

Now, however, this consensus is being tested, and in some places, ripped apart. Some people were never on board with it; for others, it was agreeable only to the extent that they didn't have to risk very much to preserve it. External challenges that could have had an integrative effect—like migration and Russian aggression—are instead having a disintegrative one. Europe's decline, however, is largely attributable to indigenous factors, not outside ones. Economic stagnation, populism, disenchantment with liberal democracy, and rising social tensions will render Europe into precisely the enervated state that Vladimir Putin seeks for it. Asked if it is "essential" to "live in a country that is governed democratically," only about 40 percent of Europeans born in the 1980s respond in the affirmative.[3] Consequently, authoritarian populist parties (of both the left and right) hold almost 20 percent of the seats in European national parliaments, nearly twice as many as they did thirty years ago, and they sit in a third of Europe's governments.[4] Today, Europeans must ask themselves: How seriously are they committed to Europe? What are they willing to sacrifice in order to preserve the greatest experiment in political cooperation in human history?

While events of the last few years make evident that Europe should once again be the central focus of American foreign policy, Washington looks the other way. After the Cold War ended, America's attention shifted to the Middle East, Asia, and beyond. Figuring that Europe was finally and forever "settled," policy makers lost interest in the region, a propensity that became even more pronounced in the wake of the 9/11 attacks. This complacency about Europe grew under the administration of Barack Obama, America's first post-European president in the sense that the continent never occupied the prominent place in his worldview that it had in those of his predecessors. In a 2009 Tokyo speech, Obama declared himself "America's first Pacific president," a title he earned through childhood experience growing up in Indonesia and Hawaii and that would take on a tangible policy caste with his much-ballyhooed "pivot" of American military and diplomatic resources to Asia. "Here, we see the future," Obama told the Australian parliament in 2011, the implicit message being that unnamed other parts of the world represented the past. Under Obama, there were no ambitious

European initiatives akin to the Marshall Plan or the EU and NATO expansions undertaken by his predecessors in the late 1990s and 2000s.

Yet just when events are proving the indispensability of American engagement, the bipartisan consensus on commitment to Europe is eroding. While campaigning for the presidency of the United States, Donald Trump repeatedly denigrated NATO as "obsolete," questioned America's treaty obligations to defend its allies in Eastern Europe, and had nothing but kind things to say about Vladimir Putin (characteristic of a broader favorable attitude toward authoritarians). Putin's regime returned the favor by actively working to get Trump elected, publicizing emails it had hacked from the Democratic National Committee and Hillary Clinton's campaign through the conduit of Wikileaks. Trump came to office on the heels of a European-style, ethnonationalist movement the likes of which most Americans never believed could take root in their country. He is part of a global wave of illiberal populists whose European adherents see a kindred spirit and strategic ally in the Russian regime. The new American president views international relations as a giant protection racket in which alliances have absolutely nothing to do with shared values and are purely transactional. In electing Trump, America has done the unthinkable: catapult an authoritarian demagogue to the most powerful position on earth. No longer can it be taken for granted that the United States will be leader of the free world; it may become a passive bystander to global struggles for liberty, or, should President Trump reach some sort of diplomatic condominium with Putin, an active opponent.

Meanwhile, the country's ascendant left wing harbors similar skepticism of American alliances; in 2010, fifty Democratic members of Congress signed an open letter complaining that "years after the Soviet threat has disappeared, we continue to provide European and Asian nations with military protection through our nuclear umbrella and the troops stationed in our overseas military bases."[5] Only 49 percent of Americans express a favorable view of NATO; the proportion of those holding unfavorable views increased from 21 percent in 2010 to 31 percent in 2015.[6]

This book represents the culmination of more than six years living in and reporting across Europe. Like most Americans, I had perceived the continent mostly through the prism of history: Europe was the place from which my ancestors fled persecution, a land of museums, castles, and empty churches. At university, I took courses on the British Empire and Cold War. Whatever was interesting about Europe seemed to lie in its past. A class I took on the EU convinced me that the only challenges on Europe's horizon concerned tinkering around the edges of munificent social welfare systems. An assumption of perpetual stability—that the continent's consensual politics, respectable economic growth, and impenetrable security arrangements would remain forever static—heavily influenced my career decisions as a journalist. Like many young people in search of adventure, I was drawn to those parts of the world where borders were still in flux and violence a facet of daily life, where dictators ruled their subjects and heroic dissidents fought for freedom, where ideologies still made a difference and people risked everything to advance them. I traveled to Southern Africa and the Middle East nurturing dreams of becoming a conflict reporter.

It took an unexpected job offer from Radio Free Europe/Radio Liberty (RFE/RL) in Prague to alter my perspective. I was familiar with RFE/RL's gallant past of "broadcasting freedom" behind the Iron Curtain. But like most of the people I later told about my new employer, I was unaware that the institution still existed. Traveling extensively across Europe and throughout the former Soviet Union, I came to understand that history had not ended, that Europe had not entered a "post-ideological" age, and that optimistic assumptions about the inevitable triumph of liberal democracy, free markets, peaceful coexistence, and political pluralism were premature even on the very continent that so prided itself in having founded and exported these values to the world.

Soon after moving to Europe, I realized that to understand the continent and how it functions, I needed to acquire some familiarity with its largest and most powerful country. In the summer of 2012 I moved to Germany, and it didn't take me long to develop the favorable impressions shared by so many foreign visitors to this remarkable land. The diligence and precision, the admirably self-critical approach to history, the thoroughness and obsessive attention to detail (applied to tasks deserving of such exactitude and those that don't), the elevated quality of public debate, the high expectations set for oneself and others—all these were attributes that I came to appreciate in both individual Germans and German society. For someone who detests "flakiness"—that mix of unreliability and presumption so prevalent among my millennial generation—Germany was a sort of paradise, a place where dependability and common sense reigned.

But if the Germans impressed me with their straightforwardness, I was equally struck by their reductionist mindset. A pacifist political culture regards even modest displays of defensive military posture as harbinger of catastrophic nationalism. Indifference toward the Khomeinist regime in Iran, whose anti-Semitic rhetoric evokes that heard not so long ago on Berlin streets, as well as a collective shrug in reply to Russia's annexation of Crimea, left me questioning what lessons Germans had learned from such diligent study of their past. Historical guilt for the crimes of Nazism inspired an open-door refugee policy as ill considered as it was well intentioned, the negative consequences of which will be felt for generations. German self-righteousness was crystallized in a conversation about the scandal over U.S. National Security Agency surveillance practices when a young member of the Bundestag insisted that Americans must be punished because "spying is illegal." The naïve earnestness of his hectoring was matched only by its axiomatic absurdity: Because espionage is illegal, my interlocutor sincerely believed, it could, and should, be prohibited.

Americans prefer not to dwell on the past; Gore Vidal, commenting on this tendency, called us "the United States of Amnesia." Our country was founded by, and continues to be replenished with, people escaping the stifling social confines and procrustean national traumas of their homelands. Europeans, sometimes for better but as often for worse, are less adept at moving beyond their painful histories. One cannot comprehend German outrage over the NSA scandal without understanding the country's status as a postwar American protectorate. Hungary's descent into "illiberal democracy" is an echo of its authoritarian past. Greece's current dysfunction does not make sense without reference to its years of military dictatorship and centuries under foreign rule. Vladimir Putin mobilizes Russians to defend the Motherland from what he portrays as a conniving and conspiratorial West by invoking their valiant struggle in the "Great Patriotic War" against fascism. Such appeals may cynically distort history for political gain, but they draw on lived experiences. Explaining why these histories, real and imagined, remain so resonant is one of the reasons I wrote this book.

The End of Europe is organized geographically and thematically into eight chapters, each a case study of a nation in crisis. None of these crises, however, are exclusive to the nations where they predominate; worrisome trends that are most visible in one country spill over borders and reverberate across the continent. My journey begins in Estonia, perhaps the NATO member most vulnerable to subversion and invasion from the East, where controversy surrounding the dismantlement of a Soviet World War II memorial reveals how Russia exploits ethnic tensions along Europe's eastern periphery to undermine the Western alliance. In Hungary, it is conversely the erection of a World War II memorial that elicits a contentious debate over memory politics and exemplifies a regional drift toward authoritarianism. Germany's response to the NSA scandal exposes the fragility of that country's strategic attachment to the West, and the chapter on the European Union explores the continent's dysfunctional handling of the greatest migration crisis since World War II as well as its long-standing failure to assimilate its Muslim citizens. In France, the exodus of Europe's largest Jewish community unmasks the protean nature of the continent's deadliest tradition, anti-Semitism. Across the English Channel, the unprecedented withdrawal of an EU member state, potential Scottish independence, and fracturing of the Labor Party portend disintegrative ripple effects for the European project and underline the parlous condition of the social democratic political tradition. Greece is the land where populism and clientelism went to war against the fiscal rectitude required by the euro. My travels conclude somewhat optimistically in Ukraine, the new West Berlin, whose people are fighting a battle for Europe the existential nature of which their fellow Europeans refuse to acknowledge. These crises share a root cause: the lack of solidarity. They can be ameliorated only by cohesion: political, economic, military, and cultural.

Where does America fit into this picture? Europe is America's most critical ally. No other region of the world shares such strong commitment to liberal democratic values. Protection of individual rights; the free flow of goods, people, and information; freedom of speech and religion; maintenance of a rule-based international system—none of these would be possible without European cooperation. When America wants to accomplish anything internationally, whether devising a response to global warming or halting Iran's nuclear weapons program, Europe is the ally it turns to first. Indeed, everything of value that America has accomplished in the world since 1945 has been done with Europe by its side. A century before Americans and Europeans would begin building the present-day liberal international order in the ashes of World War II, the great French chronicler of America, Alexis de Tocqueville, observed that "the two continents can never be independent of each other, so numerous are the natural ties which exist between their wants, their ideas, their habits and their manners."[7] Simply put, Europe's unraveling would be one of America's worst foreign policy disasters.

There is a tendency among American policy makers and pundits, particularly those on the right, to hold up their collective nose at Europe. They shudder at Europeans' deference to the state, their willingness to turn over so much of their incomes to the government, their limits on free speech, and their reluctance to pay for militaries, never mind use them. So widespread and deeply held is this conception in some quarters that "Europe" has become a dirty word in American political discourse, shorthand for a sort of feeble collectivist impulse. Americans complain that Europeans are "free-riders" whose lavish social programs are possible only through the defense umbrella thanklessly subsidized by American taxpayers.

Europeans, meanwhile, view U.S. gun culture with bewilderment at best, revulsion at worst. Americans' open religiosity gives them chills. The fact that Americans pray to God, insist on using air conditioning, and still employ the death penalty horrifies the average European. Protests against the American-led war in Iraq drew record numbers in London, Paris, and Madrid; hardly any Europeans have bothered to protest Russia's annexation of Crimea or Bashar al-Assad's gassing of children.

As an American who has lived in Europe and travels there frequently, I am well acquainted with these social, political, and cultural disagreements, but this is not a book seized with resolving them. The arguments you are about to read stem from a conviction that the values and interests uniting Americans and Europeans are far more numerous, and of greater import, than anything which divides us.

1

Russia: On Europe's Edge

Are we, day after day, to allow the ghosts of the past to seize us by the hands and prevent us from moving forward?

Vladimir Putin, 2005

Accommodating evil has, so far, never forced evil to retreat, or to become more humane; on the contrary, it has always made life easier for it. In the end, when confrontation came, the price that everyone had to pay was higher than the cost of a firm stance.

Vaclav Havel, *To The Castle and Back*, 2007

IN THE PRE-DAWN HOURS OF APRIL 27, 2007, a group of senior government officials in the small Baltic republic of Estonia assembled in their capital, Tallinn, for an emergency meeting. What compelled the gathering was not a terrorist attack, natural disaster, or the rapid mobilization of Russian forces along the border, but a seemingly quotidian task of the kind normally managed by local parks departments: the relocation of a monument. This, however, wasn't just any monument. Hours before the cabinet assembled, 1,500 ethnic Russians had begun gathering around the "Memorial to the Liberators of Tallinn," located in the city center, to prevent its transfer to a military cemetery. After two nights of rioting (the worst since the 1944 Soviet reoccupation), some 1,000 protestors were detained, more than 150 were injured, and one died.

Originally erected by the Russians in 1947, the Bronze Soldier, as the memorial is colloquially known, had become a potent symbol of Estonia's conflict over national memory. When Estonia and its Baltic neighbors Latvia and Lithuania regained independence in 1991, they immediately set out to de-Sovietize and rejoin the West. They did this by weeding out communist apparatchiks from state bureaucracies, revising education curricula to include the history of communist oppression, and tearing down monuments to Soviet icons. But unlike statues glorifying Marx, Lenin, or proletarian revolution, Tallinn's memorial to the Red Army was initially spared the trash heap, likely because of the ambiguity of its meaning. As the Russian Duma would note in a resolution decrying the statue's relocation, the Soviet Union played a decisive role "liberat[ing] Europe from fascism," a liberation that included the reversal of a three-year Nazi occupation of the Baltic States begun in 1941. Unmentioned by the Duma members, however, was the 1939 agreement their Soviet predecessors struck with Nazi Germany carving up Central and Eastern Europe, which not only launched World War II but led to the first Soviet occupation of the Baltics the following year. Only when Hitler reneged on the Treaty of Non-Aggression, also known as the Molotov-Ribbentrop Pact, by attacking the Soviet Union in 1941 did Moscow decide to "liberate" Eastern Europe from the fascism it had enabled before going on to impose its own, decades-long bloody rule.

Allied victory in the war, joyously celebrated in New York, London, and Paris, was a more complicated matter in Eastern Europe, which had been effectively surrendered to the Soviets at the postwar Yalta summit. It would take nearly fifty years of cold war before the possibility of a Europe whole, free, and at peace (as President George H. W. Bush rhapsodized just months before the Berlin Wall collapsed) could emerge. After regaining independence, Estonia and Latvia found themselves with substantial numbers of ethnic Russians: the factory workers, military officers, civil servants, and their descendants whom the Soviet Union had dispatched as part of a Russification program. Integrating these communities, which account for roughly 25 percent of the population in each country, has been an uneasy task. Just as the Kremlin invented threats to ethnic Russians in the Georgian region of South Ossetia, Crimea, and eastern Ukraine as pretexts for military intervention, the "plight" of Russian minorities in the Baltics is ripe for exploitation. These countries' geographical proximity to Russia and status as the only post-Soviet republics to join both the EU and NATO—a point of especial irritation for resentful Russian nationalists—render their domestic political and social tensions a potential proving ground for international conflict.

In his March 2014 address before Russia's rubber-stamp upper chamber, celebrating the "referendum" that reported an improbable 97 percent of Crimean citizens voting to join the Russian Federation, Vladimir Putin ridiculed the granting of independence to post-Soviet states as a "sovereignty parade" before getting to the emotional nub of the matter. "Millions of people went to bed in one country and awoke in different ones, overnight becoming ethnic minorities in former Union republics, while the Russian nation became one of the biggest, if not the biggest ethnic group in the world to be divided by borders."[1] If the "Russian nation," a unitary entity, had been wrongly "divided by borders," then presumably it is the Russian government's duty to reassemble it. With this speech, Putin dangled the possibility that Russia might attempt in eastern Estonia or northern Kazakhstan—regions with a high percentage of Russian speakers—what it had pulled off without firing a single bullet in Crimea.[2]

According to its president, Russia now reserves the right to intervene militarily wherever it likes—overturning legitimate governments, installing puppet regimes, annexing territory—if it deems the rights of ethnic Russians to be in danger. Three months after annexing Crimea, Putin announced to a gathering of Russian ambassadors his intention to "protect" the *Russkiy Mir*, or "Russian World," a broadly defined ethno-linguistic community whose "compatriots" comprise anyone with a "sense that they are a part of the broad Russian World, not necessarily of Russian ethnicity, but everyone who feels to be a Russian person." No instrument of the state would be neglected in defense of this vaguely defined principle: Putin swore to implement "the entire range of available means." To this neo-Brezhnevian assertion of a near-unlimited right to intervene militarily in former Soviet bloc countries, Putin married neo-Hitlerian blood-and-soil nationalism. Inventing claims of oppression endured by ethnic "compatriots" is precisely how the Führer justified the occupation of the Czech Sudetenland and other territories.

The events that followed the Bronze Soldier's relocation presage the sort of escalatory scenario that keeps Western leaders awake at night. Beginning on April 26, 2007, just as riots were erupting on the streets of Tallinn, a series of highly coordinated, distributed denial-of-service (DDOS) attacks were launched against websites of the Estonian state, media outlets, banks, and other important institutions. A pioneer in e-government, Estonia is one of the most wired societies on earth, one where citizens can pay taxes and vote online. It produces more tech start-ups per capita than any other country in the world (Skype being the most famous). But this reliance on the Internet left Estonia especially vulnerable to cyberattack, the first known one perpetrated against a government. Though only one ethnic Russian living in Estonia was found guilty of involvement in the three-week-long series of attacks, the Estonian government publicly accused Russia of orchestrating it.

The Bronze Soldier incident looms large as Russia reasserts itself in Eastern Europe, probing NATO for weaknesses. On September 5, 2014, two days after President Obama delivered a speech in Tallinn reassuring the Baltic States of NATO's security commitments, smoke grenades exploded in a remote wooded area near the Estonian-Russian border as an Estonian intelligence officer named Eston Kohver was kidnapped by Russian agents. Kohver had been investigating a local smuggling ring that turned out to be a trap set by Russia's Federal Security Bureau (FSB), the successor agency to the KGB. Snatched from Estonian territory, the first time an intelligence officer from a NATO country had been abducted on his home soil, and ferried to Moscow, he was paraded on television and accused of being a spy. After a show trial and a year of captivity in the notorious Lefortovo Prison, Kohver was sentenced to fifteen years in jail. Soon after his sentencing, however, he was exchanged for a Russian spy held by Estonia, the dramatic prisoner swap occurring on a bridge like a scene from divided Berlin.

In the Latvian capital of Riga, meanwhile, the Russian Embassy has recruited local ethnic Russians, including former convicts, to fight alongside Russian troops in Ukraine, and police have seized arms caches from the homes of ethnic Russian residents suspected of participating in the conflict. Lithuania, which was persuaded by the events in Ukraine to reintroduce military conscription, has distributed a manual to citizens instructing them how to behave in case of Russian invasion. "Keep a sound mind, don't panic, and don't lose clear thinking," it reads. "Gunshots just outside your window are not the end of the world."[3] When the country tried to break Russia's near-monopoly over its energy supply by connecting to Sweden's electrical grid via underwater cables and hooking up to a floating Baltic Sea natural gas plant, Moscow dispatched a group of warships to sail a symbolic but intimidating course through international waters.[4] (Since the Ukraine crisis began, Russian fighter planes have repeatedly violated the airspace of the Baltics, Sweden, Finland, and countries as far afield as the United Kingdom.) Russia understands the stakes of energy transition in the Baltics. For if these countries succeed in weaning themselves from Russian supplies, it would demonstrate that geography need not be destiny for the small nations of Central and Eastern Europe.

Since NATO's founding in 1949 in the ashes of World War II, the security of Europe (and, increasingly, that of lands beyond) has depended on the military alliance of the Atlantic democracies. Lord Ismay, the British diplomat who served as NATO's first secretary general, pithily defined its animating purpose: "Keep the Russians out, the Americans in, and the Germans down." Today, Vladimir Putin's strategy can be understood as a slight spin on this formula: Move the Russians in, get the Americans out, and keep the Germans down. His ultimate aim is to revise the outcome of the Cold War, chiefly, the notion that countries should be free to decide their own political and security arrangements. Russia considers the wholly consensual process of NATO expansion into former Warsaw Pact states illegitimate, as well as a humiliating sign of its loss of power and prestige in the lands it used to rule. Its invasion of Georgia in 2008 and of Ukraine six years later indefinitely stopped those countries' plans to join the alliance and put all other aspirant states on notice: Express interest in NATO at your own risk. Iulian Fota, former national security advisor to the president of Romania, says that Russia's repeated aggression has elevated it progressively from having a "voice" within European security discussions to a "vote" on the candidacy of potential NATO members to an outright "veto" over decisions within the alliance.[5]

Having stalled the alliance's expansion, Russia's next move may be to challenge it on its own territory, thus revealing Article 5, NATO's collective security guarantee, to be a sham. Destroying NATO does not mean getting into a shooting war with the alliance, nor does it require the conventional military invasion of a member state; Russia need only demonstrate that Article 5 is not worth the paper it's written on. For NATO collective security is as much an idea as it is the deterrence capability physically manifested in soldiers, tanks, and warships. Showing the hollowness of this idea would take little more than replicating Russia's Crimean operation, a cunning example of "hybrid war" in which disinformation, soldiers without insignia, and Soviet-style "active measures" (deception operations) were deployed to confuse Russia's adversaries, sow dissension among Western leaders, and divide the alliance from within. In recent years, senior Russian officials have raised the prospect of a lightning-quick "preventive occupation" of the Baltic countries, an ironic turn of phrase in light of how Moscow still refuses to acknowledge that its Soviet-era presence in the Baltics was indeed an occupation.[6]

Considering the rationale Putin gave for the absorption of Crimea, it's not difficult to imagine Russia carrying out a similar maneuver in the Baltics, again under the pretext of "protecting" the *Russkiy Mir*. If this action succeeds, the security order on which the Western world has depended for seven decades will collapse, and "the greatest defensive alliance the world has ever known," in the words of former NATO secretary-general Paul-Henri Spaak, will be unmasked as a paper tiger.

At his most fundamental level, Putin is a kleptocrat, committed first and foremost to the preservation of the authoritarian mafia state he helms. He is also a Russian exceptionalist who genuinely believes that his country has a unique and beneficial role to play in world affairs. Along its thousands of miles of borders, Russia desires friendly governments—as any country would—though in this case "friendly" invariably means pliant fellow dictatorships. Beyond, Russia seeks a docile West unable to challenge Moscow's prerogatives in its so-called near abroad, the absolutist affirmation of state sovereignty as a sacrosanct principle of interstate relations, and dismantlement of the rules-based liberal world order that protects small, weak countries from the predations of larger, belligerent ones. Putin does not, as some analysts and politicians have blithely asserted, want to "resurrect the Soviet

Union." He has no interest in restoring the command economy, reestablishing communism as a political movement, or reoccupying Eastern Europe. His objectives, though less outwardly ambitious, are menacing nonetheless: increase Russia's influence in the independent nations of the former communist bloc, establish a veto power over their foreign policies and alliances, overturn Europe's security architecture, and coerce the West into accepting these radical revisions to the existing world order.

The clearest articulation of the Putin worldview remains the speech he delivered at the 2007 Munich Security Conference, a few months before the Bronze Soldier incident. Dispensing a riptide of pugnacious anti-Americanism, Putin lamented that Soviet defeat in the Cold War had ushered in a "unipolar world" with "one center of authority, one center of force, one center of decision-making." The United States, he said with prescient (if unintended) irony in light of the looming Russian invasions of Georgia and Ukraine, "has overstepped its national borders in every way" and was responsible for "new dividing lines" in Europe.[7] Marking Victory Day celebrations three months later, he compared America's position on the world stage to that of Nazi Germany, declaring, "In these new threats, as during the time of the Third Reich, are the same contempt for human life and the same claims of exceptionality and diktat in the world."[8]

That same year, as part of an effort to whip up xenophobic hostility against the West, the Kremlin launched a campaign of historical revisionism that would have dangerous implications for the future. Over the ensuing decade, Joseph Stalin's reputation has undergone dramatic rehabilitation from that of a mass-murdering zealot to an occasionally over-aggressive state-builder. "We cannot allow anyone to impose a sense of guilt on us," Putin instructed a group of history teachers, lest Stalin's imperialism and brutality be cited in critique of the authoritarian Russian state Putin has constructed. Following that directive, a Kremlin-endorsed education manual describes the Soviet Union as "an example for millions of people around the world of the best and fairest society" and laments its demise. It defends Stalin's rule as the result of "circumstances of the cold war" that "demanded" harsh repression and blames reformist Soviet premier Mikhail Gorbachev, not the sclerotic Soviet system, for "the slowest economic growth in the 20th century."[9] More ominously, the guide mourns the end of Russian domination in Central and Eastern Europe: "Thus the Soviet Union lost its security belt, which a few years later would become a zone of foreign influence, with NATO bases an hour away from St. Petersburg."[10]

Perhaps the most chilling instance of Kremlin revisionism occurred at the 2015 Victory Day celebration in Moscow. At a press conference with German chancellor Angela Merkel, Putin was asked about his culture minister's controversial statement that the Nazi-Soviet Pact of 1939 represented "a huge success of Stalin's diplomacy." Putin replied that he was in full agreement, because the pact "had significance for ensuring the security of the USSR."[11] In reality, the Hitler-Stalin treaty laid the groundwork for a war that caused the deaths of tens of millions of Soviet citizens. But Stalin's official rehabilitation is a necessary precondition for hardening domestic repression: Russia needs strong leaders, new generations of children are taught, or else the country will collapse.

Extending from presidential proclamations to public monuments all the way down to school textbooks, the official Putinist narrative, in its nationalistic historical revisionism, marks a regression to the era before Soviet premier Nikita Khrushchev renounced Stalin's "cult of personality" in his famous 1956 "secret speech." Memorial, a non-governmental organization that preserves the memory of Soviet atrocities and advocates for human rights, has come under sustained assault from the Russian government, which has gone so far as to confiscate the society's meticulously collected database of oral testimonies recorded by survivors of Stalinist persecution. More recently, local officials in the city of Perm seized control of the Museum of Political Repressions, located on the grounds of a former gulag, and transformed it into an institution honoring what the newly installed head of exhibitions calls the labor camp's "contribution to victory" in World War II.[12] Russia's Supreme Court has also upheld a lower court decision punishing a blogger for writing that both Nazi Germany and the Soviet Union invaded Poland in 1939, effectively making factual statements regarding the origins of World War II illegal. Glorifying one of the twentieth century's most prolific mass murderers has worked for the Kremlin: 52 percent of Russians now believe that Stalin played an "undoubtedly positive" or "rather positive" role in the country's history, the highest level of support measured for Stalin since polling on the question began in 2006.[13] For comparison, in 1989, Russians named Stalin as the eleventh most influential person in world history; by 2013, they placed him at the top of the list.[14] Vladimir Putin has made history by changing it.

Though largely ignored by the West, which lulled itself into believing Russia had fundamentally changed after the postcommunist transition, Putin's whitewashing of the Soviet past sent alarm signals to the newly independent nations of the former Eastern bloc that had taken up the hard task of commemorating the bloody and long-suppressed history of communist crimes. When the Georgian government built a Museum of Soviet Occupation in its capital, Tbilisi, in 2006, Putin was reportedly so angry that he upbraided his counterpart Mikhail Saakashvili in a face-to-face meeting. (Considering how both Stalin and his secret police chief Lavrentiy Beria were Georgian, Saakashvili tartly replied, he would be happy to build a Museum of Georgian Oppression in Moscow.) Four years later, in a move laden with symbolism, Georgia took down the statue of Stalin that stood at the center of his hometown, Gori. "If one thinks of the modern values of Georgia and where Georgia will be tomorrow, Stalin's statue will not be a part of Georgia's future," David Bakradze, then chairman of the parliament, proudly told me at the time.[15]

For Estonians, Georgians, and other citizens of ex-Soviet republics, this repossession of the past is motivated by both geostrategic concerns and fidelity to the truth. Exposing the history of Soviet crimes signals civilizational distance from Moscow. Excavating history in this fashion inevitably provokes Russian objection, as Moscow regularly insists that countries appraising Soviet-era abuses do so as a means of suppressing their own crimes, like collaboration with the Nazis. These complaints are occasionally warranted, particularly with regard to the Baltic States, where attempts to expose Soviet persecution sometimes involve the glorification of fascist collaborators as national heroes. But Kremlin denunciations of pro-Western political factions in the post-Soviet space can never be taken at face value, as they routinely adopt the tired Stalinist tactic of labeling anyone who criticizes Russia a "fascist" (witness the Duma resolution attacking the Bronze Soldier's relocation as tantamount to "glorifying

fascism"). So frequent and indiscriminate are these attacks that it is difficult to characterize them as anything other than politically motivated.

State-directed veneration of Stalin and nationalist reappraisal of the origins of the World War II refute important declarations by Russian leaders,
Putin included. In December 1989, the Soviet Congress of People's Deputies declared the Hitler-Stalin Pact null and void.[16] Putin himself expressed
his personal opposition to the pact in 2005, ten years to the day before he
would proudly defend it in front of Merkel. Asked by an Estonian reporter
to clarify remarks he had made about her country's making "foolish territorial demands" of Russia and whether Russia would acknowledge the past
Soviet annexation of the Baltic States as an "occupation" (which it has still
not done), Putin referred her to the 1989 resolution that laid the groundwork for Baltic independence. He added that the Hitler-Stalin Pact "did not
reflect the opinion of the Soviet people but was the personal affair of Stalin
and Hitler."[17] Four years later, on the seventieth anniversary of World War
II, he wrote an article for a Polish newspaper stating that "any form of
agreement with the Nazi regime was unacceptable from the moral point of
view and had no chance of being realized."

Whatever the "opinion of the Soviet people" was in 1939, when the Hitler-
Stalin Pact was signed, today the sentiment that "there are parts of neighboring countries that really belong to us" is held by 61 percent of Russians,
up from 22 percent in 1991.[18] "The Russians see some territories like Islamists see Spain," says a high-ranking military official from a NATO country, likening the covetousness of Russian irredentists for some former
Soviet lands to the atavistic longings Al-Qaeda expresses for Andalusia.
"Society is being prepared for the idea that we might have to fight," the
Russian playwright Aleksander Gelman, who served as a delegate to the
Congress of People's Deputies in 1989, says about Putin's latter-day defense of the Hitler-Stalin pact.[19] "In reality there are no real reasons for
a world war at present, except for our own insane ideas. But we have to re-
member that insane ideas can be made real."

What are those "insane ideas"? A 2014 Russian Culture Ministry report
outlining the "Foundations of State Cultural Politics" defines the country's
identity only in negation to the West: "Russia is not Europe." By that it means
that Russia is illiberal, authoritarian, nationalistic, Orthodox Christian, and
economically autarkic, a compilation of reactionary values distilled into an

ideology known as "Eurasianism," the new doctrine of Russian imperialism. Its prime exponent is a former Moscow State University professor and
graphomaniac named Alexander Dugin, whose most famous treatise explains world conflict as a perpetual battle between "Eternal Rome" (land
powers like Russia, whose values are communal) and "Eternal Carthage"
(maritime nations like America and Great Britain, which prioritize the
rights of the individual).[20] Although Putin has not adopted the more occult
and openly racialist aspects of the professor's paranoid oeuvre, Dugin's
prominence in state media testifies to his influence.

In contrast to its Cold War sales pitch as a society of the future, Moscow
today signifies its repudiation of the West by posturing as a defender of
"traditional values" against a deluge of irreligiosity, sexual decadence, and
post-national "globalism." Putin speaks of Russia as opposing not necessarily Europe but what it has become: a place of hedonism, depravity, self-
indulgence, cosmopolitanism, and materialism. With its commitment to
nationhood, personal sacrifice, and the natural family, Russia now has the
thankless task of defending *true* European values. "It is evident that it is
impossible to move forward without spiritual, cultural, and national self-
determination," Putin declared at the 2013 gathering of the Valdai International Discussion Club, an annual confab of Russia watchers.[21] "We can see
how many of the Euro-Atlantic countries are actually rejecting their roots,
including the Christian values that constitute the basis of Western civilization. They are denying moral principles and all traditional identities: national, cultural, religious and even sexual." Such moralistic language, along
with a high-profile crusade against homosexuality, appeals to conservative
nationalists across Europe, from Hungarian prime minister Viktor Orbán
to French National Front leader Marine Le Pen to the United Kingdom
Independence Party's Nigel Farage, who all evoke a simpler, ethnically and
religiously homogeneous European past.[22]

Lacking the institutional checks on power that existed during the communist era, Russia today is a more unpredictable adversary than was the
Soviet Union. After Khrushchev, the USSR was ruled by a presidium of
aging apparatchiks who, for all their ideological bluster, were generally
risk-averse. In Putinism, Russia has reverted to the cult of personality, in
this case, a personality defined by historic resentments, national chauvinism, and a lack of concern for human life, as shown by Putin's probable

involvement in the 1999 Moscow apartment bombings that helped him secure power.[23] "Maintaining the governance of a vast territory, preserving a unique commonwealth of peoples while occupying a major place in world affairs calls . . . for enormous sacrifices and privations on the part of our people," he said in a 2008 speech, foreshadowing the hardships he would summon his people to endure after the seizure of Crimea engendered Western sanctions and diplomatic isolation. "Such has been Russia's thousand-year history. Such is the way in which it has retained its place as a mighty nation. We do not have the right to forget this." Joseph Stalin expressed this same idea less sentimentally when he likened Soviet citizens to "screws in the great machine of the state." The connective ideological thread has woven its way through Russian history from tsarism to communism to today's Eurasianism: a repudiation of Western liberalism's most essential moral claim—that a human being is not a means to state-determined ends but is an end unto him- or herself.

From its broad avenues lined with drab prefabricated apartments to the Cyrillic lettering that adorns storefronts and billboards, Narva is interchangeable with many nameless towns in Russia's great expanse. But it is Estonian, albeit just across a river from Russia. Customs checkpoints on either side of the bridge linking it to the town of Ivangorod are the only hints that this sleepy settlement is the easternmost point of the EU and NATO. Visiting Narva, one understands former Polish foreign minister Radoslaw Sikorski's observation that he felt a "historical sense of being on a tectonic plate."

Evacuated in 1944 by the invading Soviets, Narva soon became home to Estonia's highest concentration of ethnic Russians. When the USSR collapsed nearly five decades later, tens of thousands of ethnic Russians, having suddenly lost their dominant position as colonizers, moved from Estonia to Russia. In recent years, however, few have chosen to "repatriate." Most find life in a prosperous, democratic country—even as a minority—and visa-free travel throughout the world's largest trading bloc more attractive than returning to the Motherland. Nonetheless, while most ethnic Russians have voted with their feet by remaining in Estonia, Narva, which is 95 percent Russian, remains geographically and mentally closer to St. Petersburg than Tallinn. They may all live in the same tiny country, but ethnic Estonians and Russians inhabit different worlds: They largely attend separate schools, live in separate towns and neighborhoods, and consume different media. Polls consistently indicate that the two communities harbor diametrically opposing views on a variety of social and political subjects; for instance, whereas 68 percent of Russian-speaking Estonians hold the government in Kyiv responsible for the crisis in Ukraine, 78 percent of ethnic Estonians believe Moscow is to blame.[24]

To destabilize the Baltics' domestic politics, Russia aggravates these divisions through financial support to politically disruptive ethnic Russian organizations.[25] Its subversion and intimidation of the Baltics long predate the current turmoil in Ukraine and, indeed, never really ended after Baltic re-independence. On February 25, 1994, the president of Estonia, Lennart Meri, delivered a speech in Hamburg addressing the future of East-West relations. Three years after the mostly peaceful demise of the USSR and with Boris Yeltsin presiding over a newly democratic Russia, those relations were better than they had ever been. Indeed, that summer, Yeltsin would join a group of European leaders at a summit on Corfu to sign a trade agreement and hail "a truly great step toward the reunion of our continent." Meri, however, was reluctant to embrace the prevailing optimism. Russia's Foreign Ministry, he could not help but notice, had released statements announcing that, "the problem of ethnic Russian groups in the neighboring countries cannot be solved by Russia by diplomatic means alone." Senior Kremlin figures were asserting that Moscow's role in the former Soviet space would be that of "primus inter pares"—first among equals—a foreshadowing of the "sphere of privileged interests" that president Dmitri Medvedev would declare some fifteen years later. Combined with Russia's insistence that the Baltic States had not been forcefully occupied but rather "voluntarily" joined the Soviet Union in 1940 and 1944 ("little short of the statement that tens of thousands of Estonians, including my family and myself, had 'voluntarily' let themselves be deported to Siberia," Meri observed), these uncomfortable facts militated against "wishful thinking" about the West's relationship with Russia.[26]

Sitting in the room that February 1994 evening was a visibly displeased Vladimir Putin, then a senior advisor to the mayor of St. Petersburg. According to one guest, when Meri described Soviet forces in Estonia as occupiers, Putin conspicuously rose from his seat, marched loudly to the exit, and slammed the heavy steel door behind him.[27] A clue as to what so angered him, aside from the standard recitation of facts about Russian imperialism from one of the formerly subjugated, can be found in a 2009 U.S. State Department cable about a meeting U.S. diplomats held with an Estonian foreign ministry official. The Russian president, according to the Baltic envoy, "has a personal gripe with Estonia" triggered by the farmers who allegedly "betrayed" his father, then a soldier in the Red Army, to the Germans during World War II.[28]

Even without this element of personal bitterness, Russia's relations with Estonia were bound to be poor, as evidenced by the way the Putin regime deals with other post-Soviet states insolent enough to chart a Western path. As early as 2007, in a move clearly designed to intimidate newly admitted NATO members, Putin suspended Russian participation in the Treaty on Conventional Forces in Europe, an important post–Cold War legal instrument through which NATO and Russia limit and monitor the amount of heavy weaponry deployed on the continent. The following year, Russia invaded Georgia and unilaterally declared the existence of two phony republics on its sovereign territory. In retrospect, the Georgia war was more portentous than most Western leaders realized at the time. Only six months later, however, the freshly inaugurated Obama administration offered to "reset" relations with Moscow. In what would become a recurring feature of its diplomacy with rogue regimes, the administration studiously tried to ignore its interlocutor's external aggression, increasing domestic authoritarianism, and flagrant disrespect for international norms, so as to pave the way for a nuclear arms reduction treaty known as New START.

Washington's cozying to Moscow, welcomed by France and Germany, widened an already growing divide between Eastern and Western Europeans. Five months after Vice President Joe Biden announced the reset in February 2009, twenty-two distinguished Central and Eastern European leaders— former Czech and Polish presidents Vaclav Havel and Lech Walesa most prominent among them—published an open letter to President Obama warning that "Russia is back as a revisionist power pursuing a 19th-century agenda with 21st-century tactics and methods."[29] Western elites either ignored the letter or responded with derisory accusations of fearmongering. One signatory, former Czech defense minister Alexandr "Sasha" Vondra, recalled a dressing-down he received in the White House at the hands of Michael McFaul, then President Obama's director for Russia and Eurasian affairs on the National Security Council, a future ambassador to Moscow, and a key architect of the reset policy. McFaul, Vondra recalls, went "ballistic" over the letter, accusing him and his cohorts of "Russophobia."[30] Since at least the time of Napoleon, this charge has been hurled at practically anyone expressing skepticism of Russian foreign policy. But it packs a particular sting when applied to Central and Eastern Europeans, whose experience of living under Russian subjugation allegedly discounts their analysis. Balts, Czechs, Poles, Ukrainians, and others from the region—goes the usual explanation—carry too much historical and emotional baggage to be credible observers—unlike their Western counterparts, who can evaluate matters dispassionately from the safe preserves of Berlin, Paris, and Washington. In some foreign policy circles, it is a sign of sophistication to scorn the former president of Georgia, Mikhail Saakashvili, as a Russia-obsessed "hothead" responsible for bringing war to his country. For all his faults, it was the much-maligned Saakashvili who, as far back as 2009, when policy makers were confidently proclaiming a new era in East-West relations, "stressed repeatedly" to a U.S. Defense Department official that Russia would invade Crimea.[31] Given the way Russia has behaved in the quarter-century since the USSR collapsed, growing up behind the Iron Curtain ought to be considered more a marker of wisdom and prescience, not sentimentality and paranoia, in terms of one's analytical bona fides.

From the moment the reset policy was officially inaugurated in March 2009 with a clumsy photo-op featuring Secretary of State Hillary Clinton and Russian Foreign Minister Sergei Lavrov cheerfully pressing a red button mistakenly imprinted with the Russian word for "overcharge," Moscow has played the West for fools. Before Barack Obama even became president, Russia was in active violation of the Intermediate-Range Nuclear Forces Treaty, an agreement that prohibits the testing of ground-launched missiles.[32] In 2010, when the FBI uncovered ten Russian sleeper agents, some trying to penetrate the U.S. defense and high-tech sectors, the scandal was quickly swept under the rug so as not to let it puncture the positive narrative the administration had constructed. When fugitive NSA leaker Edward Snowden mysteriously turned up in Moscow three years later, Putin showed his appreciation by ignoring Obama's request that he extradite history's greatest pilferer and disseminator of American national security secrets, granting Snowden asylum. Whatever marginal gains came from getting the Russians to make symbolic reductions in their nuclear stockpile, they hardly outweigh the price: granting Moscow the diplomatic breathing space to harden domestic subjugation, refine its propaganda instruments, and invest heavily in the military modernization that laid the groundwork for the invasion of Ukraine.

The reset's central problem was that both sides had completely different understandings of its purpose. Washington invested the process with substance and optimism, seeing diplomatic rapprochement as the opportunity for wholesale enhancement of relations. By contrast, the Kremlin saw it as a means of solidifying its authoritarian rule at home and girding itself for muscle flexing abroad. A constant refrain of the Obama administration, in response to those who challenged its rosy perceptions of Russia, was to accuse critics of being ill equipped to navigate a "post-American world" of rising non-Western powers. When 2012 Republican presidential candidate Mitt Romney called Russia America's "number one geopolitical foe," Obama quipped, "The 1980s are now calling to ask for their foreign policy back." But Romney's analysis was fully consonant with that of the Central and Eastern European statesmen who had warned of Russia's resurgence. Five years after the release of their letter, a genuinely flabbergasted secretary of state John Kerry tacitly conceded its prescience while watching helplessly as Russia prepared to annex Crimea. "You just don't in the 21st century behave in 19th-century fashion by invading another country on completely trumped up pretext," he pleaded, his recognition of Putin's atavistic bellicosity an almost verbatim repetition of what the twenty-two European leaders had warned of back in 2009. Emotive congressional testimony to the contrary, countries, authoritarian ones in particular, "behave" as they wish, often in illegal or immoral ways. Declaring otherwise does not make it so. And unless a concert of rule-abiding countries prevents bad actors from doing illegal or immoral things, world order collapses. In a 2008 presidential debate, Obama telegraphed what would soon become his style of foreign policymaking-by-remonstration when he declared it "absolutely important" that the West "explain to the Russians that you cannot be a twenty-first-century superpower . . . and act like a twentieth-century dictatorship." Over the ensuing eight years, it seemed to have escaped Obama administration officials, who prided themselves on nuance, that Putin may be a man of *both* past and present, using postmodern means to achieve premodern ends in what has become the *modus operandi* of twenty-first-century dictatorships.

It was not until Russian hackers attacked the Democratic National Committee's computer servers, however, that many reset proponents belatedly conceded they had misjudged the Russian regime. According to private cybersecurity firms and American intelligence sources, two groups of Internet hackers connected to Russian military intelligence stole tens of thousands of internal DNC communications over a yearlong period beginning in the summer of 2015. They then presumably passed along the material to Wikileaks, which publicized a selection of the messages on the eve of the Democratic National Convention in a manner designed to embarrass the presidential campaign of Hillary Clinton.[33] This act of cyber-espionage signifies an audacious new stage in Russian political subversion against the West. It was no secret that the Kremlin rightly viewed the Republican nominee as more amenable to its foreign policy aims. Throughout the campaign, Donald Trump—elected to office with the full and open connivance of a hostile foreign power—repeatedly praised Putin, expressed his desire to "get along" with Russia, denigrated NATO as "obsolete" and a drain on American resources, and even suggested that, were he to become president, the United States would join those paragons of respect for international law—Cuba and Zimbabwe—in formally recognizing Russia's violent annexation of Crimea. Hacking a political party's servers and releasing sensitive information to affect the outcome of an election is the sort of meddling that the Kremlin had previously only carried out in former Soviet republics. That it has helped destabilize the United States in such fashion ought to remove any doubt Western policy makers may have about the nefarious aims and unscrupulous practices of the Putin regime.

One man to whom Russian behavior came as no surprise is Toomas Hendrik Ilves, who stepped down as president of Estonia in 2016 after having served in the job for ten years. Ilves spent the past decade traveling the world warning about the threat Russia poses not only to his country but also to the whole Western-written global rulebook. A voracious reader and technology buff who lives on a farm that has been owned by his family (with a brief respite during the Soviet occupation) for generations, Ilves would rather do other things than bang on about Russian troublemaking, but as the leader of a small country in Eastern Europe he has little choice. Born to Estonian émigré parents in Sweden, raised in New Jersey, and educated at Columbia and the University of Pennsylvania, the perennially bow-tied Ilves ran Radio Free Europe's Estonian Service in the 1980s and cheerfully describes himself as a "Cold Warrior." As adept at lecturing on cybersecurity as he is reading Latin texts and discussing classic rock music, Ilves freely dispenses the sort of brutally honest observations that most statesmen of his rank avoid saying aloud. He's probably the only world leader to liken the imperiled state of the international legal and security order to an infamous music festival gone deadly awry. "Ladies and gentlemen, Peace, Love and Woodstock is over," Ilves declared in the fall of 2014. "We've just had our Altamont."[34]

If Russia plays the Hell's Angels in this analogy, NATO is the police: underequipped, underfunded, and not visible enough to have a deterrent effect. "The Donetsk People's Republic is better armed than some NATO members," Ilves remarks, commenting on the Russian-backed rebel army waging war in eastern Ukraine. He's entitled to complain, because Estonia is only one of a handful of NATO countries that spends the minimum 2 percent of GDP on defense that the alliance requests of its members. Wherever he speaks, Ilves can be counted on to recite the litany of international security arrangements Russia has violated, from the 1945 United Nations Charter (outlawing territorial annexations) to the 1975 Helsinki Final Act (stating that borders can be changed only through "peaceful means and by agreement"), the 1990 Charter for a New Europe (recognizing "the freedom of States to choose their own security arrangements"), and the 1994 Budapest Memorandum (guaranteeing Ukraine's territorial integrity in exchange for its relinquishing what was then the world's third-largest nuclear weapons stockpile). Russia, or its legal predecessor, the USSR, signed all of these agreements: It has since violated every single one of them.

Ilves mentions these accords not to demonstrate their uselessness (most signatories scrupulously abide by them) but to stress that Russian belligerence and rule breaking, not Western "provocation" or "encirclement," are to blame for the current predicament. Since the eruption of the Ukraine crisis, a group of influential critics, led by the University of Chicago political scientist John Mearsheimer, have contended that the accession of former Eastern bloc countries such as the Czech Republic, Poland, and the Baltics into NATO justifiably frightened Russia and "provoked" it to invade and occupy its neighbors.[35] "Wasn't consolidating a democratic Russia more important than bringing the Czech Navy into NATO?" sneered *New York Times* columnist Thomas Friedman after Russia's 2008 invasion of Georgia. Reviving this complaint weeks before the annexation of Crimea, Friedman declared that NATO expansion "remains one of the dumbest things we've ever done and, of course, laid the groundwork for Putin's rise."[36]

On the contrary, it was the Russian regime's ideology, behavior, and rhetoric that provided the impulse for NATO expansion, not the other way around. Far from representing a historic error, the enlargement of NATO into Central and Eastern Europe has been one of the few unmitigated success stories of American foreign policy as it consolidated democracy and security on a continent once scarred by total war. Not only do attacks on NATO enlargement ignore the centuries-long history of Russian expansion but they also mistake victim for perpetrator—as if the Hitler-Stalin Pact, the 1956 invasion of Hungary, or the 1968 crushing of the Prague Spring had never happened. Russia's fear of "encirclement" by the EU or NATO is what's known in psychology as "projection," the phenomenon whereby one denies one's own harmful behavior while ascribing it onto others.

Yet the people running the Kremlin appear to hold these views sincerely. Released in December 2015, Russia's revised National Security Strategy paints the West as Moscow's main adversary, blaming it for "creating seats of tension in the Eurasian region" and "exerting a negative influence on the realization of Russian national interests."[37] This document only put into writing what Russian officialdom had long been saying in public. "The policy of containment was not invented yesterday," Putin averred in 2014.[38] "It has been carried out against our country for many years, always, for decades if not centuries," long before NATO was even a glimmer in Dean Acheson's eye. Putin appears to ignore the fact that the only times Russia has been invaded since 1900—in World Wars I and II—the West fought on its side and granted its postwar territorial demands. As for Russia's truncated, post-Soviet borders, they were not imposed on Russia from afar, as the terms of Versailles were enforced on the Germans; Moscow acceded to every claim of independence made by its present-day successor states, and it was the Russian Federation itself that led the USSR's dissolution.

Russian belligerence, rather, makes NATO expansion a self-fulfilling prophecy. Estonia wouldn't feel the need to join a collective security alliance if its eastern neighbor weren't so menacing. And NATO has repeatedly gone out of its way to conciliate Moscow, starting with its 1994 acceptance of Russia into the Partnership for Peace, a military-to-military cooperation program that the alliance operates for nonmember states. The NATO-Russia Council, a consultative organ, was founded in the same spirit of transparency. In 2009, when relations with Russia were tense but not nearly as bad as they are now, even Radoslaw Sikorski, the former foreign minister of Poland and the furthest thing from a dove on Russia, hypothesized about its one day joining NATO. The fault for tensions between Russia and the West lies with the Russian leadership, which refuses to acknowledge the crimes of its past, embraces a zero-sum view of the world, and respects the principle of state sovereignty only when doing so serves its own interests. Governments that don't conform to Kremlin dictates can expect to be targeted with subversion, economic blackmail, invasion, or, as of 2014, annexation. To understand why the present-day East-West tensions are not inevitable, consider how another large, formerly imperial power has earned the respect of those it once conquered. Despite its Nazi past, Germany today ranks as the most admired country in the world. None of its neighbors fear it. What is stopping Russia from earning similar trust and esteem?

Russia's post-imperial syndrome is unlikely to be cured any time soon, regardless of who rules it. The system that Putin created implicates too many dependents on its largesse, and the chauvinistic fervor whipped up by the near-monopolistic state media has so thoroughly permeated society that it's foolish to expect a liberal democratic rebirth after Putin leaves power. Until the KGB-mafia deep state withers away, Russia will remain a corrupt and predatory country.

To be sure, Russia comes nowhere close to matching the combined military strength, power projection, or technological capabilities of NATO. Russia's GDP, to take but one measure, is just 1/32 that of the United States. But such broad metrics tell us nothing about the methods by which Moscow is trying to undermine the alliance or about its chances of success. As history shows, nations in decline are often the least risk-averse. Though Russia doesn't want a conflict with NATO collectively, it can and does play members against one another to increase its leverage. One way of doing this is to instill a sense of fear and resignation by persuading some members of the alliance that other members are low-hanging fruit for Russian predation and not worth defending.

As NATO has moved eastward, its military footprint has not followed. The reason offered for this by some Western policy makers is that edging alliance forces closer to Russia is threatening to Moscow. But as a result, the region where the alliance is most vulnerable, namely Poland and the Baltic States, receive the least protection. President Ilves points to the Polish town of Suwalki, located in a narrow sliver of land between Lithuania, Poland, Belarus, and Kaliningrad (the heavily militarized Russian exclave wedged between Poland and Lithuania), as a particular area of concern. Russia could quite easily seal off the Baltic States by storming this sliver of territory.

Cold War–era "deterrence by denial," the strategy of deterring an attack by convincing an adversary that launching one would be in vain, is therefore applicable today. For such a strategy to work, however, the entire alliance must have skin in the game. Estonian army chief Riho Terras confidently asserts that were Russian special forces, sans insignia, to enter his country with the aim of stirring up trouble as they did in Crimea, the men under his command would not sit on their hands. "You shoot the first one to appear," he says.[39] That's exactly what an Estonian military chief should say, but the next logical question is what the Estonians plan to do, after having shot "the first" enemy soldier, when 100 or 1,000 more follow. A strategy of deterrence by denial would drastically reduce the chances of such a contingency by making it abundantly clear to the Russians that any attempt to undermine the sovereignty of a NATO member would entail serious repercussions.

It is largely France and Germany that have resisted meaningful eastern deployments for fear of provoking Russia. They routinely cite a clause in the 1997 Founding Act on Mutual Relations, Cooperation, and Security between NATO and the Russian Federation, which promises that NATO will avoid "additional permanent stationing of substantial combat forces" in Central and Eastern Europe. Yet they ignore the language that immediately precedes that phrase, which conditions NATO restraint on maintenance of "the current and foreseeable security environment." The "current . . . security environment" at the time the Founding Act was signed featured such conditions as "NATO and Russia do not consider each other as adversaries"; that both sides have a "shared commitment to build a stable, peaceful and undivided Europe, whole and free"; and that "Russia will exercise similar restraint in its conventional force deployments in Europe."

That the security environment in Europe has changed radically since 1997 is due entirely to Russian aggression. Russia has repeatedly violated both the letter and the spirit of the Founding Act, rendering null and void the rationale for limitations on NATO deployments and permanent bases in Eastern Europe. Nonetheless, many insist that the West should uphold its obligations under the Founding Act regardless of how Russia behaves. "Where Russia has become very unpredictable and is misbehaving, to say the least, and is tearing up the rule book, I think it's up to us to show that we are the guys who are predictable," says Jamie Shea, NATO's Deputy Assistant Secretary General for Emerging Security Challenges. "We keep to the rule book."[40] At some point, however, keeping to the rule book becomes the riskier strategy. Russia has betrayed the understanding behind the Founding Act and shows no interest in upholding it. The wholly legitimate security needs of NATO's most exposed members should take precedence over fruitless attempts to abate its irreconcilable differences with Moscow. It is far less expensive to deter aggression than to respond after territory has been seized.

Russia's invasion of Ukraine and threatening moves in Eastern Europe— challenges to NATO's core purpose of territorial defense—took the alliance by surprise. Beginning in the early 1990s, a hasty triumphalism led many to predict that NATO would have to engage in missions abroad or risk extinction. "Out of area or out of business" was the refrain one heard from the lips of Western policy makers. Heeding this advice, the alliance waged aerial bombardment campaigns to prevent genocide in the Balkans, launched a counterinsurgency war in Afghanistan, and carried out another series of bombing raids over Libya. Everyone seemed to believe that NATO's raison d'être—keeping the Russians out of Europe—had become obsolete. But as the West slashed defense budgets and relocated resources to Asia and the Middle East, Russia underwent a massive conventional arms buildup to the point that there now exists a perilous imbalance on NATO's eastern flank, where, over the past decade, Russia has conducted a series of foreboding military exercises. "*Zapad* (West) 2009" simulated a nuclear attack on Warsaw; a subsequent "*Zapad*" maneuver four years later incorporated military units from the former Soviet republic of Belarus. Today, Russia can deploy 60,000 soldiers to its western border in as little as seventy-two hours. "The image that Russian official sources convey is that they're preparing for large-scale interstate war," says Johan Norberg of the Swedish Defense Research Agency. "This is not about peacekeeping or counterinsurgency."[41]

NATO has been slow to respond. During the Cold War, hundreds of thousands of U.S. soldiers were stationed in more than 800 bases across Western Europe. Today the number hovers below 70,000, including sailors and airmen, none of whom are permanently based in the territory of new NATO members. "Steadfast Jazz," an exercise undertaken in the fall of 2013, involved only 160 American soldiers; meanwhile, NATO's "high-readiness task force," created after the annexation of Crimea to assuage the fears of the alliance's eastern members, can deploy only about 5,000 soldiers within seven days. Recent war game simulations held under the auspices of the RAND Corporation found that a Russian attack on the Baltics would be "a disaster for NATO," resulting in Russian forces "at the gates or actually entering Riga, Tallinn, or both" in as little as thirty-six hours.[42] "We need to learn to fight total war again," says the Danish colonel in charge of a new NATO command in Lithuania.[43] Philip Breedlove, who served as NATO's

Supreme Allied Commander during the Russian annexation of Crimea and the launching of its war in Eastern Ukraine, writes that "neither the United States' military nor those of its allies are adequately prepared to rapidly respond to overt military aggression."[44]

In addition to their conventional arms buildup, Russian leaders have begun to use unprecedentedly loose language about the deployment of nuclear weapons. At a March 2015 meeting, the Russians shocked their Western interlocutors by threatening a "spectrum of responses from nuclear to non-military" if NATO were to station forces in the Baltic States. When asked during a television interview the same month if he was prepared to deploy nuclear weapons during the Crimea operation, Putin responded, "We were ready to do this." This chest beating forms a key component of Russia's oxymoronically named "escalate to de-escalate strategy," in which Moscow would utilize "tactical" nuclear weapons against NATO forces in the early stages of a military confrontation in the hope that doing so would persuade the alliance to back down and limit conflict to a geographically small piece of territory that the Russians would then be able to control.[45]

Disturbingly, Russia's aggressive behavior has not translated into broader public support for NATO in the West. For reasons that are detailed later in this book, favorable attitudes toward NATO in Germany—the alliance's largest and wealthiest European member—dropped from 73 percent in 2009 to 55 percent in 2015. A poll taken that same year asking whether NATO should defend an ally under attack from Russia found 47 percent of Spaniards, 53 percent of French, 51 percent of Italians, and 58 percent of Germans saying it should not, essentially disavowing Article 5.[46] Jeremy Corbyn, the left-wing leader of the British Labor Party, refused to say whether NATO should defend an ally invaded by Russia, whereas Donald Trump, then campaigning for the American presidency, insisted only member states that pay an unspecified "fair share" to the U.S. Treasury are entitled to alliance support. This reluctance to extend solidarity to the alliance's eastern members suggests buyer's remorse after NATO's 2004 enlargement. Six years after the Baltics joined NATO, a cable from the U.S. Embassy in Berlin reported that, "Germany continues to regard proposed NATO contingency planning to defend the Balts against possible Russian aggression as counterproductive and unnecessary."[47] But what is the point of having countries join a collective defense organization if there is no plan for their defense?

With the end of the Cold War, strategists on both sides of the old Iron Curtain deemed passé a whole raft of institutions, strategic theorems, and intellectual currents born of the struggle against Soviet communism—from Radio Free Europe/Radio Liberty to NATO to the concept of nuclear deterrence. We had emerged from the age of ideology, they argued, and it was time to supplant the bipolar order with more "inclusive" and equitable arrangements. As early as 1987, Mikhail Gorbachev advocated Soviet entry into what he called "the common European home," thereby ending the "division of the continent into military blocs." Ten years later, Boris Yeltsin hoped that Russia would one day join "greater Europe," a place "without dividing lines; a Europe in which no single state will be able to impose its will on any other."[48]

Incorporating Russia, under its current regime, into "greater Europe" means transcending the Western-created, alliance-based structures that shaped the postwar world order. Downplaying or disregarding altogether the wide array of fundamental differences between Russia and the West—on matters ranging from respect for international law to individual rights—is a feature, not a bug, of such appeals. Fuzzy and vague talk about the "convergence" of national interests and global "interdependence" provides altruistic cover for what is essentially a back-door effort to right the power "imbalance" that was the result of the Soviet Union losing the Cold War. A world without political or military blocs has usually been the territory of pacifist utopians; Russian iterations of the idea, needless to say, are not part of this idealistic intellectual tradition. Complaints by Moscow regarding the "unfairness" of the current international system must be seen for what they are: attempts to restore the power and influence Russia lost when its empire collapsed.

However sincere his predecessors' assertions of Russia's natural place in the community of Western democracies might have been, Putin has barely made even a pretense of sharing their vision. Ultimately, he is motivated by a desire to divide Europe from America, and divide Europeans among themselves. Instigating a Russia-France-Germany "triangle" in opposition to the U.S.-led war in Iraq (splitting the two major continental powers from the United Kingdom, Spain, and most of Central and Eastern Europe) was an early indication of his ability to sow discord within the West. Around the same time, French president Jacques Chirac and German chancellor Gerhard Schröder proposed a "European Security and Defense Union," a military alliance that would exclude Washington, to parallel and perhaps one day succeed NATO. A 2008 speech in Berlin by Russian president Dmitri Medvedev, laying the groundwork for what later became the "European Security Treaty," expanded on this idea of diluting the Atlantic Alliance. Lamenting how "Europe's current architecture still bears the stamp of an ideology inherited from the past," namely liberal internationalism, and "a bloc politics approach that continues by inertia," Medvedev suggested a new set of institutions embracing the "unity between the whole Euro-Atlantic area from Vancouver to Vladivostok."[49] Kremlin-aligned analyst Fyodor Lukyanov praised Medvedev for issuing a broadside against a Western narrative promoting "the expansion of Western institutions rather than the creation of something new and universal."[50] The following year, Russian Foreign Minister Sergei Lavrov suggested that the Organization for Security and Cooperation in Europe (OSCE, a multilateral institution specializing in election observation and human rights monitoring of which Russia is a member) replace NATO as guarantor of a "common security space" stretching across the entire Northern Hemisphere.[51] Repeatedly invoking the phrase "indivisibility of security," by which he meant "the obligation to refrain from strengthening one's own security at the expense of the security of others," Lavrov essentially argued that any military alliance on the European continent which excludes countries from membership is by nature a threat to Russia.

Along with "indivisibility of security," another standard term in this jejune strategic vernacular is "mutual security." As distinguished from NATO's model of "shared security," by which individual members of an exclusive alliance partake in collective efforts to defend themselves from external threats, "mutual security" infers arrangements between individual nations. It is a euphemism for the concept of "spheres of influence," which gives powerful countries like America and Russia the freedom to behave as they wish in their respective regions while consigning weaker countries to limited sovereignty. As the world's largest landmass, with borders spanning from the Arctic to Eastern Europe, the Middle East, Central Asia, and the Pacific Ocean, Russia has every reason to be content with a world order that confines American power projection to the Western Hemisphere.

Like many Russian leaders before him, Putin balances naked aggression with diplomatic overtures to the West. "Our common task should be the development of a system of equal security for all states, a system that is adequate to modern threats, a system built on a regional and global, non-bloc basis," he declared at the 2015 Victory Day celebrations in Moscow. In a recent documentary aired on Russian television titled "World Order," Putin described Europeans as "vassals" following orders "from across the ocean."[52] Although "we don't expect our European partners to give up their Euro-Atlantic orientation," he said, they should "unite with Russia" to resolve "economic, political, security . . . problems. We are ready to work with them and aren't about to pout about the sanctions." In a German TV interview commemorating the twentieth anniversary of the Berlin Wall's collapse, he observed, "Germany and the German people were hostages in the struggle between the two superpowers and occupation forces both in the West and in the East. I would like to emphasize: both in the West and in the East . . . Germany became a kind of sacrifice card in the struggle between these superpowers."[53] In addition to drawing a moral equivalence between the West and the USSR, this comment sent an important, if subtle, message to Putin's German audience. Referring to them as "hostages in the struggle between" America and the Soviet Union whose unfortunate predicament was the result of forces beyond their control, he cleverly validated Germans' sense that their country is a perpetual victim of outside machinations.

These arguments are seductive to Westerners who have convinced themselves that the sort of ideological battles that defined the previous century are now permanently part of the past. In Europe and, to a lesser extent, the United States, prominent representatives of the liberal internationalist and "realist" schools of foreign policy argue that, whatever the current rift in relations between Russia and the West, it is ultimately overshadowed by the two sides' common interests. The fundamental irreconcilability of Western and Russian values and interests is downplayed at the expense of what's portrayed as being ultimately a power struggle between two blocs. Westerners seeking to tame American "overreach" have much in common with Kremlin strategists, even if they have major differences over how to achieve a post-American world order or what it would look like. When Medvedev had the gall to announce his European Security Treaty just months after Russia's invasion of Georgia, the EU's foreign minister at the time replied that the proposal "deserves to be taken seriously." On the "realist" Western side, meanwhile, Tom Graham, a Russia specialist and former official in the George W. Bush administration and currently a managing director at Henry Kissinger's consulting firm, praised the Medvedev proposal, concluding, "If this ultimately leads to the subsuming of NATO into a larger structure over the long term, we should be prepared to accept that."[54] When Barack Obama rose before the well of the United Nations General Assembly in 2009 to declare that "alignments of nations rooted in the cleavages of a long-gone Cold War make no sense in an interconnected world," he probably didn't recognize how closely his idealistic pontification adhered to the Kremlin's cynical rhetoric.

And when Russia, using the airy language of internationalism and cooperation, insists on being regarded as "an equal" in the international system, it's not asking to be the geopolitical equivalent of an adult—to sit at the proverbial big table and be treated like any other responsible member of the democratic family of nations. Earning that privilege, after all, entails measurable tasks (modernization and liberalization) and responsibilities (respecting rules and norms) that the Russian regime isn't prepared to shoulder. What the Kremlin really intends by driving divisions within NATO and eventually "subsuming" it into a broader, "pan-European" security architecture is to contest the very validity of the West's first principles, to revert to a world order where might makes right. If it cannot neuter NATO with an attack on alliance territory that will prove the worthlessness of Article 5, it can try the institutional route, diluting the West's alliance structure, legal norms, and political cohesiveness from within through bribery, coercion, subversion, and disinformation. Worse than letting the fox guard the henhouse would be letting him live inside.

It's neither an exaggerated sense of fear, nor anti-Russian prejudice, nor hankering for American global omnipotence that motivates a more robust Western response to Russian aggression. Improved relations with the West, up to and including membership in the EU and NATO, should *always* be accessible as a civilizational option for Russia, the critical word here being "option." Joining the West and embracing its liberal values, consensual politics, and humane norms is a choice Russia has had every opportunity to make. If it selects the Western path and adheres to its standards, as President Ilves, Sasha Vondra, and many other ostensible "Russophobes" genuinely wish, then Europe and the larger Western world would undoubtedly welcome it with open arms. But that welcome is contingent on an understanding that the Euro-Atlantic community is more than just a geographical space: It is a group of societies defined by shared values. And the prerequisite for Russia's entering the transatlantic community is that it demonstrate respect for those values. Embracing notions of "mutual security," "indivisible security," and other voguish concepts designed to paper over the fundamental rifts underlying Russian antagonism toward the West would sacrifice those values in exchange for improved relations with a criminal regime whose idea of peaceful coexistence includes coercion and invasion of its neighbors.

Hungary: Democracy without Democrats

Who controls the past, controls the future; who controls the present controls the past.

George Orwell, *1984*

The winners will be those who can better understand the past, and who can come to the right conclusions more swiftly and more courageously.

Viktor Orbán, Hungarian prime minister, July 25, 2015

A STONE'S THROW FROM BUDAPEST'S majestic Gothic revival parliament building, Freedom Square teems with monuments attesting to Hungary's turbulent twentieth century. Dominating the north side of the plaza is a giant obelisk constructed by the Soviet Union and dedicated to the city's Red Army liberators. A few paces south one finds a statue of Imre Nagy, the executed hero of Hungary's 1956 anti-Soviet revolt, standing on a bridge looking forlornly on parliament. At the southern end of the square, outside a Calvinist church, stares a bust of Admiral Miklós Horthy, the authoritarian regent under whose reign Hungary passed the first anti-Semitic law of twentieth-century Europe in 1920, allied with the Axis Powers, and deported some half-million Jews to Auschwitz in the largest and swiftest mass transfer of the Final Solution. In the middle of it all, a bronzed Ronald Reagan walks briskly toward the nearby U.S. Embassy.

With its abundant memorials, this one plaza commemorates the grand sweep of Europe's most influential twentieth-century ideologies: communism, nationalism, fascism, and democracy.

On the Sunday morning of July 20, 2014, police cordoned off Freedom Square while construction workers put the finishing touches on an addition to this urban tableau already brimming with historical tributes: the Memorial to the Victims of the German Occupation. From the moment its construction was announced, following an opaque artistic competition lacking public consultation, it had been the subject of heated dispute. Beginning with its very title, which labels the unimpeded movement of German soldiers onto friendly territory an "occupation," the memorial absolves Hungarians of complicity in the Holocaust. Depicting the Archangel Gabriel (described in the plans as "the man of God, symbol of Hungary") under attack from a sharp-clawed German imperial eagle, it portrays the Hungarian nation as a collective victim of Nazi predation. This distortion of history obscures both the specifically anti-Jewish nature of the Holocaust and the Hungarian state's active collaboration in mass murder. Randolph Braham, professor emeritus at the City University of New York and himself a Hungarian Holocaust survivor, writes about the role played by Hungarian authorities in the crime: "With Horthy still at the helm and providing the symbol of national sovereignty, the approximately 200,000 Hungarian policemen, gendarmes, civil servants, and 'patriotic' volunteers had collaborated in the anti-Jewish drive with a routine and efficiency that impressed even the relatively few SS who had served as 'advisors.'"[1] So able and willing were the Nazis' Hungarian accomplices that Adolf Eichmann, the SS official in charge of deporting the country's Jews to the death camps, managed to oversee the gruesome task with just 200 Germans at his command.

Had the nationalist government of Prime Minister Viktor Orbán not spent the previous four years conducting a campaign of historical distortion regarding the country's Holocaust history, one might be more charitable about its motives for constructing this monument. Through a set of government-sponsored historical institutes, publicly funded documentaries, revisions to school curricula, bestowal of state honors to extreme right-wing figures, and erections of public monuments and museum exhibitions, the Orbán administration has disseminated a narrative that minimizes

Memorial to the Victims of the German Occupation, Budapest.

Hungarian culpability in the extermination of some half-million Jews and rehabilitates Horthy's reputation from that of opportunistic Nazi ally to selfless defender of national independence.[2]

Opposition to this revisionist crusade reached a critical phase in January 2014, around the same time that plans for the occupation memorial were unveiled. After the director of a government-subsidized historical center phlegmatically referred to the 1941 deportations of Jews living under Hungarian authority as a "police action against aliens," outraged leaders of the Hungarian Jewish community announced they would cease cooperation with the government on activities marking the seventieth-anniversary Holocaust Remembrance Year. Orbán decided to postpone work on the monument until after national elections in April, at which point consultations on its design would resume. But just two days after his party, Fidesz, secured a landslide victory, Orbán reneged on his promise and workers returned to the construction site, which by then had to be patrolled by police to keep protestors at bay. In an open letter to Orbán, thirty members of the

U.S. Congress stated that while "Hungary is an important ally and partner of the United States," it should "build an appropriate memorial that tells the entire Hungarian story of the Nazi Occupation, not one that whitewashes the truth."[3] Orbán was unmoved. The Hungarian government completed its controversial memorial in the dead of night, slipping the bronze angel and eagle into the square disguised in metal foil.

Budapest's Memorial to the Victims of the German Occupation is distinguished not only by its revisionist message but also its vulgar design. Holocaust memorials tend to be solemn and subtly allegorical. Around the corner from the iconic Brandenburg Gate, Berlin's more accurately named Memorial to the Murdered Jews of Europe—2,711 black concrete stelae arranged in a mazelike pattern on a sloping plaza—immediately unsettles visitors with its figurative representation of the Holocaust's unfathomable depth. Elsewhere in Budapest, "Shoes on the Danube Bank" displays sixty pairs of iron footwear fastened to the river's stone embankment, marking the last standing place of Jews who, every day during the 1944–1945 winter, were ordered to take off their shoes before being shot by Arrow Cross militiamen, the Nazis' Hungarian accomplices.

When a noted Hungarian art historian wrote a letter to Orbán questioning the occupation memorial's meaning and artistic merit, the prime minister replied, "Didactic historical works of art, which were the norm in my youth, have more of a depressive impression on me."[4] This was a strange defense of the memorial, for it is nothing if not didactic. Indeed, it's striking how a monument built by a government that claims for itself the exclusive legacy of Hungarian anticommunist resistance so much resembles a work of socialist realism. By obscuring Jewish victimhood entirely and ascribing total innocence to Hungarians and total evil to Germans, the memorial is as factually deceptive and politically exploitative as any Stalinist icon. Just as communists downplayed or ignored the anti-Semitic intent of the Holocaust in order to claim the Nazis' victims as martyrs to the cause of "antifascism," the Hungarian right asserts that all Hungarians were equal victims of a foreign-imposed tyranny. Characterizing opposition to the memorial as deriving from "the pub counter of cheap political pushing and shoving that is practically unavoidable these days," Orbán implied that complaints about historical truth are in actuality fig leaves for domestic political opponents intent on delegitimizing his government abroad. After lecturing his correspondent that the "invaders" of Hungary were not "Nazis" but "Germans," whose collective and eternal guilt the memorial appears to endorse through its symbolic use of the eagle that today appears on the German federal government escutcheon, Orbán avoided drawing a similar conclusion about Hungarian blameworthiness, stating that "it can hardly be disputed that Germany bears responsibility for what happened in Hungary after March 19, 1944. . . . We cannot bear a responsibility that is not ours to bear."

If such a highly subjective claim as one insisting that Germany bears all responsibility for the Hungarian Holocaust can "hardly be disputed" in Hungary, it's only because the government has consecrated it in law. One of the first things Fidesz did after winning a parliamentary supermajority in 2010 was rewrite the constitution. Today, the Preamble of the Fundamental Law of Hungary states:

> We date the restoration of our country's self-determination, lost on the nineteenth day of March 1944, from the second day of May 1990, when the first freely elected organ of popular representation was formed. We shall consider this date to be the beginning of our country's new democracy and constitutional order.

By affirming that Hungary lost its "self-determination" the day German soldiers entered Budapest, the constitution pardons Hungarians and Hungarian institutions for what transpired over the proceeding forty-five years. According to Hungarian historian Eva Balogh, Germany's "occupation" of Hungary is better understood as "a troop movement within the territories of military allies" because Germany initially allowed Horthy to remain as head of state and left nearly all government functions in the control of Hungarian authorities.[5] With no notable acts of official resistance and scarcely any German officers to oversee them, Hungarian police and gendarmerie rounded up hundreds of thousands of their fellow Jewish citizens and deported them to Auschwitz. Denying that the Hungarian state bears responsibility for this crime, Orbán admits only that individual officials—

and not the Hungarian government—"collaborated," a word choice implying that Hungary was an enemy, not an ally, of Nazi Germany.

Orbán's defense of the occupation memorial was also notable for studiously dodging the fact that the main victims of the Nazis in Hungary, as everywhere else in Europe, were Jews. "The victims," he wrote, "whether Orthodox, Christian or without faith, became the victims of a dictatorship that embodied an anti-Christian school of thought"—essentially claiming that Christians were as much victims of the Nazis as were Jews, a word his letter does not use even once. Memorializing amorphous "victims of the German occupation" in this style, Braham writes, is a way to "generalize the Holocaust by homogenizing the losses of Jewry with those incurred by the military forces and the civilian population during the war. The equation of the martyrdom of armed soldiers, who died as heroes in the service of their country, and of Christian civilians, who were killed in the wake of the hostilities, with that of the Jews, who were murdered irrespective of their age or sex, is clearly politically motivated." Orbán concluded his missive with this considered opinion: "From a moral perspective and with regard to the historical content of its system of allegories, this work of art is accurate and flawless," a curious way to describe a morally and aesthetically repulsive piece of propaganda.

Immediately after the occupation memorial was finished—and presented to the public, unusually, without any public ceremony—a counter-display known as the "Living Memorial" sprang up just steps away along the opposite sidewalk. Flowers, candles, suitcases, and other personal items now cover the pavement in honor of Hungarian Holocaust victims. Black-and-white photographs of relatives lost at Auschwitz and laminated placards affixed to the metal bars of the guardrail alert passersby to the politicized abuse of history before them. It was here, in the summer of 2015, that the celebrated Hungarian conductor Adam Fischer led 1,000 people in singing the German and French national anthems, followed by those of Hungary and Slovakia—"coupling the anthems of peoples who for generations were pitted against each other as enemies, but today in the European Union live together in peace and cooperation." When I visited Freedom Square one Friday evening about a month after Fischer's recital, an eighty-seven-year-old

Holocaust survivor sat directly opposite the memorial addressing a small group of people. A rotating crew of citizens stand watch over the Living Memorial to prevent its defacement by neo-Nazis. I asked that evening's attendant, a man who appeared to be in his late fifties, a gentile, why he was spending a beautiful Budapest summer night in what seemed like lonely, futile protest. "History is more complicated than this falsifying, simplifying monument," he answered.

Second to Russia, no European country is manipulating its history for political purposes more egregiously than Hungary. In both places, rewriting the past is done with an eye to the future, as governments inculcate their citizenries with nationalism, irredentism, and intolerance and then marshal these attitudes in service of the state. The clashing historical narratives embodied by the dueling memorials of Freedom Square have engaged the wider public in a debate reaching far beyond the usual esoteric academic circles. As Hungary creeps further into authoritarianism, its revisionism has worrisome implications for Europe's future.

All societies have cleavages. Most stem from differences in class, religion, tribe, race, or ethnicity, and these cleavages are not mutually exclusive. Throughout Southeast Asia, for instance, the Chinese merchant class represents the interweaving of economic-based cleavages with ethnic ones. In the more ethnically homogeneous countries of Eastern Europe, meanwhile, political division is largely determined by both economics and geography, with competitive, liberal urban centers squaring off against conservative, rural peripheries. Although the city-country cleavage certainly applies to Hungary, there exists another, more significant, and largely overlooked one: conflicting approaches to history.

Visiting Hungary today, one is struck by the prevalence of maps, postcards, posters, bumper stickers, and other ephemera displaying an enlarged Hungarian landmass encompassing parts of present-day Romania, Serbia, Croatia, and all of Slovakia. This was the "Greater Hungary" of the Austro-Hungarian Empire. In the post–World War I Treaty of Trianon, the victorious powers divested newly independent Hungary of two-thirds of its land and one-third of its population. Although some ethnic Hungarians (known as Magyars) in these areas emigrated to the territorially diminished Republic of Hungary, more than three million found themselves citizens of other countries. For Hungarian nationalists, this loss of territory, though hardly unique in Europe, was an earth-shattering trauma that sears their collective conscience like the phantom pain of a severed limb. According to the website of the government-funded "Veritas Institute," Trianon is "20th-century Hungary's greatest tragedy, the wounds of which remain unhealed even today," a greater tragedy, apparently, than the extermination of a half-million Hungarian citizens in the Holocaust.[6]

Determination to reverse the outcome of Trianon is what prompted Hungary's doomed alliance with Nazi Germany, consecrated in 1940. Budapest joined the Axis in exchange for Berlin's support of territorial claims against its neighbors. But when the war ended in Axis defeat, Hungary was forced to surrender the territory it had invaded and occupied. The communist dictatorship that took power in 1949 ruthlessly suppressed nationalism, particularly the advocacy of territorial aggrandizement, seeing it as an obstacle to communist brotherhood. Soviet occupation could only put a lid on these deeply ingrained yearnings, however, and one of the first things Viktor Orbán did on taking power in 2010 was to name June 4—the anniversary of the Treaty of Trianon's signing—a "Day of National Cohesion." Bemoaning "the unjust and unfair dismemberment of the Hungarian nation by foreign powers," the official proclamation declared that the division of Hungary had brought "political, economic, legal and psychological problems that to this day are not solved." (Orbán allegedly once sported a Greater Hungary bumper sticker on his car.)[7]

Ignoring the reasons *why* Hungary lost two-thirds of its territory—namely, its membership in the belligerent axes of both world wars—this annual day of mourning calls on Hungarians to wallow in victimhood and nurture feelings of resentment toward the Allied victors. Apart from Russia's Special Operations Forces Day, instituted by Vladimir Putin in 2015 to mark the invasion and annexation of the Crimean peninsula, no other European country has consecrated irredentism with a state holiday; on the contrary, it is precisely such jingoistic fervor and imperial nostalgia that the European project was created to overcome. It is difficult to conceive of any other EU member, never mind a former Axis power, establishing such a holiday.

It is impossible to imagine Germany, for instance, commemorating the aftermath of World War II in this way. After its defeat, some twelve million ethnic German civilians were forcibly expelled from Central and Eastern Europe in what remains the greatest forced population transfer in human history. An estimated two million of those people—mostly women and children—died in the expulsions, a far more grievous fate than what Hungarians suffered as a result of Trianon. Even discussing this ethnic cleansing, never mind proposing a national day of remembrance of it, remains highly fraught lest one be perceived as asserting German victimhood at the expense of the millions of innocents killed in a war that Germany started. By contrast, Hungarian government statements, museums, memorials, and other instruments of its history policy seem intended to create the perception that Hungary was a victim of the conflict, rather than one of its perpetrators.

Also unlike Hungary, Germany has undertaken an honest reckoning with its history, a many-sided process known as *Vergangenheitsbewältigung,* or "coming to terms with the past." Beginning in the early years of grade school, German students are subjected to rigorous and mandatory Holocaust education that doesn't avoid addressing Nazi atrocities or the widespread support Hitler enjoyed among ordinary Germans. Most German students visit a concentration camp before graduating from high school, Holocaust-related programming airs frequently on German public television, and permanent commemorations—from the Berlin Holocaust memorial to the brushed steel *Stolpersteine* ("stumbling blocks") affixed into the sidewalks outside the last known homes of Nazi victims—can be found all over the country. Germany's federal government fully assumes responsibility for the nation's historic wrongdoing, and when the plight of German expellees is acknowledged in public debate, it usually comes with the caveat that their suffering was a direct consequence of German aggression. Hungary's official historiography, in contrast, shifts responsibility for the crimes of the past onto outside forces. Needless to say, if a German chancellor or other high-ranking official were to engage in the sort of rhetorical chicanery and historical whitewashing employed by Orbán and his acolytes, there would be an international scandal. Indeed, more than a handful of German politicians and public figures have faced withering public rebuke and social ostracism for uttering sentiments that are only mildly revisionist compared to what passes for mainstream opinion in Hungary.

Viktor Orbán obviously didn't create the Hungarian victim complex, which can trace its roots back hundreds of years. But he has recognized how nostalgia for lost national glory can be exploited politically. According to the standard tale of woe, Hungary has been repeatedly wronged by its neighbors: forced to part with a significant amount of territory and citizens after both world wars, abandoned by the West to the Russians during the Cold War, and today "singled out" for opprobrium over its democratic backsliding by sanctimonious Americans and Western Europeans. Heightening Hungarians' myopia and grievance are the obscurity of their language, which has no close European relatives, and a demographic dispensation whereby a substantial portion of their ethnic brethren lie outside the country's borders, two elements that lead the Hungarian-born journalist Paul Lendvai to call his countrymen "perhaps the loneliest people in Europe."[8]

Because Hungarian complicity in the Holocaust confounds this one-dimensional narrative of Hungarian victimhood, an effort has been made to relativize the fascist and communist regimes, if not outright claim that the depredations of the latter were worse than those of the former. Throughout Eastern Europe, where an honest accounting of communist crimes was impossible before the fall of the Soviet Union, there is a receptive audience for such historical reassessment. Certainly in Hungary, while fascist oppression disproportionately targeted minority groups (primarily Jews and Roma), communist oppression affected a wider segment of society. "For most of my compatriots, communism in the 20th century was much more dangerous and caused much more harm to the Hungarian people in general than the Holocaust," says László Csösz, senior historian at Budapest's Holocaust Memorial Center.[9] "It's easier to put yourself into the position of a victim than into the position of a perpetrator or bystander." And though fascism claimed far more corpses, communist rule endured in Hungary for much longer and is the more recent memory. For both these reasons (in addition, of course, to its ideology), the Hungarian right emphasizes the crimes committed by communists while softening or rationalizing those of the Nazi-allied regimes that preceded it.

Budapest's House of Terror museum is the institutional expression of this politicized narrative. Located on Andrássy Avenue, a wide street resembling the Champs-Élysées, the *Terror Háza* symbolically occupies the building that served as secret police headquarters under the regimes of both the Arrow Cross (the Nazi puppet state installed in late 1944) and then the communists. Established on the initiative of the first Orbán-led Fidesz government, which was elected in 1998, it was completed shortly before national elections four years later. Extending over four floors and constructed by a Hungarian-born Hollywood set designer, its interactive exhibitions lead visitors on a chronological journey through fifty years of Hungarian history, taking them from the actual cells in which both fascist and communist interrogators tortured their victims, to a Soviet tank used to crush the 1956 anti-Soviet uprising, to a re-created "People's Court" where class enemies were condemned to the gulag. Like the occupation memorial, the House of Terror has been controversial since its inception. Although it is dedicated to documenting both totalitarian regimes that ruled Hungary in the last century, the Holocaust is mentioned in just two of its twenty rooms. Many charge that the museum's ulterior purpose is to settle scores: to conflate the relatively liberal "ghoulash" communism of the 1970s and 1980s with the Stalinist regime that preceded it, and thus indict present-day leaders of the postcommunist Socialist Party for the crimes of their political forebears. At a speech inaugurating the House of Terror, Orbán declared it "a way to reach an agreement with history."[10]

Whatever the sincerity of these lofty words, the museum has been anything but a catalyst for conciliation. Before one even reaches the ticket counter, its tendentious political motives become abundantly clear. Standing at the end of the entry hallway are two large granite plinths, one black and featuring the Arrow Cross insignia, another red with the five-pointed communist star. By commemorating the 40,000 "victims of Arrow Cross terror" killed at the end of 1944 and not the more than 400,000 Jews deported to Auschwitz earlier that very year with the full connivance of the Hungarian state, the display drastically understates the number of Hungarian Holocaust victims and leaves visitors with the impression that their murder was the work of a few bad apples. When it comes to the communist

period, meanwhile, any functionary in the four-decade-long regime is considered morally compromised.

Mária Schmidt, the museum's founding director, is an historian and
longtime advisor to Orbán as well as a leading figure in the conservative
nationalist school of Hungarian history. Her intellectual project over the
past twenty-five years has been to dispute the singularity of the Holocaust
and cast it as equivalent to the crimes committed in the name of communism. "Holocausts of the 20th Century," the title of an article she wrote in
1999, gives the gist of her perspective.[11] With language that recalls the
French far-right politician Jean Marie Le Pen, who infamously called Auschwitz a "detail" of European history, Schmidt asserted, "World War II is
not about the Jews, not about genocide. However regrettable, the Holocaust
and the destruction or rescue of the Jews was of minor importance, one
could say a marginal issue, which was not among the military goals of
either side."[12] Although it's sadly true that ending the Holocaust was not
a "military goal" of the Allies, the "Final Solution" was *the* paramount goal
of the Germans, who might have won the war had they not diverted so
many precious resources to the wholesale murder of the Jews. But if the
unprecedented attempt by one of the world's most advanced societies to
direct its entire state apparatus toward the mechanized extermination of
a particular ethnic group is seen as a "marginal" aspect of World War II,
it becomes easier to sympathize with the vast majority of Hungarians
who were pro-German.

I met with Schmidt in her office on the top floor of the House of Terror.
"We never killed them," she told me when I asked why her museum largely
ignores local participation in the rounding up, ghettoization, and deportations of Hungarian Jews.[13] "It only happened because the Nazis came in
and organized it and instructed us to do it. . . . Of course they found people
who were with them, but I think without the German invasion it would
not have happened. Because it's not in the Hungarian history; we never
used such methods." This is factually incorrect. In 1941, while still a fully
sovereign state, Hungary expelled some 20,000 Jews living within the
country's newly expanded borders to Kamianets-Podolski, a town in modern-
day Ukraine then under German occupation. There, the Jews were shot

and deposited into mass graves, victims of the first, large-scale Holocaust massacre. At one point, the sheer scale of the deportations so overwhelmed the SS forces, which could not kill the Jews fast enough, that the Germans insisted the Hungarians bring them to a halt.

As to Schmidt's claim that the Holocaust "would not have happened" barring "the German invasion," she is fighting a straw man. That the Germans bore principal responsibility does not exclude Hungarian collusion; German leadership hardly absolves Hungarians, Estonians, Latvians, Lithuanians, French, and people of many other nationalities who enthusiastically assisted the process. It was, for instance, Hungarians who drew up lists of their fellow Jewish citizens, forced them into ghettoes, and piled them onto the trains. According to historian Csösz, neither German determination to exterminate European Jewry nor Hungarian participation "was sufficient to produce the murder of half a million people." Both were necessary.

Another way in which nationalist historians relativize or even trivialize the Holocaust is by explaining communism as a form of Jewish revenge for the oppression Jews endured under the Miklós Horthy regime of 1920–1944. In the tempestuous political atmosphere of interwar Europe, many Jews were attracted by communism, seeing in it an internationalist bulwark against the blood-and-soil, invariably anti-Semitic nationalist movements then sweeping the continent. Communism, they believed, would sublimate their ethnic difference under a veil of common humanity. It is important to recognize that it was the experience of persecution, not ethno-religious identification, that led these secular Jews to communism, because communists could claim to be the largest and best-organized resistance to fascism. Joining a communist party was, in fact, an explicit renunciation of Judaism and Jewish identity. Still, despite the prevalence of Jews in communist movements at the time, most European Jews were not communists nor were the leaders of communist parties disproportionately Jewish.

Hungary was an exception to this trend. The majority of commissars in the short-lived, post–World War I Hungarian Soviet Republic were of Jewish origin. Nonetheless, Jewish conspicuousness in communism was mirrored by a similar overrepresentation in the professional class, which was resolutely anticommunist. Hungary's Jewish bourgeoisie and aristocracy were larger, wealthier, and more assimilated than that in any other Jewish community in Eastern Europe. According to historian Jerry Z. Muller, however, such nuances were lost on most Hungarians: "In Budapest as in the countryside, opposition to the [Hungarian Soviet] regime, defense of the Church, and anti-Semitism went hand in hand."[14] After only 133 days, the Hungarian Soviet Republic was overthrown, and a two-year-long "White Terror," much of it openly directed against Jews, ensued. Horthy came to power in its wake, establishing in the Hungarian popular imagination a cycle of "Jewish Bolshevik" violence followed by "Hungarian" counterrevolution. By the closing months of World War II, after six million of their co-religionists had perished at the hands of the Nazis and their collaborators, Jews (communist or not) had no choice but to see the advancing Red Army as a liberating force, a stance that immediately put them at odds with their gentile countrymen. It didn't matter that Jews would be persecuted as much as everyone else under communist rule. What Paul Lendvai labels the "irresolvable dialectical relationship" between Jews and ethnic Hungarians had already hardened into place.

Today, with 100,000 citizens of Jewish origin mostly concentrated in Budapest, Hungary is home to the only real Jewish community of any considerable size in Eastern Europe. Consequently, the politics of anti-Semitism continues to have a valence that isn't apparent in places like Poland or Romania, where hardly any Jews remain. Since Hungarian Jews don't subscribe to the historical interpretations presented by the occupation memorial and the House of Terror or to the exegeses offered by Viktor Orbán and Mária Schmidt, they mostly find themselves on the left side of the political spectrum. When one adds this ideological homogeneity to the fact that Jews are overrepresented among the liberal intellectual elite, it makes the already extremely polarized Hungarian political discourse pregnant with insinuation, intended or not. For the Hungarian right, the Jewish association with communism, socialism, liberalism—essentially any cosmopolitan political persuasion—remains widespread if largely unspoken.

György Schöpflin, an eloquent Fidesz member of the European Parliament, attributes the tribal nature of Hungarian politics to an urban-rural divide that largely maps onto a Jewish-gentile rift. Hungarian political debate is roughly characterized by a "Budapest intellectual elite which is of course not for one moment purely Jewish" versus a "Fidesz leadership" that is "overwhelmingly non-Budapest."[15] For the left, communist rule was not inherently illegitimate in the way the authoritarian regimes that preceded it were, because "at the end of the day, the urbanists always felt that the communists were doing it wrong, but they were doing the kinds of things basically they approved of . . . whereas they saw the other side as airy-fairy nationalist, revolutionist, fascistoid. You have people walking around you and you know that his grandfather killed your grandfather, it's difficult. You have a kind of common culture with great politeness and courtesy and smiles, but actually you hate the bastards."

Downplaying the anti-Jewish nature of the Holocaust in the service of nationalist mythmaking represents an assault on historical memory that ironically mimics the communist politics of forgetting. Most museum directors busy themselves digging into archives, curating exhibits, and fund-raising. Mária Schmidt has never been content with such an unassuming role. Making frequent interventions into political and historical controversies, she's an activist in the manner more befitting a left-wing scholar. From her perch atop the House of Terror, Schmidt appears often on television and in the press leading the charge against those who criticize her brand of right-wing historiography. Shortly after the occupation memorial was unveiled to widespread condemnation, she published a tirade under the title "Captive of the Past" that condemned the "intellectual terror of the left-liberal opinion leaders."[16] Given that she heads a museum of communist atrocity called the "House of Terror," her choice of words sounded like an attempt to associate her critics with the perpetrators of Stalinist crimes. The essay dripped with innuendo. Variously describing the memorial's critics as "a cosmopolitan or internationalist group" and "servants to foreign interests" who are "flat-out anti-nation," Schmidt alleged that "they see empire—could be the Soviet, the European Union or the American—as fundamentally superior to the Hungarian." The disloyalty of these interlopers, she continued, leads them to harp on "the favored topics of the empires (Holocaust, racism, Roma issues, homosexual marriage, etc.)" irrelevant to true Hungarians.

Schmidt then alleged that her critics claimed possession of a biologically acquired right to eternal victimhood. Those who dispute the government-

endorsed historical narrative, she claimed, "would like to consider their ancestors' tragic fate an inheritable and advantageous privilege. They would
like this 'victim status' to bleed to generations of those who suffered no
harm." Furthermore, "by reheating the decades-old themes of 'anti-
Christianity' and 'anti-Hungarianness,'" these rootless cosmopolitans,
or "Hungarian left-liberals rooted in Marxism and internationalism . . .
have become the longest lasting plums of the side promoting 'transcen-
dence of nations,' which even in Western-Europe is shrinking." Because of
their hatred for Hungarians, which they mask as a sort of liberal open-
mindedness, "they exclude themselves from our national community."

Not all who worked for the communist regime earn Schmidt's condemnation. When I interviewed her in 2012, she was remarkably charitable
toward the many former apparatchiks who saw the light and entered the
ranks of Fidesz, a cohort including no less an eminence than Viktor Orbán
himself, who was a member of the party youth organization in the early
1980s. "In a small country like Hungary, people have the task to survive,"
she allowed. "So most of the people will not be heroes."[17] (When I mentioned
this amnesiac and inconsistent political puritanism to the former socialist
prime minister Ferenc Gyurcsány, Orbán's arch-nemesis, he scoffed. "We
have this expression: 'My communist is a good communist, your communist is a bad communist.'")[18]

Schmidt boasted to me that the House of Terror has "played a very important role because it was the first time we began to have another narrative on
the 20th century, a very successful one, and we transformed the way Hungarians think on the 20th century." Though the latter point is undoubtedly
true, the response from international observers has been almost unanimously negative. In 2012, the Nobel Peace Prize laureate Elie Wiesel, who
had been deported to Auschwitz by Hungarian gendarmerie from his home
in Hungarian-occupied Romania, announced that he would return Hungary's highest civilian state honor in protest of government officials' "encouraging the whitewashing of tragic and criminal episodes in Hungary's
past, namely the wartime Hungarian governments' involvement in the deportation and murder of hundreds of thousands of its Jewish citizens."[19]
Two years later, Randolph Braham, the leading historian of the Holocaust
in Hungary, also gave back a state prize, decrying "the history-cleansing

campaign of the past few years calculated to whitewash the historical record of the Horthy era." Requesting that his name be removed from the
library of Budapest's Holocaust Memorial Center, Braham called the Memorial to the Victims of the German Occupation "a cowardly attempt to
detract attention from the Horthy regime's involvement in the destruction
of the Jews and to homogenize the Holocaust with the 'suffering' of the
Hungarians—a German occupation, as the record clearly shows, that was
not only unopposed but generally applauded."

Such stinging criticism from abroad has had little impact on the Hungarian government; if anything, international censure seems only to have
made Budapest more truculent. In spite of Schmidt's poor scholarly reputation, Orbán entrusted her with designing a new Holocaust-themed museum, the House of Fates, which remains in the planning stages due to a
series of predictable controversies, beginning with the refusal of Hungary's
main Jewish organization to participate. (When I asked him what he thought
of the House of Terror, a prominent Budapest rabbi replied, "I've never
been there. That's what I think.") Yad Vashem, Israel's official Holocaust
memorial and research center, withdrew from the House of Fates' international advisory panel. Schmidt, impervious to outside opinion, persists in evangelizing the Fidesz version of Hungarian history, her happy
warrior contempt for critics as ardent as when I interviewed her in 2012.
"The narrative and the history-telling on the past and on the 20th century
was a monopoly" before Fidesz first came to power in 1998, she told me.
"The ways they used to tell history and used to reach the people were not
so attractive anymore. So we won, and they lost."

It should come as little surprise that a government fostering nostalgia for
an authoritarian past would prepare the way for an authoritarian future.
Since winning a landslide election in 2010, the Orbán government has
rewritten the constitution, centralized power in the executive, weakened
checks and balances, empowered an oligarchic class, dispensed state
awards and ceded cultural policy to extreme right-wing figures, rendered
parliament a rubber stamp, overhauled public media institutions into partisan outlets, harassed civil society, and reoriented Hungary's traditionally
Atlanticist and pro-European foreign policy toward Russia and other au-

thoritarian regimes. These trends accelerated even further after Fidesz won reelection in 2014, a solidification of power largely attributable to an electoral system it had gerrymandered.

Hungary's new constitution, which replaced the one accepted by multi-party consensus in 1989, was written by a small group of Fidesz parliamentarians with barely any public discussion and no parliamentary consultation. Its passage, on a partisan vote, was accompanied by the enactment of more than thirty "cardinal laws" affecting all manner of public policy that, according to the new constitution, require a two-thirds vote to amend, thus tying the hands of any future government hoping to repeal them. Fidesz instituted changes to the way judges are selected in a court-packing scheme that would have made Franklin Delano Roosevelt blush. The 2011 establishment of a Media Council (all of whose members are Fidesz appointees), endowed with the power to exact punishing fines on journalists for vaguely defined offenses, has had a chilling effect on media and persuaded Freedom House to downgrade Hungary's press freedom ranking from "Free" to "Partly Free," a highly unusual censure for an EU member state. János Kornai, a Hungarian-born Harvard economist, concludes that Hungary is the only one of the fifteen postsocialist EU members to take what he calls a "U-Turn" back toward a command economy and political authoritarianism.[20] Since the Orbán regime came to power, "the state impinges on the economy in a much more aggressive fashion than did the governments before 2010: it exerts more efforts to rule over it."

To be sure, Fidesz is a genuinely popular political force, and it was able to ram a host of illiberal measures into law because it holds an overwhelming parliamentary majority, sustained in two democratic elections. Nonetheless, the ratification of a flurry of controversial legislation in parliament (dubbed by Kornai a "law factory") is the result of a majoritarian political faction using the instruments of democracy to accomplish undemocratic ends. "Thousands (yes, the number is no exaggeration) of discrete changes, all moving in the same direction, create a new *system*" (emphasis original), Kornai writes, which is no longer democratic but not yet a dictatorship.

Another indication of Hungary's authoritarian drift is its harassment of nongovernmental organizations (NGOs). On June 2, 2014, police raided

the offices of three NGOs that had received funds from a Norwegian government program established to support civil society projects in less developed European countries. Two months earlier, Hungarian officials had
accused Oslo of political meddling, complaining that some of the grants had
found their way to a small opposition political party and a "partisan group
of political tricksters." Taking a page out of the Putin playbook, tax authorities launched spurious investigations into the groups, which ranged
from a gay rights organization to the Hungarian Civil Liberties Union to
the local branch of Transparency International, all of them critical of the
Orbán administration. "We're not dealing with civil society members
but paid political activists who are trying to help foreign interests here,"
Orbán said at the time. To many Hungarians, this hostile language sounded
unnervingly familiar. "I am old enough to say I've seen stuff like this before, but that was 30 plus years ago," said Zsuzsa Foltányi, the executive
director of the Hungarian subsidiary responsible for distributing the grant
money.[21] After a year and a half of negotiations between Norway, Hungary,
and the EU, Budapest dropped the charges, having found no evidence of
illegal activity.

A key feature distinguishing real democracies from ones that exist solely
on paper is respect for the culture and spirit of democracy, a quality defined, in the truest sense of the word, as "liberalism." Checks and balances,
a free press, individual rights, an independent judiciary, and respect for due
process: These ingredients, fundamental to a well-functioning democracy,
are meaningless if the citizens entrusted with their care disrespect the rule
of law and run roughshod over democratic norms. Democracy, in other
words, needs democrats, and it's these that Hungary lacks, beginning with
the prime minister.

For four years, Hungary fended off international criticism by insisting
that self-righteous Western Europeans, goaded by leftist Hungarian exiles
with axes to grind, were holding it to a double standard. As a government
spokesman told me in 2012, criticisms of the Orbán administration's commitment to European principles were the result of "very deeply imprinted
prejudices and stereotypes concerning European-ness, enlightenment,
cultural values."[22] Western Europeans, he said, looked down upon their

Eastern neighbors as backward and nationalistic, and it was these prejudices that explained the growing conflict between Budapest and Brussels.

But on July 26, 2014, three months after Fidesz won a second term and a week after the occupation memorial was erected, Orbán erased any doubt as to the direction in which he intended to take his country. Addressing a summer gathering of Fidesz party activists at an ethnic Hungarian town in Romania, Orbán welcomed his audience of "Hungarians living beyond our *current* state borders" (emphasis added).[23] After sarcastically thanking his political opposition back in Hungary ("without evil, how could the good be victorious?"), Orbán declared that "the new state that we are constructing in Hungary is an illiberal state, a non-liberal state."[24] Hungary would be "breaking with the dogmas and ideologies that have been adopted by the West and keeping ourselves independent from them" and would move toward a "work-based society" that "undertakes the odium of stating that it is not liberal in character." In seeking to "organize our national state to replace the liberal state," Orbán cited China, Russia, and Turkey as "stars" to emulate. Fidesz's election mandate, he insisted, proved that Hungarians wished to transcend "the liberal state and the era of liberal democracy."

When a chorus of opprobrium rained down from at home and abroad, Orbán stood his ground. "Checks and balances is a U.S. invention that for some reason of intellectual mediocrity Europe decided to adopt and use in European politics," he told an interviewer several months after the speech, adding that "Hungarians welcomed illiberal democracy."[25] Addressing the same Transylvanian conclave a year later, he made light of the contretemps, jocularly declaring, "Having searched through every available dictionary on political philosophy, I drew a blank: I could find nothing that representatives of today's western ideological mainstream could find sufficiently offensive compared with last year."[26] And adding to his many comments depicting his political opposition as fundamentally illegitimate, not to mention unpatriotic, he said that the "Hungarian left . . . do not like the Hungarian people and they do not like them because they are Hungarians."

This was not the first time Orbán argued that liberal democracy had run its course and that something more rigid and autocratic was needed to replace it. In a 2009 speech, one year before he retook power, Orbán clearly laid out his intention to transform Hungary into a one-party state built on ethnonationalist foundations. Railing against "neoliberal elites," the Fidesz leader stated his intention to rule "the Hungarian land," that is, the multinational community of Hungarians, not merely "Hungary." He then offered his vision of the glorious future:

> Today it is realistically conceivable that in the coming fifteen–twenty years, Hungarian politics should be determined not by the dualistic field of force bringing with it never conclusive and divisive value debates, which quite unnecessarily generate social problems. Instead, a great governing party comes in place, a central field of force, which will be able to articulate the national issues and to stand for these policies as a natural course of things to be taken for granted without the constantly ongoing wrangling.[27]

Fidesz, and by extension the people of Hungary, had a choice: Either "we want to prolong the two-party system with the ongoing division as to values, or we assert ourselves as a great governing party, a political force striving after permanent government." With each passing day since Fidesz regained power on April 25, 2010 (an occasion it has christened the "ballot box revolution"), the prophecy of a "central field of force" ruling the country as a "permanent government" has edged closer to fruition. According to the Yale historian Eva Balogh, "Hungary's political landscape strongly resembles the setup that existed between the two world wars," when only a "handful" of token opposition parties existed to challenge an authoritarian apparatus.[28] It also looks a lot like the Russian "managed democracy" of Vladimir Putin, who has spoken warmly of Orbán's "rethinking of values."[29]

Orbán's hardening one-party rule mirrors a foreign policy recalibration away from the country's traditional Euro-Atlantic allies toward the authoritarian East. A year after instituting a holiday commemorating the signing of the Treaty of Trianon, Fidesz passed a law giving any ethnic Hungarian abroad the right to a Hungarian passport. Thousands of citizens in neighboring countries flocked to Hungarian embassies and consulates to apply for citizenship.[30] Initially, the dispensing of passports to Hungarians living outside the country's borders appeared to be motivated by the crass demands of electoral politics, with critics accusing Orbán of cynically creating voters who would owe him for their enfranchisement. Some took the criticism further, seeing the move as an infringement upon the sovereignty of Hungary's neighbors. Slovak prime minister Robert Fico assailed the Hungarian citizenship law as a "security threat,"[31] and in 2012, Slovakia passed a measure enabling it to revoke the citizenship of anyone who even applied for dual nationality. Meanwhile, under its "Eastern Opening," Budapest has worked to increase trade and deepen political relationships with non-EU countries, in particular Russia and China. A feature of this new diplomacy is a cozying up to dictators: Orbán banned peaceful protests by Tibetan activists when the Chinese premier visited Hungary, and he called the oil-rich post-Soviet kleptocracy of Azerbaijan a "model state" when its dauphin dictator visited Budapest. In a rare step for a European leader, Orbán traveled to Iran, where he met with the fiercely anti-Western Ayatollah Ali Khamenei and announced a "new era" in Iranian-Hungarian relations.

Though this geostrategic reorientation is ostensibly being done for economic reasons, it is imbued with deeper cultural meanings. Hungarians trace their origins to tribes that lived east of the Ural Mountains thousands of years ago. What should be an obscure genealogical detail, however, is routinely exploited by nationalists who claim that ethnic Hungarians possess an intrinsically binary Euro-Asian identity that facilitates alliances with traditionally authoritarian and collectivist Eastern societies, alliances Hungary should foster to balance its relationship with the liberal and individualistic West. This atavistic cultural ambivalence partly explains Orbán's startling rapprochement with Russia. In 1989, as a 26-year-old law student, the future prime minister became the youthful face of East European anticommunist resistance when he delivered a fiery speech at a rally in Budapest denouncing Soviet military occupation. Since that fateful day, a stubborn refusal to let go of communist-era grudges is perhaps the only thread linking Orbán's early liberal anticommunism to his present authoritarian nationalism. This has made Budapest's warming ties towards Moscow all the more awkward and disturbing, especially after Russia invaded Ukraine in 2014. Despite its geographic proximity to the conflict and status as a former Warsaw Pact member, Hungary has been one of the loudest critics of EU sanctions on Russia. "We have shot ourselves in the foot,"

Orbán said of the punitive measures that August.[32] The following month, the CEO of the Russian state-owned Gazprom met with Orbán in Budapest, after which the Hungarian government stopped supplying gas via a "reverse flow" pipeline to the struggling Ukrainians.[33] Three months later, on the same day that Russian-backed separatists violated a ceasefire by shelling the Donetsk airport, Hungary awarded a contentious nuclear energy contract to Russia, further cementing Moscow's grip over its former satellite's energy supply. To cement the deal, and in a sign of just how warm relations with Russia have become, Putin chose Budapest as the site of his first bilateral state visit to a NATO country since the Ukraine crisis erupted.

Faced with criticism of its domestic and foreign policies, Fidesz leaders often tell Western interlocutors that, as much as the unabashed cultural conservatism and undemocratic methods of Hungary's dominant political party may offend them, the alternative would be much, much worse. That alternative is Jobbik, the "Movement for a Better Hungary," an explicitly racist and anti-Semitic party whose members often goosestep around Roma villages wearing uniforms resembling those of the Arrow Cross. Jobbik leaders bemoan "gypsy crime" and Israeli "occupation" of the Hungarian economy, burn EU flags at their rallies, and call the country's NATO membership a "security risk."[34] During a 2012 parliamentary debate, Jobbik foreign policy spokesman Márton Gyöngyösi—an Irish-educated accountant in his late thirties who left the international firm KPMG to pursue a career in neo-Nazi politics—called for drawing up a list of Jews in order to root out those who "pose a national security risk to Hungary."[35]

Though they advise Western visitors to save their wrath for the true enemy of democracy and pluralism—Jobbik—Fidesz partisans themselves don't seem very concerned about the far-right party. In a highly anticipated speech to international Jewish leaders in Budapest that I attended in 2013, Orbán did not once utter the word "Jobbik" during a long disquisition on anti-Semitism.[36] This hesitance to confront the far right may stem from Fidesz's having stolen much of its agenda; indeed, the parties exist on a seamless continuum. A 2015 study found that Fidesz has adopted eight of Jobbik's ten key policy proposals, which range from amending the constitutional preamble regarding Hungary's loss of sovereignty (originally proposed by Jobbik in 2007) to targeting multinational corporations for increased taxation, nationalizing the public utilities, and improving relations with authoritarian regimes.[37] According to the study's authors, rather than challenge Jobbik from the center right, Fidesz incorporated the party's main ideas while dispensing with its coarse rhetoric. It has "used Jobbik as a pioneer to explore new solutions and push the terms of the political debate to increase their own room for maneuver" in pursuit of its "long-term strategic goal of establishing a consolidated system." At points when its popularity wanes, Fidesz is wont to pull highly symbolic right-wing stunts, like mailing a xenophobic "questionnaire" about immigration to every Hungarian citizen or plastering the country with Hungarian-language billboards demanding that migrants (none of whom could be expected to understand the inscrutable language) respect the country's traditions.

As Hungary's third largest political force, Jobbik is indeed frightening. But it's also a distraction from the country's central problem, which is the threat that Orbánism poses to democracy. For foreign journalists eager to report on renascent fascism and paramilitary theatrics, Jobbik is an attractive subject. Yet the more insidious menace comes from those wearing a cloak of respectability and who actually hold power.

Orbán's ambitions extend far beyond Hungary. Since returning to power in 2010, the Hungarian prime minister has positioned himself as the greatest internal dissenter to the European project. Initially, this battle revolved around Hungary's fiscal relationship with the EU. Early in his tenure, while fighting to obtain a loan of more than €10 billion from Brussels, Orbán lashed out at EU officials who insisted on setting conditions for the disbursement. "We are more than familiar with the character of unsolicited comradely assistance, even if it comes wearing a finely tailored suit and not a uniform with shoulder patches," he declared in a National Day speech before 100,000 people. "Hungarians will not live as foreigners dictate!" During elections for the EU Parliament, Fidesz posters declared, "We are sending word to Brussels: Hungarians demand respect."

Harnessing popular fears about the stream of migrants pouring into Europe, Orbán has greatly expanded his profile across the continent. No longer is he the pit bull prime minister limited to the domestic political stage; he is now internationally renowned as the last defender of "Christian"

Europe against the Muslim hordes and ranked by *Politico* as the most influential European of 2015. In a remarkably short period, Orbán has gone from being Europe's polecat to its phenom, eagerly applauded for his uncompromising stance against Angela Merkel's immigration policy by the German chancellor's ostensible allies in both the Bavarian Christian Social Union and the pan-continental European People's Party. By anointing himself the flag-bearer of those demanding a Europe with barbed-wire fences, Orbán has neutralized scrutiny of his domestic policies and rendered his "illiberal state" model respectable.

The danger now is that "Orbánism" is proving contagious, particularly in the postcommunist neighborhood of Central Europe. After its electoral rout of the centrist, pro-European Civic Platform in late 2015, Poland's populist Law & Justice party made good on leader Jaroslaw Kaczynsi's promise to create "Budapest in Warsaw." It began with the symbolic removal of EU flags from prominent government locations, just as Orbán did after he took power. In a series of moves that precipitated a constitutional crisis, the Law & Justice-aligned president egregiously overstepped his ceremonial role by refusing to swear in Constitutional Court nominees appointed by the previous government. After the new Law & Justice-dominated parliament, in a legally specious move, retroactively invalidated these appointments and nominated a new slate of judges, the president administered the oath of office to them in the middle of the night. Law & Justice has imitated Fidesz-style historical revisionism by attempting to revoke a state award bestowed in 1996 on a professor who had written a book about postwar anti-Jewish pogroms. Though the governments in Budapest and Warsaw have differences over how to handle their neighbor to the east (Law & Justice, like every major Polish political faction, is resolutely skeptical of Russia), Orbán certainly has much advice to offer his colleague—and other aspiring national-populists in Europe—about centralizing power and merging one's political party with the institutions of the state while undermining domestic opposition and evading foreign scrutiny.

Accordingly, Law & Justice has also politicized a whole slew of government institutions, from public service broadcasting to the intelligence agencies. Following the president's pardon of the former head of the anticorruption bureau (a former Law & Justice MP found guilty of abusing his office), the prime minister quickly appointed him to head the secret services. After spending years accusing its political rivals of conspiring with Russia to bring down a plane carrying nearly 100 top Polish civilian and military leaders (including Kaczynski's twin brother Lech, the former president) in 2010, Law & Justice reopened an investigation into the tragedy. Some government officials have gone so far as to demand that charges be brought against former prime minister Donald Tusk, who after completing his second term was elected president of the European Commission. (Much as political cleavage in Hungary has its origins in competing historical narratives, belief in Smolensk conspiracy theories has become "a marker of political identity" in Poland, writes the Bulgarian political analyst Ivan Krastev.)[38] Reacting to the political chaos in his country, former Polish president and Nobel Peace Prize laureate Lech Walesa remarked that he was "ashamed to travel abroad."[39]

Once admired as the heart and soul of "New Europe," the Visegrád Four regional alliance of Hungary, Poland, the Czech Republic, and Slovakia now shows signs of developing into a populist, neo-authoritarian rump within the EU. In Prague, populist president Miloš Zeman is the most pro-Russian head of state in Europe, a worrying development in a country once brutally invaded and occupied by Soviet troops. He is the only president of a NATO country to deny a Russian military presence in Ukraine (calling the conflict there a "civil war") and has opposed EU sanctions on Moscow since their imposition. Illustrating the role that Russian money plays in European politics, Zeman's campaign was funded by executives of Lukoil, the Czech subsidiary of the Russian state-owned Gazprom.[40] The country's finance minister is the second wealthiest man in the country who has used his vast fortune to buy up a significant share of the country's media, leading some to speak of the "Berlusconization" of Czech politics, after the Italian prime minister who at one point owned six of the country's seven main television channels. In neighboring Slovakia, meanwhile, the left-wing populist prime minister Robert Fico has responded to the migrant crisis by stating that "Islam has no place" in his country, a sentiment that made palatable coalition with the ultranationalist Slovak National Party. After meeting with Putin in August 2016, Fico said that the EU should drop sanctions on Moscow in spite of its continued occupation of Ukraine. Across Central Europe, the "spirit of 1989" is being reversed through xenophobia, populism, and accommodation to Russian imperialism.

Trends in East Central Europe complicate the thesis famously advanced by Francis Fukuyama in his seminal 1992 work, *The End of History and the Last Man*. In our postcommunist, post-ideological age, Fukuyama argued, no viable alternative exists to a liberal democratic political system married to regulated free-market capitalism; the only foreseeable political disputes concern how best to manage this arrangement. While the past two decades have proved Fukuyama's thesis to be premature when applied to less developed parts of the world, recent trends in Europe show that not even Western democracies are immune to serious regression. In both Hungary and Poland, two countries that have benefited enormously from political liberalization and open markets, strong voting blocs have approved governments that explicitly reject basic liberal values. Once the paradigmatic example of transition to liberal democracy and market economies, the Visegrad Four are slowly becoming models of regression to illiberal democracy and economic autarky.

Orbán's hard-charging nature and intolerance of dissent suggest that it's largely exogenous factors that have arrested Hungary's slide into authoritarianism. Agnes Heller, a prominent liberal Hungarian philosopher, sees Orbán as having descended from Europe's "Bonapartist" tradition of authoritarianism. He is a budding strongman who, were it not for the external constraints provided by the EU's open internal borders and proscription of capital punishment (two policies that Orbán has toyed with flouting), could become an actual autocrat. "Under these conditions, he cannot become a dictator," she told me in her academically messy apartment overlooking the Danube, where I met her in 2012. "He has all the capacities and all the inclinations to be one." Thirty-five years after she was expelled from communist Hungary, Heller found herself the target of a Fidesz-instigated smear campaign that accused her of stealing research grant money (which resulted in no official charges of wrongdoing). The late Mark Palmer, who got to know Orbán well while serving as American ambassador to Hungary during the transition to democracy but later fell out with him, told me before he passed away that "when [the Hungarians] get to the point where objective organizations view them as not free, the EU would have to suspend them." Hungary is not far from reaching that point, if it isn't there already. If Hungary applied for EU membership today, it probably wouldn't be admitted.

One person who has watched Orbán's reign with particular dismay is Karel Schwarzenberg. A grand old man of *Mitteleuropäisch* politics and society, descended from a long line of Austro-Hungarian aristocracy, Schwarzenberg fled Czechoslovakia with his family after the 1948 communist putsch. He spent his years of exile in Austria as a fierce advocate for the human rights of East Bloc dissidents, efforts that brought him close to the playwright Vaclav Havel. When the Velvet Revolution catapulted the soft-spoken, chain-smoking, pub-crawling Havel to the presidency, Schwarzenberg returned to Prague to work alongside the newly ensconced philosopher king. He later set out on his own political career, eventually becoming foreign minister. Putting the promotion of human rights and defense of liberal values at the center of his work, he crisscrossed the world, imparting the lessons of the Czech experience to all who would listen; he was once deported from Cuba for trying to arrange a meeting with dissidents. His 2013 campaign for the Czech presidency (featuring artwork that depicted him sporting a hot pink Mohawk) inspired hope in a younger generation apathetic about their country's seemingly intractable corruption, political anomie, and failure to live up to the lofty humanist ideals Havel espoused. Often seen smoking a pipe, his potbelly hanging prominently before him, and speaking Czech with a thick Hapsburg accent, Schwarzenberg initially seems like an odd figure to strike the common touch.

Schwarzenberg's blunt, self-deprecating honesty, reminiscent of Havel's, is what makes him so appealing. Infamous throughout the land for a tendency to doze during parliamentary sessions, Schwarzenberg turned this perceived weakness into a strength: "I fall asleep," his campaign billboards declared, "when others talk nonsense."[41] More substantial was the stand he took during the heated presidential race, when he stated that the Benes Decrees (the postwar laws expelling Germans from the Sudetenland) were morally unjustifiable. For his honesty and courage, Schwarzenberg was targeted with a deluge of abuse from his opponent, the Russian-backed Zeman, who depicted him as a crypto-Austro-Hungarian imperialist bent on returning the Sudetenland to Germany. Schwarzenberg was ultimately defeated, in large part due to xenophobic hysteria over his response to this seven-decade-old controversy.

Schwarzenberg has known Orbán since the latter was a young, shaggy-haired liberal firebrand, and when I asked him about the Hungarian prime minister's transformation into an apostle of illiberalism, he replied, "As famous Lord Acton said, power corrupts and absolute power corrupts absolutely. And if you win absolute power. . . . He does all the politics which destroyed the old Hungary and reduced Hungary to a nation of only Magyars, and is repeating all the mistakes of the Hungarian upper class between, let's say, the 1870s and World War II. I mean it's really astonishing, putting up monuments for Horthy and all this national drumbeating."[42]

Why does it matter if a country consciously lies about its past? Inculcating in future generations a litany of myths about national innocence, perpetual victimhood, and lost honor grants license to irresponsible and dangerous behavior. Today's fight over memory politics in Hungary echoes the mid-1980s German *Historikerstreit,* or historians' controversy. That dispute centered on whether the crimes of Nazi Germany were singular evils or comparable to other mass atrocities, in particular those of Stalinism. The intellectual combatants of the *Historikerstreit* brought no new facts to bear, but only argued over how to interpret what was already widely known. In the words of the German essayist Peter Schneider, so heated was the argumentation, so deeply did it impinge on Germany's understanding of itself, that the fusillade of polemics in the *feuilletons* attracted "a level of curiosity among the general public normally aroused by photos of the British royal family in swimsuits."[43]

The opening salvo was an essay by the historian Ernst Nolte in the *Frankfurter Allgemeine Zeitung* titled "The Past that Will Not Pass: A Speech that Could Be Written but Not Delivered."[44] Citing the Zionist leader Chaim Weizmann's entreaty to world Jewry that it support Britain in its war effort against Nazi Germany, Nolte argued that "Hitler had good reasons to be convinced of his enemies' determination to annihilate him much earlier than when the first information about Auschwitz came to the knowledge of the world." In light of this "reaction born out of the anxiety of the annihilating occurrences of the Russian revolution," Nolte contended, Auschwitz should be viewed primarily as a preemptive defense against Soviet "Asiatic barbarism," rather than the culmination of centuries of anti-Semitism. Furthermore, other than the "sole exception of the technical process of gassing," there was nothing unique about the Nazi mass murder. "Was not the 'Gulag Archipelago,'" he asked, "more original than Auschwitz? Was not the 'class murder' by the Bolsheviks logically and factually prior to the 'racial murder' of the National Socialists?" Far from being sui generis, Nolte argued, the Holocaust was best understood as a defensive reaction to Bolshevism.

Nolte's provocation intended to contextualize Nazism within the broad array of national crimes perpetrated throughout history. Nearly every major power, he argued, has gone through something like a "Hitler era." Nolte's error was to begin with a political goal (the assuagement of German guilt) and work backward from his conclusion. He hoped to restore national pride by popularizing a version of German history that sees nothing uniquely evil or exceptional about the Holocaust. Though he later insisted he wasn't defending the Holocaust as a defensive response to Stalinist terror, he undermined his argument repeatedly with assertions such as his claim that Hitler's invasion of the Soviet Union was a "preventive war."

After much back and forth, Nolte and his confrères were soundly refuted in the court of German public opinion. Among Germans today, it is a consensus view that the Holocaust was a singular event and that Germany has a duty to preserve the memory of the Holocaust and impart it to future generations. Germans have so thoroughly imbibed the awful lessons of their history that their country is one of the more immune in Europe to far-right populism.

Hungary, by contrast, has undertaken no such reckoning. In the same way that Ernst Nolte wanted ordinary Germans to feel a straightforward patriotism, uncomplicated by guilt over the Nazi past, Viktor Orbán and Mária Schmidt wish to muddy the distinctions between victim and perpetrator in order to present a simplistic view of Hungarian history. Nolte's complaint that preoccupation with the Holocaust served "the interests of the persecuted and their descendants in a permanent, privileged status" sounds indistinguishable from Schmidt's allegation that the progeny of the victims of Hungarian fascism "would like to consider their ancestors' tragic fate an inheritable and advantageous privilege." It is inconceivable that a German chancellor today would express a desire to "preserve Germany for the Germans." Yet this is precisely the sort of language, redolent of the 1930s, that Viktor Orbán uses today about Hungary.[45] Convinced that Hungarians are perennial victims of global machinations—abetted by his "evil" domestic opponents—and unencumbered by comprehension of, or a sense of humility about, where heedless nationalism has taken his country in the past, Orbán feels emboldened to advance a chauvinist political agenda.

High in the Buda hills, a collection of Soviet-era monuments stares down on the capital below. Memento Park, as it's called, is an open-air museum of communism's sculptural detritus. Opened to the public in 1993, it features a collection of towering busts, sculptures, and memorials that once graced the streets and squares of Budapest. A giant bronze re-creation of Stalin's boots—the only remaining part of a statue cut down by protestors during the 1956 uprising—sit atop the grandstand where party apparatchiks reviewed May Day parades. Spread out across the park stand a variety of works crafted in the highly expressive styles of socialist realism: elongated profiles of Marx and Engels that resemble stone heads from Easter Island; bas-relief Stakhanovites reaching joyously into the air; two giant, muscular comrades holding hands and staring confidently (and not a little homoerotically) into each other's eyes. Sterling specimens of brutalist political kitsch, these monuments are also painful reminders of the historical mendacity and punishing ideological conformity compelled by the communist dictatorship. One day, we may hope, the Memorial to the Victims of the German Occupation will be uprooted from Freedom Square and transported to Memento Park, where it belongs.

3

Germany: The Return of Rapallo?

We cannot become wanderers between worlds.

Hans Dietrich Genscher, foreign minister,
Federal Republic of Germany, 1983

WHEN A GERMAN DEFENSE MINISTRY official known to the public only as Leonid K. entered his supervisor's office and saw a group of officials from the Federal Prosecutor waiting for him, he realized his day, and perhaps his life, would not proceed as planned. Leonid K. worked in the Bendler-block, the Berlin building complex where, seventy years earlier, a group of Wehrmacht officers plotted the daring but unsuccessful assassination attempt against Adolf Hitler known as "Operation Valkyrie."[1] That morning, July 9, 2014, he had been about to call his mother to wish her a happy birthday when the summons arrived from his boss.

Prosecutors confronted Leonid with evidence indicating he was a spy. From 2012 to 2014, they alleged, he had passed secret government documents to an agent of another country's intelligence service. The two men had first met six years earlier in Kosovo, where Leonid had been seconded to the United Nations peacekeeping force and where his supposed handler, a rule of law expert, was his supervisor. The German and his foreign acquaintance became fast friends, staying in touch after their Balkan tours ended.

A four-line message sent in 2010 changed both of their lives forever. That year, an anonymous source contacted the Bundesamt für Verfassungsschutz

(BfV), Germany's equivalent of the FBI, claiming that Leonid was spying for Russia. Trips he had made recently to Hungary and Turkey were not vacations, the informant revealed, but rendezvous with his handler, an agent of Russia's Federal Security Bureau (FSB). The BfV passed the tip to Germany's Military Counterintelligence Service (Militärische Abschirmdienst, or MAD), which immediately placed Leonid under surveillance.

For the next three and a half years, Leonid's behavior did indeed raise suspicions that he was working as a spy—but for Washington, not Moscow. Military counterintelligence officers soon came to believe that Leonid's supervisor in Kosovo, an American professor working as an USAID contractor, later identified in the press only as "Andrew M.," was in fact an operative for the CIA, not the FSB. Andrew had paid for Leonid to fly to Istanbul, lent him €2,000, and conducted conversations with him over Skype—which is harder to monitor than normal cell phone calls—all of which indicated to MAD that the two men's relationship was more than that of two friendly work acquaintances.

Confronted with these allegations, he would later recall, Leonid was shocked. "It is a fatal misinterpretation of a friendship," he told the Süd-duestche Zeitung two weeks after the claims of his spying for America were leaked to the media. He was never arrested, however, and after his interrogation at the Bendlerblock, he was allowed to return home by train to the Berlin suburb of Potsdam. There he found several BMWs parked outside his apartment building; police had already ransacked the place and confiscated his computer. So enormous was the public outcry at this discovery of American perfidy that the German government ordered the CIA station chief in Berlin to leave the country or face the prospect of being declared persona non grata. It was an extremely rare move on the part of an American ally (the last time such an expulsion had occurred was in 1995, when France ousted the Paris station chief for attempting to buy information from government officials), doubly so for Berlin's having announced it publicly.

The exposure of Leonid K. was the final straw in a yearlong series of embarrassing revelations regarding American espionage in Germany, a scandal that continues to strain relations between the two countries. Outrage initially erupted in the summer of 2013, when fugitive National Security Agency contractor Edward Snowden publicly revealed the extent of American surveillance practices domestically and overseas. An explosive story *in Der Spiegel,* co-written by Snowden's Berlin-based American accomplice Laura Poitras, revealed how Germany's foreign intelligence service, the Bundesnachrichtendienst (BND), had collaborated with the NSA to compile the telephonic metadata (basic information like numbers dialed and call duration) of German citizens. Subsequent exposés described NSA bugging of the European Union legation in Washington and claimed that antennas on the roof of the U.S. Embassy in Berlin were used to intercept phone calls. The German press coverage was as breathless as it was naïve; American spies, *Der Spiegel* indignantly reported, "are officially accredited as diplomats," as if this were not standard practice all over the world.[2]

But the most explosive allegations were yet to come.

Edward Snowden announced himself to the world on June 9, 2013, in Hong Kong and flew to Moscow two weeks later on June 23. To this day, the circumstances of Snowden's travel to and eventual residence in Russia are the subject of great speculation. Snowden and his defenders insist that he was a conscientious whistleblower who intended all along to settle in one of the several Latin American countries that had offered him asylum. That plan was ultimately foiled after the United States revoked his passport on June 2, the same day that Snowden apparently walked into the Russian consulate in Hong Kong, where he spent the night. Yet it's hard to believe that a man who had been planning his escape for months and managed to elude the entire American intelligence community while stealing nearly two million secret government documents wound up under the protection of the two greatest nation-state cybersecurity threats to the West—China and Russia—by accident.

More likely is that Snowden, consciously or unconsciously, arrived in Russia as the result of an operation controlled by Moscow via "cut-outs," espionage parlance for mutually trusted interlocutors who may or may not know the ultimate purpose they're serving. No government, least of all that of the Russian Federation, grants asylum to a "walk-in" (an agent from a foreign intelligence service who literally walks into another country's diplomatic post promising to spill the beans) a mere month after encountering him. A great deal of circumstantial evidence suggests that the Russians cultivated Snowden as a potential defector for years before he defected, through channels disguising their involvement. "Given the right initial direction and a favorable propaganda environment, political movements in the West can serve the Kremlin's purpose without hands-on control," writes *The Economist* journalist Edward Lucas, an expert on Russian espionage. "It would not be hard for Russian intelligence to conceal an intelligence officer or agent of influence somewhere in the background, or for that person to broker an introduction between Snowden and his future allies."[3]

One such "agent of influence," in all likelihood, was Wikileaks, the "anti-secrecy" collective that dispatched a representative to help spirit Snowden out of Hong Kong and bring him to Russia. Since its emergence nearly a decade ago, Wikileaks has directed nearly all of its efforts at exposing the intelligence operations, military plans, and misdeeds of Western governments while all but ignoring those of the world's worst human rights abusers. Wikileaks' founder, the Australian-born computer hacker Julian Assange, once hosted a show on the Kremlin-funded Russia Today network, and one of the organization's associates, an anti-Semitic conspiracy theorist by the name of Israel Shamir, provided U.S. diplomatic cables to the dictatorial regime of Belarus, a Russian ally, which in turn used them to crack down on pro-democracy activists. Wikileaks has since claimed that it advised Snowden to seek shelter in Russia from the very beginning of its interaction with him, putting another hole in Snowden's claim that his extended sojourn in Russia is entirely inadvertent.[4] "He preferred Latin America," Assange himself said in August 2015. "But my advice was that he should take asylum in Russia despite the negative PR consequences, because my assessment is that he had a significant risk he could be kidnapped from Latin America on CIA orders. Kidnapped or possibly killed."[5] On his arrival at Moscow's Sheremtyevo Airport, Snowden miraculously acquired the services of Anatoly Kucharena, a Muscovite lawyer who sits on a board overseeing the FSB and who helpfully offered to assist in the fugitive American's asylum claim on a pro bono basis.

Russia's government isn't just highly selective in granting asylum to agents of rival intelligence services, only doing so after a thorough background check and establishment of the potential defector's legitimacy. It also expects something in return. In that respect, Snowden has been a boon. A still unresolved inconsistency in Snowden's story is what happened to the documents he stole. Two days after going public, Snowden told the *South China Morning Post* that he had not handed over all of the information to Poitras and Glenn Greenwald, her journalistic collaborator, "because I don't want to simply dump huge amounts of documents without regard to their content."[6] That directly contradicts the claim, issued later to the *New York Times*, that he "gave all of the classified documents he had obtained to journalists he met in Hong Kong, before flying to Moscow, and did not keep any copies for himself."[7] It also contradicted his assertion to the BBC that he "gave all of my information to American journalists and free society generally."[8] Despite Snowden's insistence that he had encrypted the documents to prevent any intelligence service from accessing them, a British government source revealed in June 2015 that China and Russia had gained access to at least part of his data, forcing MI6 to evacuate its agents from both countries. "British intelligence have worked on the assumption that Russian and Chinese spies might have access to his full cache of secrets," the BBC reported.[9]

Had Snowden limited his leaks to disclosures concerning the NSA's surveillance of his fellow American citizens, it might be appropriate to call him a "whistleblower." But once he began leaking sensitive information concerning his country's *foreign* intelligence operations—as he did from the very beginning by claiming in an interview with the *South China Morning Post* that the NSA hacks Chinese computers—he lost any claim to such patriotic distinction. Whatever one thinks about the morality of foreign espionage, in no way is it limited or proscribed by the U.S. Constitution or any U.S. statute, and to reveal such sensitive information aids and abets America's enemies. And so, once Snowden, having disclosed this material, accepted protection from one of his country's chief adversaries, he became a defector, if not a traitor. Irrespective of his initial intentions, Snowden has been an FSB asset from the moment he landed in Moscow, where his revelations, released in drip-drip fashion, have been carefully calibrated to ensure the maximum damage to Western interests. It was not until nearly three years after Snowden went public that the head of the BfV admitted the obvious: Snowden was likely working all along at the direction of Moscow. "Leaking the secret service files is an attempt to drive a wedge between western Europe and the USA—the biggest since the Second World War," agency head Hans-Georg Maassen told *Focus* magazine.[10] "It's remarkable that there were no publications about countries like China or Russia, which are main targets for intelligence work by the NSA." The following year, the deputy chairman of the Russian Duma's defense and security committee all but admitted that Snowden is now a double agent. "Let's be frank," he told NPR. "Snowden did share intelligence. This is what security services do. If there's a possibility to get information, they will get it."[11]

That damage Snowden caused is inestimable. "The vast majority of the documents that Snowden exfiltrated from our highest levels of security . . . had nothing to do with exposing government oversight of domestic activities," Joint Chiefs of Staff chairman Martin Dempsey told the House Armed Services Committee in 2014. "The vast majority of those were related to our military capabilities, operations, tactics, techniques and procedures."[12] Mitigating the harm—devising new "operations, tactics, techniques and procedures," as well as methods of communication, to replace those that Snowden revealed to the FSB—will cost billions of dollars. Snowden's disclosures almost certainly assisted the Russians in evading U.S. surveillance and may have played a role in their stealth invasion and annexation of Crimea. One of the first documents Snowden leaked, in 2013, revealed how the NSA had spied on Russian president Dmitri Medvedev at the G-20 summit in 2009, alerting Moscow that its communications network was insecure.[13] By the time of the Crimean operation the following year, Washington was taken by surprise. "Some U.S. military and intelligence officials say Russia's war planners might have used knowledge about the U.S.'s usual surveillance techniques to change communication methods about the looming invasion," the *Wall Street Journal* reported.[14] In addition to the highly prized information that Snowden's revelations offered to nation-state actors, his actions might also have abetted the rise of the Islamic State of Iraq and the Levant (ISIS). "Within weeks of the leaks, terrorist organizations around the world were already starting to modify their actions in light of what Snowden disclosed. Communications sources dried up, tactics were changed," says former CIA deputy director Michael Morrell.[15] After the November 2015 attack in Paris by homegrown jihadists took the lives of 130 people, the EU counterterrorism coordinator said that Snowden's revelations had helped the terrorists avoid detection.[16]

Harder to quantify is the reputational harm done to America and its alliances. Other than embarrassing the French government, it was hard to see what justification existed for Wikileaks' decision in July 2015 to publish the NSA intercept of a meeting French president François Hollande held with German Social Democrats to discuss the Greek debt crisis three years earlier. The leak's timing—amid some of the most contentious negotiations between the Syriza government and its creditors—as well as its content—exposing backdoor negotiations conducted by the French government with German chancellor Angela Merkel's domestic political opposition—seemed designed to provoke maximum discord between the EU's two largest members.

In Germany, the most reputationally harmful leak came on October 23, 2013. *Der Spiegel,* citing Snowden's material, reported that the NSA had tapped Merkel's personal cell phone for the previous decade, since before her tenure as chancellor. Thus "Handygate" (employing the German slang term for mobile phone) was born. With few exceptions, the press, public, and political class responded with righteous indignation. "Asylum for Snowden!" screamed the cover of *Der Spiegel,* in whose pages fifty prominent Germans demanded that their government provide refuge to the wanted American. "Goodbye friends!" declared *Die Zeit,* which angrily lamented that U.S.-German relations "have to be put on a realistic footing."

Merkel, who clearly wanted to handle the matter discreetly, could do little to stem the outrage. In March 2014, the German parliament convened a committee to investigate the NSA's activities. No corresponding effort was made to examine the intelligence operations of any other foreign power; reading the German-language press, one could hardly be blamed for thinking that the United States is the only country to conduct espionage in Germany. (A six-month cyberattack against the Bundestag in 2015, alleged by German intelligence sources to have been the work of the Russians, barely registered in the German media or political discourse.) America's reputation would take a further hit in July 2014, when prosecutors arrested a 31-year-old employee of the BND, "Markus R.," on charges that he had passed along information about the parliamentary committee to the CIA in exchange for cash. To add insult to injury, the arrest was announced publicly, and the

U.S. ambassador was summoned to the Foreign Ministry for a reprimand, on the same day the city of Berlin was preparing to celebrate seventy years of postwar German-American friendship.

The weight of all these allegations, collectively comprising what's become known as the "NSA skandal," has damaged American-German relations to a point not seen since the 2003 Iraq War. It was in this atmosphere of outrage, distrust, and betrayal that Berlin—having concluded just a week after nabbing Markus R. that Leonid K. was too a spy—expelled the CIA station chief.

Over the following weeks, a steady stream of leaks from the German government characterized the matter of Leonid K. as an open-and-shut case. "If I were the Attorney General, I would press charges, the evidence of espionage activities is very strong," an unnamed German intelligence official told *Die Welt*.[17] "His biography smells of spying activities," said another. Leonid meanwhile defended his innocence. "It's sad that a friendship between a German and an American now burdens the German-American relationship," he told the *Süddeutsche Zeitung*, a perceptive observation. For geopolitical rupture was precisely what this accusation of espionage was intended to inflict.

Less than two months later, however, the investigation into the curious case of Leonid K. and Andrew M.—deemed by the *Süddeutsche Zeitung* to be even "more serious" than that of Markus R.—was showing serious cracks. Though prosecutors had once spoken of "reasonable suspicion" that Leonid was passing along secrets to the CIA, no incriminating evidence was ever found on his computer, cell phone, iPad, or in any of the 19,000 emails examined by authorities.[18] Some aspects of the investigation seemed to have been conducted by Inspector Clouseau. In one intercepted mobile phone communication between the two men, Andrew told Leonid to switch to Skype because talking on an ordinary line was "bad Opsec," intelligence jargon for "operational security." German investigators took this joking remark about poor cellular reception as a sign that the two were engaged in clandestine conversations.

In January 2015, Leonid was completely cleared of the charges against him, the recipient of a "first class acquittal" in the words of one investigator.[19] "The Spy Who Never Was" is how *Der Spiegel*, which has done more than any other news outlet to fan the flames of German hysteria about the NSA, titled its story on Leonid's exoneration.[20] But the damage was done. Few other media outlets followed up their initially wild claims. (Nor did they report the station chief's return to Germany just a month after he or she was forced out, as I heard from a well-informed source.) "If you ask on the streets, people will tell you there was an American spy at the Ministry of Defense," a German intelligence official told me months after the matter had been resolved.

In this age of militant opposition to smoking, there was something disarming about the late Helmut Schmidt's stubborn refusal to break the habit. Cigarettes were practically an appendage of the 97-year-old former German chancellor—what jelly beans were to Ronald Reagan. Hamburg state authorities once investigated Schmidt and his wife for lighting up in a public theater, and when the EU threatened to ban menthols several years ago, he reportedly stockpiled several years' supply, some 200 cartons. Schmidt's indifference to the admonitory aspect of public opinion extended to more philosophical matters as well. Whether in the columns of *Die Zeit* (the venerable weekly he co-published), during television interviews, or in the live panel discussions he joined with impressive frequency for a man approaching 100, Schmidt dispensed the sort of unvarnished opinions that come easily to a former world leader freed from petty constraints like political calculation or concern for popular approval. Sometimes the views he expressed were as unfashionable as the Reyno brand menthols he sucked down at an alarming rate.

One intervention that set many eyes rolling was the piece he published in *Die Zeit* on November 1, 2013, a week after the Handygate scandal broke. Chancellor Merkel's schoolmarmish assertion that "friends do not spy on one another" did little to sate the widespread public anger, tinged with vulnerability, which had left Germans seeking validation for their outrage. They would get none from Schmidt, who advised his countrymen to cool it. "During my decades in politics I had always assumed that my telephone conversations were recorded by foreign hands," he began, with typical world-weariness. "I advise the chancellor to remain calm."[21]

Schmidt was not the only former German leader who assumed he was targeted by foreign spy agencies. According to German journalist Josef Joffe, Schmidt's successor, Helmut Kohl, kept a mason jar full of deutsche marks handy to place calls from a phone booth in the countryside whenever he needed to conduct especially sensitive conversations.[22] Gerhard Schröder, Merkel's Social Democratic predecessor, was also allegedly a target of NSA eavesdropping. "I was against the Iraq War and therefore should have assumed that it was a given for the Americans to find out what my motives were and whom I was scheming with," Schröder said in response to a 2014 news report.[23] So there was nothing particularly new about American spying on the German chancellery. And unlike Caesar's wife, the German government itself was hardly above suspicion regarding such matters. Weeks after expelling the CIA station chief, reports surfaced that the BND had been spying on Turkey, a fellow NATO ally, for years, and had also intercepted phone calls from secretaries of state Hillary Clinton and John Kerry.[24]

Nor are all leaks created equal. Since the eruption of the Ukraine crisis in 2014, a series of embarrassing statements—privately uttered by Western diplomats who just happen to be staunch Kremlin detractors—have been leaked to the media. While spying on foreign leaders is obviously nothing new, the purpose of such intelligence collection has always been to inform the political leadership of the country doing the intelligence collecting. Rarely, if ever, have such exchanges been aired to the public with the intent of humiliating the target. Notwithstanding what former secretary of state Henry Stimson famously said, gentlemen have always read each other's mail. What they hadn't done, until very recently, was read the contents of that mail aloud from the rooftops.

When audio recordings of Polish foreign minister Radoslaw Sikorski calling his country's alliance with the United States "worthless," "harmful" and "bullshit" were leaked to the media around the same time the CIA's Berlin station chief was expelled, few in Germany looked to the most likely source of the eavesdropping. The West had just placed sanctions on Russia for its behavior in Ukraine, and Sikorski was one of the loudest diplomatic advocates for dealing harshly with the Putin regime. Though the party responsible for recording Sikorski was never exposed, it was not difficult to guess who might have been behind it. The resources and knowledge required to bug the conversations of a group of Polish politicians meeting at several Warsaw restaurants over a yearlong time period pointed squarely at Moscow. Partly as a result of these remarks, the EU passed over Sikorski, one of Russia's most high-profile critics, for the job of EU foreign minister.

At the height of the pro-European Maidan protests in Kyiv, a recording of a phone call between U.S. assistant secretary of state Victoria Nuland and the American ambassador to Ukraine was posted on YouTube. After expressing her preference for the United Nations over the EU as a mediator between various Ukrainian political figures, Nuland casually remarked, "Fuck the EU." Her cursing earned ferocious headlines around the world, with critics likening her to a haughty official in the British Imperial Service choosing favorites among the natives. The Russians barely even tried to conceal their responsibility for the leak: The first person to post a link of the conversation on Twitter was an aide to a Russian deputy prime minister. Moscow's motivation was obvious: attack the top American diplomat responsible for Europe in order to drive a wedge between the United States and its EU allies. The following month, another private conversation, this one between the Estonian foreign minister and his EU counterpart, was also posted online.

Public dissemination of such remarks was unprecedented. For all the European hue and cry over American surveillance activity—something in which the Russians (and many others) are also engaged—the United States has never publicly leaked the contents of surveilled conversations, not even those of its adversaries. (According to Merkel's chief of staff, there is no evidence that the NSA even recorded any of the phone conversations within the German government's communications network it allegedly tapped.)[25] Nearly three years after Nuland's offhand remark, Moscow and its Western sympathizers continue to smear her as a scheming puppet master pulling strings in Ukraine. Merkel, apparently forgetting her principled objection to eavesdropping on private conversations, also joined the attacks on Nuland, decrying her comments as "totally unacceptable."

Yet as with Leonid K., the initial claims about NSA spying on Merkel were also shown to have been overstated, if not outright false. In June 2015, nearly a year and a half after *Spiegel* reported that the NSA had been tapping

Merkel's phone, Germany's federal prosecutor dropped his inquiry into the matter. His office had been unable to prove that the document leaked by Edward Snowden and seized on by the media as solid evidence of American perfidy amounted to "an authentic eavesdropping order from the NSA or another US intelligence agency." Nor did it "contain any concrete evidence of surveillance of the mobile telephone used by the chancellor."[26]

Edward Snowden unveiled NSA operations around the world, but it's in Germany where the scandal has generated the loudest public fury and severest political consequences. From 2013 to 2015, the percent of Germans agreeing with the statement, "The U.S. government respects personal freedoms," dropped from 81 percent to 43 percent, both the sharpest decrease and lowest number in Europe.[27] The only other countries where majorities disagreed with that statement are Argentina, Turkey, and Russia. Snowden is one of the most admired men in Germany, more popular even than President Obama, who introduced himself to the country in 2008 with a Berlin speech before 200,000 cheering people. In view of how Snowden's documents revealed that America conducts more espionage in Germany than in any other European country, this disproportionate response might have been expected. Yet the leaks also struck an emotional chord. It's likely that Snowden's handlers in the FSB (who—up to and including former Dresden KGB resident Putin—are extremely well acquainted with German politics and society) executed the release of his documents so as to manipulate deeply rooted German national neuroses. For instance, though Snowden's documents alleged that the NSA had monitored the phones of thirty-five world leaders, Merkel's name was the first to be released. In addition, one of the first Western politicians to visit Snowden in Russia was Hans Christian Ströbele, a Green Party member of the Bundestag, a longtime committeeman on that body's intelligence oversight panel and a fierce critic of the United States. Such a meeting could not have taken place without the direct involvement of the FSB. On his return to Berlin, Ströbele—a radical left-wing lawyer who defended Red Army Faction terrorists in the 1970s—demanded Germany grant Snowden asylum.

This heightened outrage, however, has less to do with the specific disclosures than with cultural and historical legacies exclusive to Germany. Even if the highly orchestrated release of the NSA files was undertaken without any particular plan for Germany in mind, the reaction there was bound to be stronger than in most other countries. To understand the special qualities of the German response, consider that of neighboring France. When stories about NSA mass surveillance and targeted eavesdropping of President François Hollande and two of his predecessors became public, the French reacted with insincere shock, followed by studied insouciance. France has a formidable intelligence apparatus that it has long deployed against both adversaries and allies. The French government's surveillance of its own citizens, meanwhile, rivals any invasions of privacy that the NSA has been accused of. On top of this, France is notorious for engaging in economic espionage—stealing the secrets of foreign companies that compete with French firms—a taboo in the intelligence world. Aware of all this baggage, the French government registered a perfunctory complaint about how eavesdropping *entre amis* was "unacceptable." After a day or two of angry headlines, the French media and public lost interest.

Germany's intelligence services, unlike France's, were created by the United States after World War II and remain heavily dependent on American tutelage and cooperation. As in personal relationships, dependence can breed resentment, and such feelings contributed to the wrath over the NSA. "In the eyes of the Americans, we were a US aircraft carrier in the middle of the Continent," a German government official complained to *Der Spiegel*, which ruefully observed that it would "scarcely have been possible for the country to emancipate itself from the US" given its intelligence services' technological inferiority.[28] But the dramatic disparity between the French and German responses goes beyond mere gaps in intelligence-gathering capability.

The ongoing Snowden saga is hardly the first exposure of sensitive American intelligence operations, but two circumstances peculiar to the digital age have given it staying power. First is the extent of surveillance: Today, pervasive Internet and cell phone usage leave ordinary citizens exposed like never before and have made it easier for governments to collect massive amounts of data. Second, the web provided Snowden and his enablers a platform the likes of which his Cold War forerunner, CIA defector Philip Agee,[29] could have only dreamed. (Though the German government

has resisted demands to offer Snowden asylum, its treatment of Agee—
who found shelter in West Germany after both Britain and the Netherlands
deported him—suggests historical precedent for how its current deference
to America could evaporate.)

Hardly any news story about German attitudes to government surveillance lacks reference to the Nazi regime and East German communist dictatorship, both of which violated individual rights and privacy as a matter
of course. There exists in Germany a deep uneasiness about the entire enterprise of intelligence gathering, and this historical trauma feeds into the
country's unique sensitivity. Germany has some of the world's most stringent data protection laws; its 2011 national census was the first in twenty-
five years and was taken only at EU behest. While it's understandable that
Germans, given their history, would be warier of government espionage
than other European publics, there are radical differences between the
NSA and the Gestapo or Stasi, not the least of which are the political envi-
ronments in which these intelligence services operated. Nothing presented
by Snowden thus far indicates that information collected by the NSA has
been used to harm a single innocent German citizen. German indignation over the NSA is indeed more a product of collective memory than a
proportionate response to the NSA's actual behavior, but it's not the recol-
lection of Nazism and communism that informs public attitudes so much
as Germany's complex relationships with America and Russia, as well as
Germans' conception of their country's place in the world.

Consider again the indifferent French response: Collecting secrets, the
French understand, is what states do, especially states that consider themselves world powers. Herein lies the heart of the dramatically different
reaction in Germany, which, seven decades after the end of World War II,
ardently resists the trappings of power. This aversion exhibits itself most
clearly in widespread skepticism toward defense spending, let alone the
use of military force, but it also extends to other realms. Stealing information from another country conflicts with the gauzy and idealistic virtue of
multilateralism that, along with pacifism, ranks as the most important
value of postwar German foreign policy.

More than a quarter-century after the collapse of the Berlin Wall, an event
stamped onto our consciousness with images of joyous citizens sur-

mounting that horrible monument to oppression, it's easy to forget some prominent Europeans' deep unease about German reunification. Both French president François Mitterand and British prime minister Margaret Thatcher were among the skeptics, their thoughts on a reunited Germany pithily captured by the novelist François Mauriac: "I love Germany so much I'm glad there are two of them." Within Germany, a small but vocal element of left-wing intellectual opinion opposed reunification out of fear that a large, powerful, and confident Germany would inevitably throw its weight around the continent as it had to such disastrous effect in the past. The birth of the Berlin Republic in 1990 was hardly a foregone conclusion and was achieved only with great diplomatic coaxing chiefly on the part of Chancellor Helmut Kohl and his foreign minister, Hans Dietrich Genscher (crucially assisted by President George H. W. Bush and Secretary of State James Baker). Uniting his country, Kohl promised, would lead to a "European Germany" rather than a "German Europe." His passionate support for dropping the beloved deutsche mark in exchange for the euro was taken as concrete evidence of this commitment; adoption of the common currency, it was optimistically believed at the time, would lessen German dominance by integrating it economically with France.

In the 150 years since Bismarck confederated a smattering of principalities into a single empire, "the German problem" has taken many guises, from the totalitarian menace of the Third Reich to the economic hegemon of the twenty-first century. Berlin today threatens nobody militarily. But the "German problem" is more fundamental, deriving from the power intrinsic to Europe's largest and most populous country. A laudable effort to atone for the nation's historic crimes and a heightened sensitivity to how it is perceived abroad have instilled cautiousness and deference in German foreign policy. For instance, when German president Horst Köhler paid a visit to German troops stationed in Afghanistan and remarked that "military deployments are necessary in an emergency to protect our interests . . . for example when it comes to preventing regional instabilities that could negatively influence our trade, jobs and incomes," the criticism from the German public was so overwhelmingly negative that he resigned in shame. That a German political leader—however clumsily and thoughtlessly— would describe a negative impact on "trade, jobs and incomes" as an "emergency" justifying foreign military intervention summoned disturbing memories of *Lebensraum* (literally "living space," a term Hitler used to justify Nazi Germany's eastward expansion) and the extraction of gold-capped teeth from concentration camp prisoners. German leaders are careful to present themselves as the ultimate team players and their foreign policy as exceptionally selfless. "The Foreign Ministry still likes talking about 'responsibilities' rather than 'interests,'" observes Friedbert Plüger, a former foreign policy spokesman for Merkel's center-right Christian Democratic Union (CDU).[30] In the media, politics, and the think tank community, the "strategic class" consists of just a few individuals; the very word "strategy" conjures fearsome images of war rooms and pieces on a global chessboard. Most foreign policy conversations in Berlin lean to "soft" subjects like human rights and development.

Along with a hesitance to embrace tools of statecraft reliant on military force and espionage, a complex relationship with the United States contributes to the German penchant for neutrality. More than any other country in Europe, Germany understands itself in relation to America, which, in the words of political scientists Andrei Markovits and Philip Gorski, has been Germany's "creator, liberator, occupier, role model, ally, rival, and bully all rolled into one."[31] From the end of World War II to the fall of the Berlin Wall, West Germany was an American protectorate. That role often earned America admiration, never more so than during the Berlin Airlift, when, for 462 days, a constant stream of British and American planes delivered food, coal, and other vital supplies to the city's Soviet-blockaded Western sector. But Germany's dependence on and subservience to America also bred feelings of vulnerability and bitterness. It took forty years before a German president called May 8, 1945—the date of German surrender to the Allies—"a day of liberation." When Richard von Weizsäcker spoke those remarkable words, he offered the many countrymen of his generation who still felt ambivalent toward their erstwhile enemies a clear moral example. Germany and Germans, he declared, must be eternally grateful to America for having saved us (and the world) from ourselves. That sentiment was, and for some still is, a bitter pill to swallow, especially in light of all the chaos and disorder America is perceived to have caused in the seventy years since its victory over Germany brought it to the heights of global power.

The intrinsically secretive nature of espionage has made American officials reluctant to provide a defense of their intelligence-collection activities in Germany. This opened the field to a variety of anti-American voices, mainly Russia and its many German sympathizers, to capitalize on the revelations and depict the United States as uniquely perfidious. But there are plenty of good reasons for U.S. surveillance in Germany. To start, both countries have a vital interest in preventing Islamist terrorism. Mohamed Atta, who piloted one of the two airplanes that struck the World Trade Center, formed a cell in Hamburg while evading the suspicion of German security services. As the city that once stood at the epicenter of East-West tensions, Berlin has long been a nest of international espionage. According to intelligence expert Matthew Aid, the CIA's Berlin Operations Base "opened all German mail going to and from the Soviet Union and Eastern Europe."[32] In 1973, Social Democratic chancellor Willy Brandt's government collapsed after it was revealed that Brandt's top aide, Günther Guillaume, was an East German spy. That the man closest to Brandt was a communist agent was testament not only to the weakness of West German counterintelligence but also exemplifies why the CIA might want to have its own eyes and ears in the chancellor's office.

It seemed never to have crossed the minds of the outraged German press and public that a substantial portion of American spying in Germany has been directed not at their government but at adversarial powers like China and Russia. Much of the CIA's and NSA's work in Germany aims to ferret out agents from rival intelligence services who have eluded the BfV and BND—like the aforementioned Guillaume—not to abscond with German secrets. "The BND was not a very good service for many years," a former senior CIA case officer told *The Daily Beast*. "We always worried that they had moles working for the Soviets and later the Russians."[33] Laura Poitras, the Snowden collaborator and filmmaker, openly boasts of how sources in German intelligence tell her that their American counterparts have Poitras "lit up like a Christmas tree," fully monitoring her communications.[34]

One hopes that the heads of German intelligence agencies would be appalled to hear about their agents chummily consorting with an accomplice of Edward Snowden, revealing to her the operational details of an ally's clandestine activities.

This speaks to a rationale for spying in Germany that's difficult for American officials to address: Berlin's dependability as an ally, or lack thereof. Long after the end of the Cold War, Russia continues to penetrate German politics, industry, media, intelligence, and armed forces. German businesses have cozy relationships with a variety of anti-Western regimes; until very recently, German defense contractors trained the Russian military and sold weapons to Moscow. A. Q. Khan, the father of Pakistan's illicit nuclear weapons program, obtained crucial technology from employees of a German company. In 1996, Germany expelled a CIA officer who sought information on nuclear equipment sales to Iran, with which Berlin has long had strong trade ties. And there are individuals within German politics whose behavior rightly arouses concerns. Gerhard Schröder is perhaps the most prominent example.

In late 2004, around the time Viktor Yanukovych was attempting to steal a Ukrainian election with Moscow's help (an effort that included the dioxin poisoning of the lead opposition candidate), Chancellor Schröder declared Putin "a flawless democrat." The following year, less than a month after departing the Chancellery, Schröder accepted a post as chairman of the shareholders' committee of Nord Stream, the Kremlin-backed gas pipeline where Matthias Warnig, a former Stasi agent and Putin friend from their Dresden days, serves as managing director. A project of the Russian state-owned energy concern Gazprom, Nord Stream was built underwater rather than over land, at considerably greater expense, for a very important reason: By traveling straight from Russia to Germany via the Baltic Sea and bypassing the countries in between, Nord Stream allows the Kremlin to halt energy supplies to Central and Eastern Europe while keeping the gas flowing to Germany and beyond. Over the past decade, Russia has repeatedly shut off gas supplies to Europe as a way of exacting political influence, and Nord Stream has enhanced its leverage. While chancellor, Schröder backed a loan guarantee for the controversial project, which former Polish foreign minister Radoslaw Sikorski likened to the Nazi-Soviet Pact of

1939.[35] Nord Stream has since handsomely rewarded Schröder with a €250,000 annual salary.[36]

The most concerning aspect of the Nord Stream affair is not necessarily that Schröder has behaved, in the words of late Democratic congressman Tom Lantos, like a "political prostitute." For what it's worth, Schröder denied ever having been offered the Nord Stream position while in office. Regardless, it would require more than the support of the German chancellor to approve such a massive project. At the time of its proposed creation, support for Nord Stream was widespread among German business executives, think tank experts, major political figures, and members of the media. Schröder and his chief of staff, Frank-Walter Steinmeier (who later became foreign minister in Merkel's first grand coalition government of 2005–2009 and her second, formed in 2013), presented the project to the German public as a key element of Germany's bilateral relationship with Russia, under the slogan "transformation through trade." Premised on the notion that increased economic exchange with Russia would inevitably lead to its democratization, the Schröder-Steinmeier agenda recalled, in both name and substance, a previous Social Democratic chancellor's opening to the East: Willy Brandt's Cold War–era *Ostpolitik,* which sought "transformation through rapprochement." Connecting Russia to Germany with yet another oil pipeline (as Brandt himself had done in 1970), along with weapon sales to Moscow, the pair argued, would bind Russia more closely to the West and thus speed its "modernization." Yet Nord Stream puts the perceived national interest of Germany before solidarity with its democratic NATO and EU allies to the east by allowing Russia to restrict gas supplies to Eastern Europe while causing no pain to Western Europe.

Since leaving the Chancellery, Schröder has been an enthusiastic advocate for the Kremlin. When the Estonian government relocated the Bronze Soldier in 2007, Schröder saw fit to emerge from retirement and condemn Tallinn for violating "every form of civilized behavior." A month after Russia's annexation of Crimea, which Schröder defended, the former chancellor was seen smiling and embracing Putin at a lavish seventieth birthday party in St. Petersburg thrown for him by the Russian president. If the purpose of espionage is to gain a clearer understanding of other countries' intentions, then alleged NSA spying on Gerhard Schröder was a perfectly valid attempt to protect the interests of the Western democratic community against the selfish concerns of one prominent and occasionally narrow-minded member.

Judging by the warm reception he received at the party's 2015 convention, most Social Democrats seem not at all troubled by their former leader's defense of the Russians. Indeed, "Schröderism"–cold-blooded economic nationalism and strategic neutralism disguised as high-minded realism—remains the guiding foreign policy impulse of the German center left. Sigmar Gabriel, vice chancellor in Merkel's coalition government, has followed in the footsteps of many Social Democrats by advocating another pipeline project to further entrench Russian dominance over Europe's energy supply. Nord Stream 2, which the European Commission reports will increase Russia's share of the German energy market from 30 percent to 60 percent, is unnecessary, considering that the existing Nord Stream pipeline operates at only half its capacity. Given that the EU has already accused Gazprom of engaging in price-gouging practices, increasing energy dependence on the Russian state-directed firm would only further hold Europe hostage to the Kremlin's whims.[37]

When it comes to presenting a united front against Russian aggression and subversion, Germany's Social Democrats are one of Europe's weakest links. In March 2015, Gabriel presented a journalism prize to Glenn Greenwald, chief disseminator of Snowden's stolen NSA files, who later claimed that the vice chancellor told him that the United States threatened to withhold information about potential terror plots in Germany if Berlin offered the leaker asylum, an accusation denied by the Obama administration.[38] Whether or not Gabriel ever said these things, why in the first place was he honoring the activist "journalist" who had collaborated with a man identified by Germany's own intelligence agencies as a Russian agent? In the fall of 2015, Gabriel advanced a key Kremlin aim when he argued for lessening or eliminating altogether sanctions on Russia in exchange for its cooperation in quelling the Syrian civil war, this despite the fact that Moscow and the West differ fundamentally over the Assad regime.[39] Social Democratic foreign minister Frank-Walter Steinmeier has proven just as helpful to Moscow's manipulations. After a June 2016 NATO exercise in Poland, undertaken to reassure the alliance's eastern allies and in which his own country participated, Steinmeier complained that such maneuvers constituted "saber-rattling" and "warmongering," the sorts of words one might expect to hear in a Russian propaganda broadcast.[40] If these statements are what leading German Social Democrats say in public, can you imagine what they say privately?

Signing a deal with an extortionist Russian energy concern and then taking a job on its board, lauding Vladimir Putin as a "flawless democrat," garlanding those who facilitate the exposure of America's national security secrets, attacking NATO as a bunch of "warmongers"—such is the recent foreign policy record of German Social Democracy. Although no information has come to light alleging American monitoring of Sigmar Gabriel or Frank-Walter Steinmeier's communications, the NSA would be remiss not to do so.

For six decades, Germany has been formally committed to European integration, NATO membership, and the transatlantic alliance. But its strategic orientation is not irreversible. Given that it is located in the center of Europe and imbued with a national identity largely shaped in opposition to Anglo-French conceptions of individualism and political liberty, Germany's Western anchoring is, in the words of scholar Jeffrey Herf, "a novelty in the context of modern German history since the Reformation."[41] For most of its history, Germany pursued a *Sonderweg*, or "special path," a sort of German exceptionalism that translated geopolitically into a middle course between East and West. The postwar Bonn Republic's attachment to a transatlantic Western community of nations was externally imposed, a result of Allied occupation and fear of Soviet encroachment. Yet even with the Red Army occupying the eastern half of their country, West Germans were far from unanimous in supporting NATO membership.

The 1949 division of Germany into Western and Eastern states set the terms for what would become the central issue of German—indeed, European—politics over the next four decades: reunification. Though consensus in the Federal Republic of Germany (FRG) favored reunification, fervid disagreement over how, under what terms, and at what cost this goal could be achieved emerged as the major disagreement between the Christian Democratic Union and the Social Democratic Party (SPD). Postwar

CDU chancellor Konrad Adenauer renounced Germany's prewar *Schaukel-politik,* or "seesaw policy" between East and West, arguing that such balance-of-power games had led the country to destruction. *Westbindung*—binding the Federal Republic politically, economically, and militarily to the West—took precedence over the unification of Germany along the "neutral and demilitarized" lines that Stalin would offer in 1952. For Adenauer, political division with American-guaranteed freedom for West Germany was preferable to reunification with Soviet-guaranteed "neutrality." The chances that Moscow would actually allow the latter were slim to none because Stalin's understanding of "neutrality" almost always meant the eventual imposition of a Soviet-friendly dictatorship.

Nevertheless, many Germans—understandably conflict-averse after having been at the center of the most destructive war in human history—hoped that such a scenario might be feasible. Surveys reveal that it was not until the fateful year of 1961—when leaders of the German Democratic Republic (GDR), after years of pestering, finally persuaded their Soviet patrons to construct a wall dividing Berlin—that a majority of West German citizens expressed a preference for establishing "good terms with Americans" over the options "good terms with the Russians" and "act neutrally towards both." For almost the entire decade before the wall's erection, a plurality of West Germans favored neutrality; in 1956, the year of the Soviets' brutal crackdown in Hungary, an astonishing 62 percent stated their wish that Germany stay neutral.[42] That same year, under the leadership of Kurt Schumacher, the SPD initially opposed German rearmament and membership in NATO, believing that these moves, and not Soviet imperialism, were the main impediment to German reunification. In its campaign rhetoric, the SPD went so far as to label Adenauer "Chancellor of the Allies" and charged that he valued good relations with the West above reunifying his country.

German conservatives often tarred the left-wing opponents of *Westbindung* as crypto-communists and fellow travelers. But many Germans who expressed such sentiments did so out of a sincere belief that neutralism, or at least a more accommodating policy toward the Soviet Union, was in the best interests of Germany and world peace. One such person was Willy Brandt. As a young socialist journalist exiled to Sweden during the war, he had impeccable anti-Nazi credentials, unlike many of the conservatives who would later challenge his patriotism. He also had no illusions about communists, having seen many of them denounce Weimar-era Social Democrats as "social fascists," thus deriding the anti-Hitler popular front. As mayor of West Berlin, Brandt protested loudly against construction of the Wall, fruitlessly urging the Americans, British, and French to put a halt to this blatant violation of East-West agreements allowing freedom of movement within the city. "We now have a state of accomplished extortion," he wrote in a public letter decrying Western impotence in the face of Soviet aggression.

Brandt's *Neue Ostpolitik* (so named to distinguish it from Adenauer's earlier policy, which established diplomatic relations with the Soviet Union) was largely born from this sense of helpless resignation with Western fecklessness and a "conviction," in the words of German historian Hans Peter Schwarz, that "Moscow held the key to reunification."[43] When he became the Federal Republic's first Social Democratic chancellor in 1969, Brandt implemented a series of measures aimed at reducing tensions between West Germany and the Eastern Bloc. In 1970, he struck a deal with Moscow paying for the construction of pipelines to transit gas from the Soviet Union, laying the groundwork for Europe's contemporary energy dependence on Russia. That same year, Brandt's famous *kniefall* at the memorial to the victims of the Warsaw Ghetto Uprising—expressing contrition on behalf of a nation many of whose citizens preferred not to be reminded of its past—earned him international acclaim, including from the judges of the Norwegian Nobel Committee, who awarded him their 1971 Peace Prize. When he signed a treaty the following year recognizing GDR sovereignty, Brandt abandoned twenty-five years of West German diplomatic isolation of East Germany.

Just as profound as these diplomatic initiatives was the change in SPD rhetoric. Brandt's *Ostpolitik,* shorn of the strident anticommunism of his earlier career, created space in German culture, academia, and media for a creeping moral equivalence between East and West. Criticism of the Soviet Union and its satellites became increasingly taboo; talking about these regimes' human rights abuses could get one labeled an "ideological" "Cold Warrior." Government money was directed to "peace research," a pseudo-academic field of inquiry concerned with exposing the perils of Western armament. A feature of this discourse was to overlook the political conditions, military buildup, and human rights abuses of the communist regimes, because such "obsessive" focus on value differences between East and West hindered diplomatic normalization.

But Moscow's 1975 deployment of medium-range, SS-20 nuclear-tipped missiles in Eastern Europe confronted Germans with the brute realities of Soviet domination. Since the postwar settling of Europe into bipolar blocs, the Warsaw Pact had maintained conventional military superiority on the continent due to the Soviet Union's geographical proximity and massive army. The hundreds of thousands of American troops stationed in Western Europe acted as something greater than a "trip wire," but less than an actual deterrent against Soviet aggression; it was America's nuclear arsenal that ultimately maintained the equilibrium of forces. With the signing of the Strategic Arms Limitation Treaties (known by their acronym SALT), the United States and Soviet Union had achieved parity on strategic nuclear weapons—the long-range nuclear warheads each had aimed at the other. By stationing "tactical" nuclear weapons that could be used to destroy targets in the European theater, however, the Soviets upset the overall military balance in their favor. The controversy that erupted over how the West should respond to this provocation revivified a German neutralist movement that came perilously close to endangering the transatlantic alliance.

Social Democratic chancellor Helmut Schmidt ignited what would become known as the "Euromissile" debate with a 1977 speech to the International Institute for Strategic Studies in London. Deployment of the SS-20s, he argued, threatened to invalidate "mutually assured destruction," the fearsome logic that had prevented a war between the two Cold War blocs. Schmidt worried that a Soviet tactical nuclear strike against a European NATO member state would *not* trigger a U.S. strategic nuclear response against Soviet territory, hence undermining the West's deterrent power by "decoupling" the United States from the continent's security and leaving Europe vulnerable to attack. The SS-20s, Schmidt later said, were intended as "a weapon of political intimidation directed against the nonnuclear Federal Republic of Germany." What was needed in response was the deployment, on West German soil, of American intermediate-range nuclear weapons capable of reaching the Soviet Union. These weapons would eliminate what West German defense officials called the "grey zone" between U.S.-Soviet and Soviet-European nuclear forces.[44] Only then would Moscow be disabused of the notion that it could wage a successful war against NATO by limiting it to Western Europe. In 1979, NATO foreign and defense ministers agreed to the "two-track" decision, announcing the deployment of American medium-range nuclear arms to Europe by 1983 unless the Soviets abandoned their own arsenals.

For a six-year span, beginning with Schmidt's London speech and ending with the 1983 Bundestag vote authorizing deployment of American Pershing II and cruise missiles, widespread German opposition to the NATO decision confronted the West with the gravest challenge to transatlantic unity since the early days of the Cold War. *Der Spiegel* publisher Rudolf Augstein registered a typical antinuclear critique. Foreshadowing arguments that would be made decades later to rationalize Vladimir Putin's aggression against Russia's neighbors, Augstein assailed the two-track decision as "encirclement" of the Soviet Union.[45] A group of prominent intellectuals, led by Nobel laureate Günther Grass, signed an open letter to Schmidt warning against Germany's being "drawn into a policy of the American government—that at the latest since Vietnam, has lost every right to moral appeals—which could have as its consequence the destruction of all life on this planet." Opposition to the two-track decision extended far beyond elites. To this day, the largest demonstrations in German history remain those against Pershing missile deployment when 300,000 people descended on Bonn in October 1981; the following year, 400,000 protested a NATO summit and President Ronald Reagan's speech to the Bundestag. (By contrast, when Soviet premier Leonid Brezhnev visited the West German capital in 1981, there were no mass protests.) A 1983 survey revealed that, even among supporters of the CDU-Free Democratic Party (FDP) coalition government, which had been elected on a platform in favor of missile deployment, 54 percent of CDU members and 70 percent of FDP members actually favored postponing the placement out of fear that that the ongoing Intermediate Nuclear Forces Treaty (INF) negotiations with the Soviets would collapse.[46]

The arguments of the West German peace movement were specious in two respects. First, by attacking the two-track decision as an American-instigated attempt to scupper détente, antinuclear advocates obscured the origins of the endeavor. It was a West German Social Democratic chancellor, "fed up" with the Carter administration's refusal to recognize the Soviet deployment of SS-20s as "political blackmail" against Europe, whose public pleading spurred the track-two decision, not right-wing American Cold Warriors.[47] Second, peace activists branded the track-two deployments a self-serving exercise on the part of Washington—"No Euroshima through Pershings" was one rallying cry—ignoring the fact that it was the Soviets, not the Americans, who had introduced the prospect of "limited" nuclear war on the continent by dispersing tactical weapons across Europe. Washington, by checking Moscow's deployment of medium-range nuclear missiles with its own warheads, reestablished its deterrent power and reduced the chances of Soviet aggression by binding itself existentially to Europe's security.

Though leaders of the West German peace movement liked to think of themselves as committed to the fate of humanity, it was impossible not to notice the nationalistic sentiments underlying their arguments. "No German can accept this unconditional subordination of the interests of our people to foreign interests," declared the Protestant pastor Helmut Gollwitzer at the October 1981 anti-NATO rally, "or accept this surrender of the determination of the existence of our people to a foreign government." Germany, he said, was "colonized."[48] In debates over the Euromissiles and *Ostpolitik,* it was common to hear Germans speak of their country and fellow citizens as "hostages" and "sacrificial victims" of American "occupation."[49] Günther Gaus, the first West German representative to the GDR, who went slightly native while stationed there, returned from his post claiming that the deployment of American missiles in the Federal Republic would make Germany an "American province in the meaning the term 'province' had in the Roman Empire." Petra Kelly, a young co-founder of the Green Party, warned that Germany would be transformed from a "forward-based colony" of America to a "nuclear launch pad." In the minds of many on the left, write Markovits and Gorski, the Federal Republic's image had evolved from that of "accomplice" to "victim."[50] Prior to its adoption by the pacifist left, the contention that America "occupied" Germany was almost exclusively confined to Germany's far right, who harbored residual bitterness over having lost World War II. Karl Kaiser, a German Social Democratic academic and advisor to Brandt, observed that the peace movement was "national in the guise of anti-nuclear."

For the many Germans who saw their country's division as a consequence of American Cold War hysteria, Euromissile deployment appeared to threaten the promises of détente—namely, decreased superpower tension, increased trade with the East, forgiveness of historic German sins, and, most of all, reunification. America, with its obsessive Russophobia, stood in the way of Germany becoming "normal." In 1984, 53 percent of West Germans expressed support for reunification in a "bloc-free" Germany—essentially the offer Stalin had made to them thirty-two years earlier.[51] According to the logic of *Ostpolitik,* once the countries of the world overcame their clannish instincts, Cold War military alliances would dissolve and the mechanisms of "collective security" would take their place. As early as 1973, Bahr predicted that "a security system for all of Europe will replace" NATO and the Warsaw Pact.[52]

Ultimately, the Bundestag approved Pershing II and cruise missile deployment on a party-line vote. Nonetheless, the strenuousness of the debate, the radicalism of the opinions expressed, and the hair's breadth by which the Federal Republic escaped issuing a decisive setback to transatlantic unity provoked fears about the country's long-term strategic orientation. In 1985, the Hungarian liberal philosophers Agnes Heller and Ferenc Feher published an essay speculating that the Federal Republic might opt for "confederation" with East Germany, an arrangement that would compel its departure from NATO and eviction of Western military bases from its territory. All of this could have been done by democratic means—through votes in the Bundestag—and the United States would have been helpless to stop it. (Unlike Soviet forces in East Germany, the hundreds of thousands of American troops stationed in the Federal Republic were there by the consent of a democratically elected government.) Heller and Feher titled their essay "Eastern Europe under the Shadow of a New Rapallo," a reference to the 1922 treaty between the Weimar Republic and Bolshevik Russia that (like the Molotov-Ribbentrop Pact seventeen years later) included a secret annex. According to this confidential side agreement, Germany was allowed to drill its army on Soviet soil (in contravention of the post–World War I Treaty of Versailles) in exchange for training the nascent Bolshevik army officer class. In a "New Rapallo," Heller and Feher wrote, Bonn would abandon the peoples of Eastern Europe as well as its alliance with the West on the altar of reunification. "Once the path leading to a new Rapallo is taken," they warned, "the consequences cease to be exclusively German, for it will be Eastern Europe that pays the bill."[53]

Those living in the lands wedged between Germany and Russia had the right to feel that *Ostpolitik* shunted them aside. By attempting to go over the heads of the "captive nations" and deal directly with their unelected overlords in Moscow, Brandt, Bahr, and other West German leaders signaled a preference for change from the top down rather than the bottom up. What they most prized was "stability" in interstate relations, the reassuring consistency of which was hampered by the demands of popular democratic movements. Poland's imposition of martial law in 1981, for instance, confronted the practitioners of *Ostpolitik* with a quandary: continue doing business with the communist regime or heed the Polish people's cries for freedom. Their performance was far from admirable. "In order to survive, Western Europe needs stability in Eastern Europe," wrote Günther Gaus, essentially telling the Polish people to cool it.[54] "The Poles' national ambitions must also be subordinated to the interests of the preservation of the peace," remarked Egon Bahr. "I must admit," the great Polish freedom fighter Adam Michnik wrote in 1984, "that it made me angry that Willy Brandt had so quickly forgotten how bitter is the taste of that prison food, on which in his youth the German Social Democrats had been fed." The following year, on a visit to Poland in his capacity as president of the Socialist International, Brandt refused to see Solidarity trade union activist Lech Walesa. Meeting with his fellow Nobel laureate would, after all, upset the fragility of détente.[55]

However well intentioned, this faith in what might be called "trickle-down democracy" was misplaced. *Ostpolitik* hinged on the assumption that the communist bloc governments were dependable actors. Poland's crackdown and the Soviet invasion of Afghanistan, however, proved definitively that these sclerotic regimes required no "provocation" from the West to behave violently to keep themselves in power. *Ostpolitik*, guided by its nostrum of "change through rapprochement," ultimately amounted to, in the words of Jeffrey Herf, "rapprochement without change, with the separation of the issue of peace in Europe from that of political freedom in Eastern Europe."[56] What finally brought down the communist regimes of Central and Eastern Europe was a combination of the people-powered movements from below (Solidarity in Poland, the Velvet Revolution in Czechoslovakia, the Peaceful Revolution in East Germany), Soviet Premier Mikhail Gorbachev's decision not to use force to batten them down, and communism's irresolvable flaws.

To the extent that Western policies aided communism's downfall, it was by exploiting these flaws. The two-track decision, armed backing of anti-communist insurgencies around the world, vocal support for human rights, and a surge in defense spending—all of these moves kept the Soviets and their clients on the defensive. Where Western hawks saw opportunities to take advantage of the enemy's weaknesses in hopes of bringing about its demise, the preachers of *Ostpolitik* saw openings to buttress an interlocutor's position. West German aid propped up East Germany, enabling it to become the most politically repressive yet economically prosperous regime in the Eastern Bloc. Initiatives like the "deal of the century" in 1981, when West Germany paid for the construction of pipes to transfer gas from the Soviet Union, sustained Moscow's ruling gerontocracy. "It often seemed as if *Ostpolitik* was a system of outdoor relief for Eastern bureaucrats," writes historian Gordon A. Craig.[57] The notion that Eastern Europeans would ever be unshackled not by a willing Kremlin but by themselves was alien to advocates of *Ostpolitik*, whose concern for the dissidents of the East consisted mainly of nervous worry that they would "destabilize" the political situation. So invested was the SPD in legitimizing the GDR that in 1987 it released a joint declaration with the Socialist Unity Party (SED) affirming that "criticism, even in sharp form, may not turn into interference in the internal affairs of the other."[58] Such collaboration would have been unimaginable to an earlier generation of Social Democrats, who watched in horror as the GDR dictatorship sent many of their East German comrades to prison.

After the fall of the Wall, the collapse of the USSR, the dissolution of the Warsaw Pact, and the demise of the geopolitical confrontation that divided

the continent, worries that Germany would sell out Eastern Europe for better relations with Russia faded, at least temporarily. Yet the concerns Heller
and Feher expressed about Germany's Western orientation did not crumble
with the collapse of the Berlin Wall. Many Europeans, and Germans especially, erroneously believe that it was détente which brought about the
peaceful unraveling of communism, a historical misreading that today
recommends accommodation toward Moscow. By removing the role of
American hard power and anticommunist moral fervor from the story of
German reunification, the narrative of 1989 becomes, as German journalist
Richard Herzinger has put it, "We continued and never gave up and then the
Soviet Union became nice."[59] As a result of "the belief that Gorbachev gave
us German reunification as a present," much of the German foreign policy
establishment shows greater sensitivity toward the Kremlin than it does
toward ordinary Russians or Central and Eastern Europeans. When communism collapsed, the strategic imperative of *Westbindung* was rendered obsolete, and the myth that *Ostpolitik* won the Cold War became widely
accepted. With Germany reunified, surrounded by friendly democracies,
and no longer on the frontlines of East-West confrontation, the desire for
strategic equidistance between East and West remains a powerful force.

Russia's reemergence as a revisionist state has revived the long-running
contestation between *Westbindung* and *Sonderweg*. Sentiments that animated the West German neutralism of yore—aversion to military power,
opposition to "bloc politics," fear of conflict with Russia, and suspicion of
America—resonate in contemporary debates concerning Germany's world
role. The deep-seated desire for neutralism, though hardly dormant during the 1989–2014 interlude that signified a sort of holiday from history,
has once against risen to the forefront of German politics.

   One of the sacrosanct principles of postwar German policy is a commitment to multilateralism. Because nationalism had led to ruin, Germany
had no choice but to submerge its interests within those of supranational
structures. German politicians of both right and left validated their policies with the language of multilateralism. For Adenauer, who accepted the
reality of bipolarity, *Westbindung* would ensure Germany's democratic path
while strengthening the European peace order; for Brandt, who believed

bipolarity could be transcended, *Ostpolitik* would reconcile Germany with the nations to its east and lead the divided continent to harmonious convergence. Hans Dietrich Genscher spoke for the broad spectrum of German foreign policy thinkers when he famously said, "The more European our foreign policy is, the more national it is." Despite this rhetorical modesty, however, postwar German leaders have not been immune to naked self-interest; they just dress it up in the language of altruistic multilateralism.

In the early months after the Berlin Wall collapsed, hoping to quell Moscow's fears about a reunified Germany, both Genscher and Kohl claimed in private meetings with their Soviet counterparts that the countries of Central and Eastern Europe would never be admitted to NATO. However, as leaders of but one member state in a multinational alliance, this was a promise they lacked the authority to make. (Deft negotiating by President George H. W. Bush, ensuring that NATO membership would be open to any country that met the alliance's requirements, averted the potential damage of Kohl's and Genscher's freelance diplomacy.) Yet to this day the myth that NATO "promised" not to expand eastward in exchange for German reunification is widely believed.

In the first test of its post–Cold War foreign policy, the Gulf War, Germany offered only lukewarm support to Bush's carefully assembled international coalition against Saddam Hussein. Rather than send troops or provide logistical aid, Germany wrote a check to the allies for $11 billion. Protest against the war, according to Markovits and Gorski, was "quantitatively and qualitatively more pronounced than in any other country in the advanced industrial world."[60] In 1999, after hard-fought debate, Germany deployed the Bundeswehr for its first mission abroad as part of NATO's campaign to avert ethnic cleansing in Kosovo. The mission not only tested Germany's commitment to multilateralism but also forced a reckoning with the Nazi past. The recurrence of genocide on European soil presented a challenge for the 1968 generation of German leftists, whose political awakening had been motivated by pacifism and antifascism. Many of these activists had gone on to form the Green Party, which entered government for the first time in 1998 as part of a "red-green" coalition with the Social Democrats. Joschka Fischer, an erstwhile radical street activist and Green parliamentarian, became the coalition's improbable foreign minister. "I believe in two principles," Fischer told a rowdy Green Party convention. "Never again war and never again Auschwitz." He properly understood that, although "Never again war" and "Never again Auschwitz" were both worthy maxims, there were moments when they might contradict each other. Sometimes war would be necessary to stop another Auschwitz. The red-green government's decision to back NATO intervention marked a decisive point in the maturation of German foreign policy.

Berlin's abstention from the 2011 Security Council vote authorizing NATO's use of force to prevent genocide in Libya—thereby abandoning traditional allies Britain, France, and the United States to vote alongside China and Russia—signaled a decisive break with Germany's multilateral pretensions. "A serious mistake of historic dimensions," was how a former defense minister described his country's nonparticipation in the mission.[61] "A clear renunciation of the multilateral policies of former German governments," echoed a former UN ambassador. Fischer declared himself ashamed of those left-wing politicians who "initially welcomed this scandalous mistake." At the very least, critics said, Germany could have voted in favor of the operation to provide it diplomatic legitimacy and then decline active participation. Yet Berlin went out of its way not to be seen as offering even the appearance of support, promptly withdrawing hundreds of military personnel stationed in the Mediterranean. Then-NATO Secretary General Anders Fogh Rasmussen accused Germany of abandoning alliance solidarity and called Berlin's position "absurd."

Like most other Western Europeans, Germans were utterly taken aback by the return of conventional warfare to the European continent in the form of Russia's 2014 annexation of Crimea and invasion of Ukraine. (Though Germany has sent soldiers to Afghanistan as part of the NATO mission, their rules of engagement were heavily circumscribed, and their deployment has always been unpopular among the German public.) In the immediate aftermath of the Crimea annexation, a survey found 49 percent of Germans supporting a political stance "between the West and Russia" and only 45 percent for one "firmly in the Western alliance."[62] Those numbers shifted when Russian-backed separatists, using Russian-supplied weapons, shot a civilian airliner out of the sky several months later. Had that not taken place, it's likely that German public opinion would have remained at least roughly split between support for a Western political orientation and neutralism, a microcosm of the *Westbindung* versus *Sonderweg* dichotomy.

Seven decades after the end of World War II, fear of war permeates German society, and Russia's invasion of a sovereign European country appears to have frightened Germans even further into a conciliatory crouch.[63] A 2015 Pew poll showed that only 25 percent of Germans believe their country "should play a more active military role in helping to maintain peace and stability in the world."[64] Russia exploits these pacifist sentiments through appeals to Germans' historic war guilt, predisposition for a simplistic notion of "peace," and distrust of the United States. In the early months of the Ukraine crisis, a vocal faction of German commentators, politicians, and industrialists sympathetic to Moscow became so conspicuous that they earned the label *"Russlandversteher,"* literally, "Russia understander." They included not just predictable faces like Gerhard Schröder but also his predecessors Helmut Schmidt and Helmut Kohl, the latter of whom has complained about a "lack of sensitivity with our Russian neighbors, especially with President Putin."[65] Foreign Minister Steinmeier, himself frequently painted with the *Russlandversteher* brush, has owned the term and openly questioned why it is considered pejorative.[66] In her steadfast support for sanctions, Merkel has also had to contend with resistance from the powerful Committee on Eastern European Economic Relations, a lobby association representing the many German businesses with operations in Russia. As for public opinion, there exists an emotional undercurrent of sympathy for Russia, mixed with genuine trepidation of how Western "provocation" could lead to war.

Moscow's cynical exploitation of World War II, a potent feature in its disinformation war against the West, has been orchestrated largely for a German audience. According to an early Kremlin narrative, the Maidan revolution and the government it brought to power in Kyiv were not the achievements of ordinary Ukrainians fed up with corruption and mismanagement, but the work of "Nazis" intent on eradicating ethnic Russians and Jews. Though the far right did play a role in the protests that drove the pro-Russian president Viktor Yanukovych from power, Moscow grossly exaggerates both their significance and popularity, as evidenced by the lackluster performance of extremist parties in Ukrainian national elections.

In the parlance of the Kremlin and its Western sympathizers, "Nazi" does not denote an admirer of German National Socialism so much as it does an opponent of Russian foreign policy. In this sense, it is no different from the way the Soviets and their apologists tarred critics as "fascists." If the specter of Nazism has been intended to put Ukrainians in bad odor with the Europeans whose political project they desperately wish to join, it is the German public, innately sensitive to accusations of renascent fascism, who are the prime audience for this particular element of disinformation. "We are very concerned about any possible ethnic cleansings and Ukraine ending up as a neo-Nazi state," Putin said in a rare interview with a German public broadcaster in 2014.[67] Frequent allusions to Ukrainian Nazism are designed to remind Germans of their historical debt to Russia, and their intended effect on German attitudes is similar to that engendered by *Ostpolitik*. Accentuating Russian victimhood benefits Russians and Germans alike: It gives Germans license to disregard any obligations they might feel (or, in the case of the NATO charter, actually have) to Central and Eastern Europe, and it lets Russia behave with impunity. By tarring Ukrainians as Nazis, Russia offers Germany a chance to atone for its past by joining a new popular front against "fascism."

Never mind that this bargain absolves Moscow for its unprovoked aggression against a neighbor. The argument presented to Germans—that Russians are their historic victims and Ukrainians their historic collaborators—conflates the present-day Russian state with the Soviet Union, in whose service many Ukrainians died. This is not a semantic matter. Portraying Ukrainians as eternal fascists ignores how "the vast majority of Ukrainians who fought in [World War II] did so in the uniform of the Red Army," writes Yale historian Timothy Snyder. "More Ukrainians were killed fighting the Wehrmacht than American, British and French soldiers—combined."[68] To the extent that Germans wish to shape their foreign policy as compensation for historic crimes, they owe as much solidarity to Ukrainians as Russians.

Like the proponents of *Ostpolitik* before them, Europe's *Russlandversteher* dogmatically elevate "peace"—and a very circumscribed definition of it—above any other consideration. For Brandt and Bahr, "peace" with the East didn't preclude a massive Soviet military buildup, martial law in Poland, or an invasion of Afghanistan—not to mention the daily denial of basic liberties to East Bloc citizens. None of these actions, the reasoning went, could justify a robust Western response lest it "provoke" the Russians. Such restraint allows one's authoritarian adversaries to get away with a lot. "The prerequisite for peace is that people are not murdered, that people are not expelled, that women are not raped," Joschka Fischer declared to the Green Party delegates in 1999, revealing just how low the bar was set.

None of this is to discount the effort that countries should make to avoid armed conflict. German revulsion for war is not to be belittled. But a crucial task for any democratic society is to balance competing values. How to maximize equality *and* individual liberty, for instance, is a question that has occupied political theorists for generations. The flaw in the German obsession with "peace" is its unconditional quality. The aspiration to achieve peace to the exclusion of all other considerations—such as freedom, both for oneself and one's neighbors—derives from a variant of German philosophical idealism in which societal adherence to one value is decreed absolute. An open letter published in *Die Zeit* in December 2014, signed by sixty prominent Germans ranging from the film director Wim Wenders to the cosmonaut Sigmund Jähn to Gerhard Schröder, typifies this sentiment. Titled "War in Europe Again? Not in Our Names," the letter incongruously cited the Iraq War as a reason to accommodate Russian belligerence in Ukraine and apocalyptically invoked the specter of World War III as a rebuke to anyone advocating a tougher stand against Moscow.[69] Citing "the success of the détente policy" in bringing about German reunification, the letter spread blame for deteriorating East-West relations among "the Americans, Europeans and Russians," who had "all lost, as their guiding principle, the idea of permanently banishing war from their relationship"—obscuring that it was Moscow, and Moscow alone, that had resorted to war on the continent by invading its neighbor. Reminding the German government of its "responsibility for peace in Europe," the signatories called for "a new policy of détente."

Merkel, who grew up in the East German communist dictatorship, has no illusions about Putin, but her firmness doesn't extend beyond a like-minded few. Social Democratic Foreign Minister Frank-Walter Steinmeier's references to "both conflict parties" in diplomatic communiqués concerning the Ukraine crisis paint a picture of two sides with equal moral and political standing and overlook Russia's role as instigator and aggressor. Steinmeier, who helped devise the "rapprochement through trade" policy when he was chief of staff to Gerhard Schröder, also tried to position Germany as a diplomatic middleman between America and Russia in the Syria conflict. After Moscow initiated airstrikes mostly targeting pro-Western rebels fighting the Syrian government, Steinmeier took to the floor of the Bundestag to "urgently admonish the United States and Russia" to abstain from "military engagement" in Syria, conflating Washington's tepid support for a handful of proxy forces with a full-blown Russian military operation.[70]

Accommodationist views toward Russia characterize much if not most of the German foreign policy establishment. According to Green Party Bundestag member Marieluise Beck, a not insignificant portion of the German elite and public have deliberately buried their heads in the sand about Russia's activities in Ukraine and its aggression more generally, so terrified are they of the consequences that admitting the truth might entail. "Not wanting to know provides an opportunity for equidistance" between East and West, she says.[71] There exists in Germany a "fear and fascination" with Putin, whose "propagandists in the Kremlin know us better, our sensibilities better, than we know ourselves." In 2015, Germany's outgoing ambassador to NATO complained that the alliance has been "very one-sided" in its approach to the conflict in Ukraine, faulting in particular the "reassurance" measures it offered to the Eastern states (which consisted of little more than temporary rotations of several hundred soldiers and increased airspace policing) while neglecting "dialogue" with Moscow.[72] But what is a collective security alliance if it's not "one-sided"? This high-ranking German diplomat, who is hardly alone in his views, appears to believe that NATO is an international arbitration forum and not a military alliance committed to defending the security needs of its members. When NATO's Supreme Allied Commander, General Philip Breedlove, released evidence of Russian military involvement in Ukraine—a heavily documented fact that Berlin, along with other European capitals, has been loathe to admit—

anonymous German government sources told *Der Spiegel* that Breedlove was spreading "dangerous propaganda."[73]

Recrudescent nationalism should not be underestimated as a factor in another recent controversy roiling German-American relations: the Transatlantic Trade and Investment Partnership (TTIP), a proposed free trade agreement between the United States and Europe. TTIP would create the world's largest free trade area and boost the EU's GDP growth by a half-percent a year, not insignificant for a continent experiencing years-on-end zero growth and high unemployment. TTIP's opponents, whose rhetoric regularly depicts Germany as a subjugated colony of the American imperium, evoke the left-wing nationalism of the West German peace movement. "We should not render ourselves vassals to the United States and ignore the rights of the Bundestag," declared SPD secretary general Yasmin Fahimi (echoing antinuclear activist Petra Kelly's observation that Germany was a "colony" and "nuclear launchpad" of the United States).[74] Dire warnings of "chlorinated chicken," just one of many tainted American products guaranteed to poison unsuspecting German consumers, dominated news coverage of the trade deal. An October 2015 demonstration against TTIP in Berlin drew a quarter-million protestors; it's hard to imagine that most of these people were motivated to such a feat of civic participation by a highly complex trade agreement thick as a doorstop. The rhetoric and signage of the demonstrators (iconic images of Uncle Sam pointing an outstretched finger above the text, "I WANT EUROPE") suggest that it is TTIP's strategic context, not minutiae concerning tariffs, that unnerves so many Germans. "The U.S. push for world domination is unacceptable," one anti-TTIP protestor told Reuters. "Obama sends out drones to kill people and wins the Nobel Peace Prize. This has to stop."[75] What the targeted assassinations of terrorists had to do with a trade package, the man did not say.

"The memory of states is the test of truth of their policy," Henry Kissinger once wrote. "The more elementary the experience, the more profound its impact on a nation's interpretation of the present in the light of the past."[76] Kissinger's subject was the early nineteenth-century Congress of Vienna, but his conclusion about the centrality of history to a nation's definition of itself is timeless and universal. Though the legacy of totalitarian rule is frequently invoked to explain German anger over the NSA revelations, it's not so much Nazi and communist depredations that inform popular reactions to the scandal as it is another historical phenomenon: the utopian yearning for neutrality. Intense outrage and complaints of American betrayal are less the result of sensitivity to surveillance than they are products of longing for a nonpolar world. Nonaligned states, after all, should have no need to spy on one another, or be spied upon.

A new German *Sonderweg* would not necessarily entail a full-scale reversion to the dark German past. Germany can maintain its domestic liberal political culture while extricating itself from the Western alliance. Opposition to *Westbindung,* support *for Ostpolitik,* resistance to the Euromissiles, obliviousness to Russian revanchism, hysteria over imported chicken—all these phenomena share, at root, a desire for Germany to situate itself so that it no longer need take a side. For the largest country in Europe, located at the heart of a divided continent, that was an unrealistic wish during the Cold War. It is no less so today.

4

The European Union: Trouble in Paradise

If we extend unlimited tolerance even to those who are intolerant, if we are not prepared to defend a tolerant society against the onslaught of the intolerant, then the tolerant will be destroyed, and tolerance with them.

Karl Popper, *The Open Society and its Enemies*, 1945

TRAFFIC IS NORMALLY BRISK ON THE Øresund Bridge connecting Copenhagen to Malmö, Sweden's third largest city. At five miles, Øresund is Europe's longest combined road and rail link, with 20,000 commuters passing over it on a normal day, and a majestic symbol of Europe's internal open borders. Codified by the 1985 Schengen Agreement, the most tangible and, until very recently, popular aspect of European integration, Schengen allows for visa-free travel within twenty-six of the Union's twenty-eight member states.

Long before Schengen was signed, Sweden and Denmark had established an open border between their two countries in 1958. That freedom of movement suffered a major setback on January 4, 2016, however, when Stockholm announced mandatory identity checks for anyone entering the country from its southern neighbor. A tide of migrants mainly from North Africa and the Middle East had been pouring into Europe by land and by sea, arriving in such massive numbers that even Sweden's once-limitlessly compassionate refugee policy had to be supplanted by practical considerations.

Hours later, in response to the Swedish announcement and hoping to stanch the northward flow of migrants, the Danish government declared its own passport controls on the country's southern border with Germany, whose government many had come to blame for the crisis. By effectively opening its doors to anyone claiming Syrian citizenship, a unilateral suspension of the EU migration rule mandating that individuals apply for asylum in the first member state onto which one sets foot, Berlin accelerated an already large wave of migrants into Europe whose numbers would exceed one million by the end of 2015. As countries across the continent began fortifying their borders, the dawning realization that accommodating such a massive number of people would be substantially more difficult than expected hit most heavily in Sweden, long proud of its reputation as the world's most welcoming country to refugees. In 2013 alone, according to the Organization for Economic Cooperation and Development, Sweden took in more than twice as many asylum seekers per capita as any other nation.[1]

For decades, Sweden's open-door policy to refugees, economic migrants, and asylum seekers—important distinctions between the three are often blurred—was politically untouchable, unanimously accepted by the country's ruling parties, and rigidly protected from criticism by a media and societal elite that forbade even the slightest dissent. Except for a far-right party called the Sweden Democrats, whose origins lay in neo-Nazi and skinhead groups, few Swedes ever publicly questioned the country's immigration dogma. When, in November 2015, the deputy prime minister announced at a press conference that Sweden would have to reduce the number of migrants it accepted that year due to the heavy strain they imposed on public services, she broke down into tears.[2]

This weepy concession to reality, however, only acknowledged the migrant crisis's material challenges. In Sweden, Germany, and elsewhere, the tension created by the Great Migration of 2015–2016 was initially characterized as a demanding but manageable burden on European welfare states and physical infrastructure. Money could be moved around and resources could be reallocated; all that was needed was creativity and determination. When IKEA, Sweden's most iconic brand, announced it was running out of beds to supply local authorities tasked with housing the newcomers, the solution was simple: Build more beds.[3] Likewise, Sweden's foreign aid budget—

representing a higher percentage of gross national income than that of any other country in the world—could be cut by 60 percent to pay migrant resettlement costs in country.[4] Conceiving of the problem as solely a matter of resources inevitably generated a resource-dependent solution: spend more money, something that rich, generous countries like Sweden and Germany could afford.

But by assessing the crisis exclusively in quantitative terms, Europeans neglected to consider how the *nature* of the migration might present cultural challenges that no amount of social welfare spending could alleviate. To begin with, there is the massive gender imbalance of the migrants: Of the 1.5 million asylum seekers who came to Europe in 2015, 73 percent were male,[5] a disproportion significantly greater than the current population of China, the most sex-imbalanced country in the world, which in 2015 abandoned the one-child policy that for so long aggravated the disparity. Vast amounts of sociological research (not to mention common sense) show that as populations grow more male dominated they become increasingly prone to conflict, violence, and sexual assault, the latter the entirely predictable result of young men competing for a smaller pool of women. To avoid this fate, George Washington University anthropologist Barbara Miller argues that governments should consider the maintenance of balanced sex ratios a "local and global public good" like the provision of potable water and sewage removal.[6] Nonetheless, media images of the European migrant wave emphasized women and children, who represented a minority of the new arrivals.

Letting such a massive, lopsidedly male cohort into Europe would have brought enormous challenges no matter where the migrants came from. It only aggravates the situation that nearly all these men hail from majority Muslim countries where the legal status of women and popular attitudes about gender roles and human sexuality differ greatly from those in the West. A comprehensive 2013 Pew Research Center survey of worldwide Muslim public opinion found that majorities in twenty of twenty-three countries "believe a wife must obey her spouse," a view that is, needless to say, not au courant in modern Europe, especially Scandinavia, which prides itself on being the most progressive region of the world on the matter of gender equality.[7] "Solid majorities" of Muslims also support the establishment of Sharia, and 75 percent or more in thirty-three of thirty-six countries believe homosexuality is wrong. According to the World Economic Forum's 2014 Global Gender Gap Report, which assesses women's status in health, education, the economy, and politics, Islamic countries comprise sixteen of the twenty worst nations to be a woman; Syria, the source of a plurality of the migrants, is fourth on the list. On its website, the International Women's Travel Center advises that it "cannot recommend travel to any country in the Middle East."[8] In the words of Algerian novelist Kamel Daoud, the Arab Muslim world has "a sick relationship with women" that, among other evils, produces forced veiling, clitoridectomy, and reconstructive surgery for broken hymens.[9]

The predictable consequences of allowing so many young, low-skilled, unattached men into Europe became clear in the aftermath of New Year's Eve 2015 when Europeans were finally forced to nurse, in addition to hangovers, their shattered illusions about immigration. The previous evening, a mob of about one thousand Arab and North African men perpetrated mass, coordinated sexual assaults on German women outside Cologne's main train station. All told, more than 650 people filed criminal complaints detailing abuse ranging from groping to rape. "Suddenly I felt a hand on my bum, on my breasts, I was grabbed everywhere, it was horrific," one victim recalled. "I was desperate, it was like running the gantlet. Over the space of 200 meters, I think I must have been touched about 100 times."[10] Some 150 similar attacks were reported in Hamburg, and in the ensuing days and weeks, a trickle of stories appeared in local newspapers across the country detailing migrant sexual assaults not only against German women but immigrant ones as well.[11] In the liberal university city of Freiburg, a group of clubs and bars collectively decided to bar admission to refugees after a series of pickpocketing incidents and sexual assaults.[12]

No woman who has ever walked the streets of a major Arab city—nor any man who has ever accompanied one—could have expressed shock at this turn of events. Blatant street harassment is simply the norm in much of the Arab world. A 2013 study conducted by the United Nations Entity for Gender Equality and the Empowerment of Women found that 99.3 percent of women in Egypt—the most populous Arab country—have experienced sexual harassment, half of them on a daily basis.[13] So prevalent is mass, participatory sexual assault in this part of the world that there is a word for it, *taharrush,* one with which Europeans have become painfully acquainted as this distinctly Arabian pathology has been imported to their streets.

Of course, sexual violence is not exclusive to this part of the world, as the behavior of certain American football players and presidential candidates, not to mention the Catholic Church child sex abuse scandals, well attest. Nor did the various assaults occur *because* the culprits were Muslim; indeed, it is impossible to know the extent to which the perpetrators even adhere to Islam or consider themselves followers of the faith. What's undeniable, however, is that these men came from cultures that foster attitudes and behavior toward women utterly divergent from prevalent European notions of gender equality. Ironically, religion would come more into play in the defensive reactions of European policy makers and media, who rushed to claim that the Muslim milieus from which the migrants came were irrelevant. Understandably afraid of popular backlash toward migrants, they attempted to downplay these scandals to prevent public opposition to their immigration policies. Their denial of reality, however, unwittingly fueled the very populist, right-wing recriminations they tried to avoid.

Accounts of migrant men partaking in sexualized anarchy in the heart of one of Europe's grandest cities struck a discordant contrast to the *Willkommenskultur* proudly declared by the German government, political parties, media, and civic organizations just a few months earlier. "We can do it"—Angela Merkel's partly encouraging, partly enjoining announcement to Germans about the colossal task of feeding, clothing, housing, employing, schooling, policing, and integrating more than one million migrants—was starting to look less like her famous pragmatism, and more like the improvisation of the East German official whose fumbled answer to a question about border checks at a press conference led hours later to the collapse of the Berlin Wall. And it looked even more imprudent when, in January 2016, the vice president of the European Commission reported that 60 percent of the migrants entering Europe had come not in flight from war and political oppression, as had been reported by sympathetic media and NGOs, but for economic reasons.[14]

Merkel's decision would have consequences for the whole of Europe. By unilaterally suspending the EU's "Dublin rule" mandating that asylum seekers to the EU register with the member state they enter and declaring instead that any Syrian who could make it to Germany would automatically receive asylum, Merkel wasn't just welcoming more than a million migrants into Germany: She was welcoming more than a million migrants to Europe. For whether you're a tourist or a migrant, once you enter the Schengen zone you can move about its multinational area unhindered. At least, that's how it used to be before Schengen members started throwing up border checks in late 2015—a process that intensified after it emerged that at least two of the assailants in the November 13 Islamic State terrorist attacks in Paris had entered Europe via Greece as part of the largely undocumented migrant wave from the Middle East.[15] Europe's failure to devise a common approach to asylum and migration, its propensity to adopt nationalist solutions in response to this shared problem, and its sorry record in assimilating Muslim residents augur that the dilemma of social cohesion brought about by mass immigration will only grow worse.

Europe's modern experience of immigration began in the 1950s and 1960s, when a postwar rebuilding boom and labor shortage created a need for millions of guest workers. In Germany, these *gastarbeiter* were mainly Turks, welcomed with the tacit understanding that they would return home after their labor was no longer required. That understanding was never fulfilled, however, and by the mid-1970s the purpose of immigration to Europe shifted from serving the needs of European labor markets to satisfying the wants of migrants themselves. In many countries, family reunification replaced economic requirements and even asylum as the chief drivers of immigration, even though European countries, with a view toward their histories, already had some of the most liberal asylum laws in the world. According to Christopher Caldwell, a keen observer of the continent's immigration saga, "Europe solved temporary economic problems through permanent demographic change."[16]

Once they've settled, immigrants often face societies that do not know what to do with them. Whether they are economic migrants, asylum seekers, or refugees fleeing violent conflict, immigrants to Europe (and even their European-born children) are often viewed as guests. Competing with the French model of stringent immigrant assimilation has been a policy, pursued most visibly in Britain and Germany, of "multiculturalism," which in the European context means a rejection of the notion that immigrants must adhere to a core culture. Unfortunately, both social contracts have led to the establishment of parallel societies.

Some commentators have argued that whatever social challenges the new immigrants might bring with them, they present a supply of young, cheap workers that is desperately needed to revitalize the continent's sluggish economy and replenish its shrinking labor force. Declining birthrates and an aging population require an influx of workers to boost economic growth and maintain generous welfare states. This argument might have made sense fifty years ago, when Europe lacked unskilled laborers and had to rebuild its entire infrastructure after a devastating war nearly destroyed everything. But it is less convincing in the era of double-digit unemployment—an era that, in some European countries, has lasted for decades—and of globalization, when Europe needs educated workers to maintain its competitiveness. German industry's want for skilled young labor could far more easily be met by hiring some of the millions of unemployed Spanish, French, and Italians than importing untold numbers of difficult-to-assimilate and poorly skilled Middle Easterners and North Africans. Harvard economist Martin Feldstein has calculated that were Spain—whose ratio of workers to retirees is declining sharply—to instantly add two million foreign-born workers (equal to 10 percent of the workforce), it would produce a 2 percent net increase in GDP after subtracting the state expenditures consumed by the immigrants and their dependents. Although the immediate GDP boost from such a population influx, in light of Spain's persistently sluggish economy, is significant, it pales in comparison to the attendant long-term fiscal costs that would result from Spain's high health care and pension obligations, owed not only to the added workers but also their dependents.[17]

Unlike those in the United States, which features one of the world's most dynamic and entrepreneurial economies as well as a less generous welfare state, immigrants to Europe are not nearly as economically productive as native-born Europeans. Across the EU, 15 percent of non-EU immigrants are unemployed, compared to just 5.8 percent of immigrants in the United States.[18] Whereas in Europe the figure of foreign-born unemployment is 5 percent higher than that of the native born, in America it is

1 percent *lower.*[19] Listening to some major American political figures and commentators, you would not believe that immigrants have a higher labor force participation rate than native-born Americans. In Europe, however, they do not, and the disparity between foreigners and native born is even more extreme among youth. There are many reasons America does a better job assimilating immigrants than Europe, and the relative availability of work is one of the more overlooked ones. The cultural dynamics of America's immigrant success story are unique, intertwined with the country's origins as an immigrant-created society, and therefore hard to emulate, and most of the factors hindering Europe's ability to integrate immigrants are deeply rooted and resistant to change. Jump-starting economies so that they provide more economic opportunities is one of the easier things European governments could do to improve social harmony and ease the difficulties posed by mass immigration.

Still, though reducing joblessness among immigrants should be a priority for its own sake, by itself it will not solve the problems of assimilating Muslim communities or reducing the lure of Islamic radicalization. What made Merkel's decision to open Europe's gates to an untold number of Muslim migrants so problematic is that the continent has done such a poor job integrating the Muslims who already live there. A study conducted in Germany, for instance, found that "Muslims living in areas with a lower unemployment rate seem to display a higher sense of [religious] identity," precisely the opposite of what conventional wisdom dictates about religious extremism and an unfortunately common theme across the continent. "Muslims do not seem to assimilate with the time spent in the UK, or at least they seem to do so at a much slower rate than non-Muslims," a 2007 report on Muslim integration in Britain concluded. "Also, education does not seem to have any effect on the attenuation of their identity, and job qualification as well as living in neighborhoods with low unemployment rate[s] seem to accentuate rather than moderate the identity formation of Muslims."[20]

When it comes to questions of basic values, there exists a broad divergence in Muslim and non-Muslim European public opinion. A poll conducted ten years after the Mohammed cartoon controversy reported that 93 percent of Danish Muslims still believe it was wrong to publish the cartoons, the same figure reported when the crisis led to worldwide riots in 2006.[21] Elsewhere in Europe, 80 percent of Spanish, 79 percent of French, 73 percent of British, and 71 percent of German Muslims blame "Western disrespect" as opposed to "Muslim intolerance" for the cartoon uproar.[22] Another poll found 27 percent of British Muslims expressing sympathy for the "motives behind the attacks on *Charlie Hebdo*," the French satirical newspaper, with 24 percent supporting violent attacks against those who publish images of the Prophet.[23]

A more recent study in Britain, conducted by the former chairman of that country's Equality and Human Rights Commission, Trevor Phillips, was even more disturbing. While noting that the "vast majority" of British Muslims are not extremist, Phillips concluded that a "chasm" exists between Muslim and non-Muslim Britons. For instance, 52 percent of Muslims surveyed in a face-to-face poll (making the results more reliable than other, impersonal survey methods) believe homosexuality should be illegal (compared to just 22 percent of non-Muslims), 39 percent of Muslims say women should always obey their husbands (versus 5 percent of non-Muslims), and 35 percent believe "Jewish people have too much power in Britain" (contrasted to 8 percent of non-Muslims). Wide disparities in Muslim and non-Muslim opinion were also found on attitudes toward polygamy, the imposition of Sharia law, and violence toward blasphemers. "Liberal opinion in Britain has, for more than two decades, maintained that most Muslims are just like everyone else, but with more modest dress sense and more luxuriant facial hair; any differences would fade with time and contact," Phillips wrote.[24] "But thanks to the most detailed and comprehensive survey of British Muslim opinion yet conducted, we now know that just isn't how it is." Describing a sizable minority of British Muslims as constituting a "nation within a nation," Phillips, ironically the commissioner of a 1997 report that sympathized with the plight of Muslim minorities and even popularized the term "Islamophobia," woefully wrote nearly two decades later that "for a long time, I too thought that Europe's Muslims would become like previous waves of migrants, gradually abandoning their ancestral ways, wearing their religious and cultural baggage lightly, and gradually blending into Britain's diverse identity landscape. I should have known better."

To understand the gravity of the burden Europe has undertaken in open-ing its doors to Muslim migration, consider that Germany, the continent's largest country, admitted four million asylum seekers in the six decades between 1953 and 2014, in addition to some 2.6 million mostly Turkish *gastarbeiter* from 1961 to 1973.[25] That amounts to slightly more than one million people per decade, roughly the number Germany absorbed in 2015 alone. Such a sudden and immense spike in the number of migrants ought to have generated at least a modicum of controversy. It wasn't just the sheer scale of the migration, however, that should have induced skepticism about the chancellor's exhortations that Germany could "do it." In light of Merkel's much derided but prescient 2010 speech declaring that multiculturalism had "failed, utterly failed," her decision to let in an unlimited number of Syrians was perplexing, to say the least. But except for the populist, anti-Muslim protest group PEGIDA (Patriotic Europeans against the Islamiza-tion of the West), whose torchlight rallies in downtown Dresden and clownishly reactionary leadership repelled most Germans, as well as some blatantly xenophobic messages posted anonymously to online comment boards, there were, at least initially, scarcely any public expressions of skep-ticism toward Merkel's move. The handful of mainstream commentators who did voice concern—such as *Die Welt*'s in-house skewerer of German conventional wisdom Henryk Broder—were condemned along with the ex-tremists and written off as cranks. One simply didn't question the policy.

The sense that only cranks and racists could dissent from Germany's heroic migrant story was reinforced less than two months before the mass sexual assaults of December 31, 2015, when an anti-immigrant fanatic stabbed Cologne mayoral candidate Henriette Reker, a backer of Merkel's asylum policies. For a people who overcame a history of disastrous political violence and birthed an exemplary democratic culture, the attack came as a shock. In response, even more rallied in support of a cause that, by late 2015, had assumed the salvific character of a mass national duty, not unlike a blood drive following a natural disaster. When *TIME* magazine declared Merkel "Person of the Year" several weeks after the stabbing, right-thinking people everywhere felt vindicated in their endorsement of the chancellor's humanitarianism. An influential example of this intellectual conformity could be found in the pages of *Bild,* the tabloid jewel of the conservative

Springer media empire and Europe's largest-selling newspaper, which took to Merkel's "We Can Do It" entreaty with unquestioning gusto. *Bild*'s initial coverage of the migrants was uniformly positive, including, for instance, a full-page copy of the German constitution in Arabic as a welcoming gesture. Given the way right-wing populist tabloids all over the world have traditionally treated the topic of immigration, such earnestness in the service of hospitality was certainly better than its opposite, though a more discerning approach would have been preferable.

The dearth of such discernment in the European conversation over migration and Islam—caused in no small part by the reflexive disparagement of critical voices as racist and beyond the pale—is its central problem. Either one accepts unrestricted immigration, the nostrums of multiculturalism, and the claim that Muslims integrate just as well as any other group, or one risks being branded an incorrigible bigot. Images of overcrowded boats sinking in the Mediterranean naturally affected the European public conscience and demanded a humanitarian response. Yet the only morally acceptable one seemed to be a policy granting asylum to anyone daring enough to board a rickety vessel bound for Europe, thereby encouraging more and more dangerous journeys. "We invite catastrophe when we confuse the obligation to rescue a person who is drowning with that person's right to become a citizen of our country," says the French political scientist Pierre Manent.[26] Policies designed to dissuade further smuggling missions or mass migratory waves, like deporting those people who arrived illegally on European shores, were immediately deemed racist and inhumane.

For instance, in Germany, "The mood in the country is akin to a drunken rage of the kind last seen in the beer halls of the 1920s Weimar Republic," an editorialist for *Der Spiegel* intoned after the Reker stabbing, conflating all those critical of Merkel's immigration policies with Nazis. It was an apt illustration of elite piety regarding Muslim immigration.[27] No doubt the Holocaust bore heavily on the minds of Germans as they weighed their country's response to the migrant crisis, as it should. Yet this commendable appreciation of history quickly developed into an "excessive self-righteousness," in the words of German historian Heinrich August Winkler, as crucial differences between the two situations were tossed aside so that Germans could justify a policy that was hardly so black and white.

"Any attempt to deduce from the most terrible chapter of German history a special German morality, is misleading and doomed to failure," Winkler wrote. "We cannot promise more than we can deliver."[28] Winkler was saying that Germans, motivated by a laudable sense of historical restitution, felt a need to be more "moral" than anybody else. Indeed, many Germans seem to believe that, having condemned their grandparents' generation as the evilest in all mankind, they are themselves now the most morally upright people in the world. This caused them to embrace an unrealistic humanitarianism utterly oblivious to other considerations, the deleterious consequences of which they have only come to appreciate well after the fact.

So, for instance, when the mayor of Sumte, a village of 102 people in northern Germany with no shops, police station, or even a school, was told by the district government that he would have to find space for 1,000 asylum seekers—ten times the town's population—he said he was given two options, "yes, or yes."[29] Writing in the *Financial Times,* influential foreign affairs commentator Gideon Rachman proclaimed that because "mass migration into Europe is unstoppable" and "post-imperial, post-Holocaust Europe is much more wary of asserting the superiority of its culture," there would be a "battle between nativists and liberals" in which the latter would prevail. But if the European debate over immigration remains bifurcated between open-border multiculturalism and far-right extremism (the latter category into which Rachman lazily places all who oppose Merkel's worldview), it's far from certain that the liberals will win. We already see why this is the case as, across Europe, once-marginal, anti-systemic parties increase their popularity at the expense of mainstream ones almost entirely because of their absolutist stance against immigration.

Take Sweden, where in 2010, the Sweden Democrats barely entered parliament for the first time with 5.7 percent of the vote as the only party promising to cut immigration. In an effort to treat them as pariahs, Swedish authorities denied the Sweden Democrats state resources customarily given to other legal political parties, such as advertising space on buses or permits to hold events in public parks.[30] A 2012 police study found that half the party's politicians reported threats or assaults in the preceding year; some candidates were beaten with iron bars and had bombs detonated in their cars. Rather than debate the merits of immigration with the Sweden Democrats, left-wing activists adopted bullying tactics like exposing the personal details of rank-and-file party members and dispatching television crews to ambush them at their front doors.

Stigmatizing the Sweden Democrats in the hope that no self-respecting Swede would contemplate voting for them, however, had the opposite of its intended effect. At the height of the migrant crisis in the fall of 2015, a mere five years after it entered parliament, the Sweden Democrats had become the most popular party in the country. A poll commissioned around that time found that 41 percent of Swedes supported reducing the number of migrants allowed into Sweden. In a healthy democracy, a view held by 41 percent of the population in regards to an issue as crucial as immigration would command representation from mainstream political parties. But in Sweden and elsewhere, the parties of the center left and center right long ago decided to adopt a political consensus favoring near-limitless immigration. Offering no room for legitimate dissent, they abandoned the issue to the most unscrupulous and distasteful political forces. Any call to reduce immigration, however modest, was portrayed as yielding to neo-fascism; any criticism of immigrants was cast as racist. It was only a matter of time before a group like the Sweden Democrats—for its entire existence the target of unanimous vituperation from the Swedish media and political establishment—emerged as a serious political force.

Rising support across Europe for xenophobic, populist parties is partly the result of a constricted political discourse in which decent, ordinary people are told not only that plainly visible social phenomena don't exist but also that voicing concerns about these allegedly nonexistent phenomena is racist. By stifling discussion on questions related to migration and national identity, European elites have only fed the monster they hope to destroy. Rather than decrease support for extremist movements, the wholesale branding of legitimate opinions as illegitimate prejudice drives voters into the arms of the far right. This is why Sweden, the country that not long ago was the most accepting of refugees—so accepting that its left-wing government was forced to announce in early 2016 that it had no choice but to deport 80,000 migrants—is now witnessing a populist backlash led by a party with neo-Nazi roots that's only been in parliament for six years. It's why in Austria's most recent presidential election, the candidate from the Freedom

Party, founded by former SS officers, nearly became the first far-right president of a European country since World War II, defeated by less than one
percentage point in the initial runoff. With Pew finding strong majorities
opposed to the EU's handling of the migrant crisis in all ten of the countries it surveyed in spring 2016 (a figure that reached 88 percent in normally pro-EU Sweden, for instance), support for far right parties is only
bound to increase.[31]

In Germany, where Merkel's grand coalition government (commanding
more than 500 seats in the 630-member Bundestag) effectively smothers
political resistance to an open-door immigration policy, opposition is chan-
neled to a right-wing populism that, until recently, the country was unique
in postwar continental Europe for having avoided. Franz Joseph Strauss,
the legendary premier of Bavaria, used to say that no legitimate democratic
force could exist to the right of his Christian Social Union (CSU), the
CDU's Bavarian sister party. Germans have diligently respected that unof-
ficial guardrail at the national level: No party to the right of the CSU has
ever made it into the Bundestag. But that preference for a moderate politics
of consensus, expressed through recurring popular support for the traditional "people's parties" of the center right (CDU/CSU) and center left
(SPD), will likely be upended at the next federal election, when Alternative
for Germany (AfD) is expected to become the first far right party to enter
the German parliament (the party already registered a shock to the political
system when it won 21 percent of the vote—enough to earn it second place—
in the 2016 provincial elections in Merkel's home state). Founded in 2013 as
a club of white-collar, anti-Euro academics keen on bringing back the
deutsche mark, the party shifted focus and broadened its appeal by seizing
on anti-immigration sentiment. In addition to its calls for leaving the common currency, AfD, like most other European parties obsessed with halting immigration, is deeply suspicious of America, supports German
withdrawal from NATO, and advocates normalized relations with Russia.

AfD is hardly the most worrisome political movement to have gained
steam from the migrant crisis and elite disconnect with popular opinion.
Since October 2014, a year before the immigration wave hit its peak, thousands of people have gathered in the center of Dresden to demonstrate under
the banner of PEGIDA. The street movement's rhetoric is often crude and

chauvinistic; intriguingly, it has appropriated both fascist and antiauthoritarian motifs. Waving flags of the anti-Nazi resistance movement and chanting *"Wir sind das volk"* ("We are the people"), a chant made famous by the East German citizens' movement, PEGIDA leaders speak of the German government as if it were a dictatorship and regularly refer to the "traitor" Merkel and the *lügenpresse*, or "lying press," epithets last heard in Germany when the Nazis attacked their critics. All that's missing from this rhetorical assault is the accusation that the country's leaders have "stabbed Germany in the back."

Like the Sweden Democrats, PEGIDA's emergence was greeted with widespread condemnation in Germany and beyond. In her 2014 New Year's message, issued just weeks after the group publicly emerged, Merkel warned that PEGIDA's leaders have "prejudice, coldness, even hatred in their hearts." By the following summer, PEGIDA's very existence was in doubt. Merkel's condemnation and the surfacing of old photographs showing the organization's founder dressed up as Adolf Hitler severely damaged the brand, and weekly attendance at the Monday night rallies dropped from a high of 30,000 to just a few hundred. Then the migrant crisis reenergized the moribund protest group. Now, for an increasing number of Germans, PEGIDA is the only organization that gives voice, however crudely, to their anxieties about mass immigration. "The fact is," a 62-year-old unemployed computer scientist and PEGIDA demonstrator told the *Guardian*, "this is the only place I have to go—no one else represents my frustrations better than PEGIDA does."[32]

It's easy to dismiss PEGIDA'S hysterical attacks on the *lügenpresse* as neo-Nazi rhetoric; harder to discount is the poll finding that 43 percent of Germans do not feel free to express their opinions about the migrant crisis.[33] That figure was recorded before the attacks in Cologne, where it appears that high-ranking members of the police force as well as the media hesitated to reveal the truth of what had occurred. According to a police report leaked after the incident, officers couldn't even record all the crimes being committed that night because there were "just too many at the same time." After local officers wrote an internal memo entitled, "Rape, Sexual Harassment, Thefts, Committed by a Large Group of Foreign People," they allegedly received a phone call from the provincial-level police, acting on the orders of its interior ministry, instructing them to take down the report or at least remove the word "rape."[34] It stands in stunning contrast to the message conveyed by the department's New Year's Day press release, however, entitled "Festive Atmosphere—Celebrations Largely Peaceful." It would take days before what *Der Spiegel* later described as "a protocol of a massacre" found its way into an official police report, an act of conscious deception that led to the forced early retirement of Cologne's police chief.[35]

Nor was it just law enforcement officials who, however well intentioned, failed in their public duty by avoiding unpleasant facts in the service of protecting a political agenda; the German public broadcaster ZDF waited four days before reporting on the incident and later apologized for what a former interior minister dubbed a "news blackout."[36] It was not until July, with a leaked document from the Federal Criminal Police, that the full scale of the horror became apparent: All told, some 2,000, mostly North African assailants sexually assaulted 1,200 women across Germany at New Year's Eve festivals.[37] "Germany has isolated itself with its refugee policy," an unnamed government official told *Der Spiegel*. "The population is polarized and becoming radicalized—not just on the fringes. And we shouldn't forget that we have hundreds of thousands of people in the country, and we don't know for sure who they actually are and how they will turn out."[38]

A comparable dynamic has been at play across the continent. In Sweden, police covered up a spate of sex crimes committed by young Muslim migrants at a major Stockholm music festival. "This is a sore point," the police official in charge of security at the festival admitted in 2014. "Sometimes we dare not tell how it is because we think it plays into the hands of the Sweden Democrats." There is even a Swedish word for the narrow remit of acceptable discussion pertaining to hot-button issues like immigration: *asiktskorridor*, meaning "opinion corridor."[39] "The fact that you can now mention immigration, culture differences and rape in one sentence is a completely new phenomenon," says Swedish journalist Paulina Neuding.[40] Her country was essentially forced into making this recognition when a series of violent attacks on women, Christians, and gays at migrant asylum centers compelled a public conversation about the need to create "safe zones" for select minority groups. "How will individuals who cannot share a shelter with gays and Christians without harassing them be able to integrate into liberal European societies?" she asks.[41]

In Germany, the government has cracked down on "hate speech" about migrants, which is so vaguely defined as to possibly include criticism (albeit heated) of government policy.[42] Institutional whitewashes of sexual abuse in Germany and Sweden echoed a similar scandal in the northern British town of Rotherham, where authorities hid the existence of a Pakistani "grooming" ring whose members sexually abused some 1,400 children over fifteen years. Local officials, according to a government inquiry, resisted bringing these men to justice for fear of " 'giving oxygen' to racist perspectives." But it's this willful deception of the public, treating them like a herd of incipient fascists on the verge of perpetrating anti-migrant pogroms, that "plays into the hands" of extremists, not speaking truthfully about migration and its challenges. In France, home to the largest Muslim population in Europe, 76 percent of citizens have positive views of Muslims, hardly an indicator of widespread "Islamophobic" sentiment.[43] Lying about the problems immigration poses and refusing to acknowledge those who question the consensus simply inflame peoples' worst fears: that a conspiracy exists to favor the interests of one group over those of the native population.

A more prudent approach to immigration is the one adopted by Denmark, whose government has placed advertisements in Lebanese newspapers distributed in refugee camps warning people not to make the dangerous journey to Europe and confiscates valuables brought by migrants valued at more than 10,000 Danish krone (about $1,500). Though this latter measure was initially derided as cruel and inhumane by many journalists and self-styled humanitarians, some of whom went so far as to compare it to Nazi seizures of Jewish property, it was demonstrative and not punitive in intent—meant primarily to dissuade migrants from making the dangerous trek to Denmark—and now looks eminently sensible. Unlike neighboring Sweden, Denmark has pursued a more restrictive immigration policy and has a culture of open debate on issues like Islam and assimilation; it was a Danish newspaper that published the infamous Mohammed cartoons. Largely for this reason, it has been spared the sort of far-right backlash sweeping the rest of Europe. Because their country does not have a sizeable Muslim immigrant underclass and the problems attendant to it, Danes have not resorted to the extremist political parties and movements that so many of their neighbors now find attractive. "The only sustainable solution is to get these people integrated into Danish society," the country's ambassador to the United States told me, "to get people onto the job market."[44]

Despite growing support for populist, xenophobic, anti-European parties, many elites hesitate to address valid worries about immigration and national identity. And too often when they do take up these concerns, they brand them as motivated solely by racism or anti-Islamic hysteria. Talking to citizens without automatically assuming them to be bigoted, insisting that Muslims adhere to the same set of core, liberal precepts as everyone else, and rigorously defending the secular public square from Islamist infiltration could deflate the appeal of extremists on all sides. The more properly liberal reaction to seeing a woman covered head to toe in a burka—particularly on a sweltering hot French beach—is not smug self-satisfaction with multicultural "diversity" but unease, if not revulsion. Those put off by the importation into Europe of desert Arabian mores and practices cannot all be written off as "racists." Should democratic governments (such as France) choose to prohibit the wearing of such religious garb in public institutions, it is not necessarily "Islamphobic" of them to do so. Of course, there may be women who voluntarily choose to don such garments in the heat of summer, though the heavy hand of a husband or male relative can never be ruled out: One should always be skeptical of claims regarding female agency in violently patriarchic cultures. Either way, there are vast regions of the world where subjugating the female sex in such fashion is enshrined as state policy; Europe, the birthplace of the Enlightenment and the very concept of human rights, need not be a place where such practices flourish.

Instead of standing firmly for liberal principles, however, too many European leaders enter into a haze of cultural relativism—one of the chief nostrums of which is that it is a good idea to import millions more Muslims to an economically stagnant Europe that has failed to assimilate the millions of Muslims who already live there. In response to the Cologne sexual attacks, now-mayor Reker declared that any intimation the assaults might have been perpetrated by migrants was "absolutely impermissible" and suggested that women keep an "arm's length" of distance between them and other men in crowded public places. "Perhaps it was a bit helpless," she later said of her tone-deaf proposal, which seemed to put the responsibility for avoiding sexual assault on women, not their assailants. "But it also shows how helpless our society is when it comes to dealing with such incidents."[45] That a code of silence on the subject of pervasive Muslim misogyny, one that she helped enforce, might have contributed to this "helpless" condition eluded her. In that same interview, she admitted that "until now, I had been of the belief that the generation of advanced men rejected such inhuman practices," a rather stunning admission of naiveté. A female leader of the Green Party, meanwhile, downplayed the magnitude of the sexual attacks and said that what happened in Cologne, however unfortunate, was little different from the drunken tomfoolery of annual Oktoberfest celebrations. "This form of violence in Germany unfortunately is an old phenomenon," she said.[46]

In general, the guardians of *bien pensant* opinion were more concerned with how their political adversaries might take advantage of the outrage than with the outrage itself. "After Cologne, we can't let the bigots steal feminism," opined a writer for Britain's *New Statesman*. Celebrating the Muslim woman in Europe who wears a veil in defiance of her secular surroundings while ignoring those who don them due to the coercion of their male family members is an all too common reflex. Proud to wear their militant secularism on their sleeves when confronting anything Judeo-Christian, these progressives abandon their ostensibly universalistic principles the minute Islam or its adherents enter the picture. Despite the German Interior Ministry's report that "people with a migration background were almost exclusively responsible for the criminal acts in Cologne" (a delicate way of noting that the perpetrators were men of Muslim extraction), the European Commission—the executive arm of the EU—insisted that the attacks were simply "a matter of public order."[47] When Barack Obama told the United Nations General Assembly that "the future does not belong to those who slander the prophet of Islam," he not only disparaged those who have deigned to draw images of a seventh-century warlord; he also reinforced the Islamists' narrative that they will one day triumph over their secularist adversaries.

In his controversial novel *Submission*, the French satirist Michel Houel-lebecq envisions France in the year 2022, when a candidate from the newly formed Muslim Brotherhood party succeeds in capturing the French pres-idency with the assistance of the Socialists, the political inheritors of the secular French republican tradition. Published on the day of the murder-ous attacks on *Charlie Hebdo* and a kosher bakery, *Submission* was imme-diately misconstrued by some critics as a xenophobic attack on French Muslims. Though Houellebecq is not particularly fond of Islam, the real object of his critique is a bourgeois Western nihilism willing to make an accommodation with religious fundamentalists. According to the French philosopher Alain Finkielkraut, in the moral and spiritual vacuum that is Houellebecq's contemporary Europe, a highly protean, sociopolitical form of Islam has become an "anchor of identity" for many young people with a migration background.[48] While those who have participated in the various episodes of mass unrest in Muslim-majority neighborhoods throughout Europe rarely make appeals to Islam a part of their remonstrations, it is their embrace of a pan-Islamic cultural identity—distinct from that of the societies in which they live—that informs and exacerbates divisions. Euro-peans may be post-national, post-ideological, and atheist; the same can hardly be said of the Muslims who have lived there for generations or are now flooding its shores. Dalil Boubakeur, rector of the Grand Mosque of Paris, was not trying to sound triumphalist when he suggested that France convert its empty churches into mosques to accommodate the city's grow-ing Muslim population; he was simply proposing a utilitarian solution to a real problem.

Fourteen hundred sexually abused children in Rotherham, 1,200 sexu-ally assaulted women across Germany, vast Muslim ghettoes dotting the continent—these are not the only consequences of Europe's moral equiva-lence, cultural self-abnegation, and outright cowardice on the question of Islam. What ought be of utmost concern for those entrusted with high of-fice are the effects that such a massive act of social engineering will have on the continent's long-term future. Europeans need to consider whether the benefits of bringing more migrants to their countries outweigh the consequences that such a flood—bound to exacerbate preexisting problems like ghettoization and high unemployment—will inevitably have on their societies.

When Margot Wallström, Sweden's Social Democratic foreign minister, announced on her first day in office—October 3, 2014—that her country would henceforth pursue a "feminist foreign policy," many observers saw it as quixotic Scandinavian moral posturing. But when she followed up her declaration by condemning Saudi Arabia's subjugation of women and its "medieval" flogging of a secular blogger, the response was no laughing matter. Deploying a brand of multiculturalist doublespeak reminiscent of a Western university sociology department, the Organization of Islamic Cooperation, representing nearly sixty Muslim-majority countries, condemned Sweden's lack of respect for the world's "multiple cultures, diverse social norms, [and] rich and varied ethical standards." Saudi Arabia withdrew its ambassador from Stockholm, and Wallström was barred from delivering a speech to the Arab League in spite of her government's being the first EU member to recognize Palestinian statehood. Tensions escalated to the point where Sweden—the world's twelfth largest arms exporter, a rather dubious honor for a neutral country that brags of being a "humanitarian superpower"—stopped selling weapons to Saudi Arabia, once one of its largest clients.

Wallström's plainspoken advocacy for a values-based approach to world affairs, and her willingness to pay a cost in terms of cancelled weapons contracts, was a welcome breath of fresh air in European diplomacy. Too typical is the bowing and scraping displayed by the Italian government, which, in advance of a historic visit in January 2016 by Iranian president Hassan Rouhani, covered up and carted away ancient statues of naked bodies so as not to offend him during a tour of Rome's Capitoline Museum. It shouldn't surprise us that societies so willing to placate religious fanatics abroad would take a kid-glove approach to dealing with similar sentiments at home. That appeared to be the motivating principle when it emerged that the Swedish government, ostensibly committed to a "feminist foreign policy," had tried to hide a spate of sexual assaults committed by migrant men against its own women. It never seemed to dawn on people like Wallström that the hard-won gains achieved by women like herself might be jeopardized by inviting into Sweden a cohort of people whose views on gender equality are little different from those of the Saudi monarchs she so vociferously criticized.

There will be no respite from these quandaries, however, as long as Europeans continue to view nationalism as their original sin. Like immigration, the conversation over nationalism offers little middle ground: Asserting the superiority of "European values" over those of the cultures from which migrants come is the sort of morals-based language many Europeans have difficulty speaking. But it is precisely these values that have created and sustained the prosperous, peaceful, and tolerant societies that have proven so attractive to the rest of the world. While they should always be vigilant toward ethnic chauvinism and xenophobia, Europeans should also create a space for a healthy nationalism—patriotism—that refuses to let the crimes of their past be used as a sort of moral bargaining chip over its future.

Like the war in Ukraine, instability in the Eurozone, and democratic backsliding in Hungary, the migrant crisis has exposed Europe's preference for muddling through; buck-passing is the common response. Whether advocating that anyone who wants to come to Europe be allowed to do so or insisting that fences be erected to keep them out, few propose solutions that address the problem at its root. Many of the migrants coming to Europe (though not nearly as many as originally claimed) are fleeing countries like Libya and Syria whose collapse could have been prevented, or at least alleviated, by serious, committed Western intervention. Although the origins of the migration crisis lay in the dysfunctions of Arab Muslim societies, its prolongation is a damning verdict against Europe's lack of a coherent foreign policy. Had Europe (as well as the United States) decided to act as something other than a passive bystander in Syria—by assisting the moderate opposition, creating safe zones, and destroying President Bashar al-Assad's air force in the early months of the rebellion, years before Iranian and Russian troops hit the ground—there was a chance that the conflict might not have dragged on for so long. Reflexively citing the Iraq experience as a counterargument to any and all methods of military intervention is not sufficient, because in both Libya and Syria—unlike Iraq—war against civilian populations was ongoing and the prospect of impending genocide was apparent.

But so allergic are Europeans to the use of military force, and so anemic are their resources, that the thought of picking a side and seeing it through to victory was unimaginable. When Britain and France raised the issue of air strikes against ISIS in the fall of 2015, Germany's foreign minister scolded that "it cannot be that important partners are playing the military card." After the outbreak of World War II, thousands of Czech and Polish refugees fled to the West and fought Nazism in the service of the Royal Air Force and Free French Forces. Yet even suggesting that Syrian refugees, the majority of whom are able-bodied young men, be conscripted to fight against Assad and ISIS is considered ludicrous. Maybe Europeans' resistance to projecting force abroad—of creating something akin to a European Foreign Legion—is so great that it outweighs, in their minds, the consequences of inaction. Maybe Europeans are more comfortable playing the role of altruistic humanitarians, caring for refugees after they've fled, than that of global power players ready to intervene overseas in pursuit of national (and supranational) interests. If that is the case, then they will be dealing with an unending wave of migrants and instability on their borders for years to come as the Middle Eastern political order continues to disintegrate.

Such vacillation has costs. Because of its inability to develop a coherent and robust foreign policy that would tackle the migrant crisis at its source, Europe finds itself in hock to autocrats like Vladimir Putin and Turkish president Recep Tayyip Erdogan—the former offering himself as a "partner" against ISIS while bombing Western-backed opponents of Russia's client Assad (whom the vast majority of refugees are fleeing), and the latter demanding political concessions in exchange for reducing the outflow of migrants languishing in Turkish refugee camps. By entertaining Putin's cynical proposal of an "anti-ISIS coalition," Western leaders willfully ignore how Moscow's Syrian intervention is fueling the very migrant wave they supplicate him to help plug. Russia's interest is very clear: In exchange for its supposed help in fighting ISIS, the West would lift sanctions on Moscow and effectively give a green light to its ongoing subversion of Ukraine. Astonishingly, many in the West apparently support this idea. A late 2015 survey of seventy-six diplomats, elected leaders, and advisors from across Europe and the United States found 53 percent supporting cooperation with Russia in Syria, while listing migration, Islamist terrorism, and the rise of populist parties as the most critical threats to Europe—three problems Moscow is actively aggravating by its intervention in Syria.[49] Maintaining Bashar al-Assad in power will only prolong Syria's misery by driving the Sunni majority that detests him even more into the arms of ISIS, therefore prolonging the conflict as well as the stream of refugees whose presence in Europe is driving up support for the far-right politicians Russia abets in numerous other ways. While the Russians have repeatedly demonstrated their overreliance on hard power to achieve their aims, Europe's overconfidence on soft power, far from keeping the world's problems at bay, has imported them into Elysium.

Throughout Europe, and especially in Germany, the refugee crisis has proven ripe for exploitation by Russian disinformation efforts. Russian media organs regularly promote the most extreme nationalist voices in the migration debate, with the clear intent of destabilizing Europe. In the most sensationalistic and politically consequential example, Russian state television, viewed widely by ethnic Russian citizens of Germany, falsely reported that migrants had abducted and raped a 13-year-old Russian German girl in Berlin. (It was only several weeks later, after the story had permeated German society, that authorities revealed the entire episode to be a hoax.) Although he surely knew the story was concocted out of whole cloth from the very beginning, Russian foreign minister Sergei Lavrov raised the manufactured scandal in his annual press conference, accusing the German government of "paint[ing] over reality with political correctness."[50] In several German cities, "spontaneous" protests of ethnic Russians popped up, demanding Merkel's resignation. (A year earlier, Germany's domestic intelligence service reported that Russia was increasing its espionage efforts in the country, leading many to suspect that Moscow had a hand in organizing these demonstrations.)[51] The following week, Putin hosted Bavarian premier and CSU president Horst Seehofer, Merkel's loudest domestic adversary on the migrant issue. Smiling for the cameras alongside the Russian president, Seehofer criticized EU-wide sanctions against Russia as a burden on the Bavarian economy.[52]

Nor is it just the lack of cohesive and robust foreign and security policies that allows instability to fester along Europe's southern Mediterranean and Middle Eastern peripheries; short-sighted and protectionist trade policies exacerbate the problem as well. To fund the care of migrants at home, for instance, Sweden has drastically cut its overseas development aid budget, eliminating programs that improve conditions in the very places so many migrants are fleeing. EU trade policies—protecting heavily subsidized domestic agricultural interests at the expense of third-world farmers hoping to export their goods to the common market—similarly increase migratory waves to Europe by pricing out producers from underdeveloped economies, exacerbating poverty and economic stagnation. "From the perspective of trade policy, the European Union has put the former colonies in a worse position than they were in during the colonial period," writes Basel University historian Andrea Franc.[53]

If a suite of common strategies designed to stem the refugee flow at its source is not in the offing, then a common policy at home is the second best option. Though Hungarian prime minister Viktor Orbán is correct in asserting that Europe must have external borders if it wishes to do without internal ones, he is wrong in claiming that the crisis is "not a European problem, but a German problem." Migrants were coming to Europe long before Angela Merkel opened her country's doors, and they will continue to come if they believe they will be welcomed without questions and therefore have nothing to lose. Frontex, the EU border agency, is woefully underfunded, and peripheral members like Hungary, Greece, and Italy have little incentive to beef up what is effectively Europe's external border security if most migrants have no intention of staying on their territories, hoping instead for greener (and better funded) pastures in Germany and Sweden. Asking the peripheral countries to handle the burden of guarding Europe's borders is like the U.S. federal government insisting that Arizona and New Mexico pay exclusively for patrols along America's southern frontier.

In the summer of 2015, Angela Merkel joined a group of schoolchildren in the city of Rostock for a televised discussion. Reem Sahwil, a 14-year-old Palestinian who had been living in Germany for four years and was the child of economic migrants, explained to the chancellor that her family's temporary asylum had expired and they faced deportation. Could she and her family stay? "You're a very nice person," Merkel responded, "but you know that there are thousands and thousands of people in Palestinian refugee camps in Lebanon and if I say 'you can all come,' and 'you can all come from Africa,' and 'you can all come,' we just can't manage that," the exact opposite of what she would proclaim just six weeks later.

Facing such a loaded question from a teenager on live television, most leaders in Merkel's position would lie or at least evade the issue. They would assure the girl that, of course, she and her family would never be deported, or would talk around the subject, or offer some vague promise to look into the case. In short, even the most hapless local politician knows that one should never say or do anything that would give the appearance of being indifferent to the entreaties of a teenager on live television. Merkel, however, told the girl the truth: Germany is a nation of laws and finite resources, and it cannot accommodate every person in the world who wishes to live there. As the chancellor explained these cold facts, the girl began to cry, and Merkel, who is childless, awkwardly walked over and started stroking her hair. Immediately, clips of the cruelly hardheaded Christian Democrat, depicted as some sort of Grimm Brothers witch, went viral. The great and the good decried Merkel for epitomizing the heartless German, an image further validated by Berlin's seemingly inflexible position in the Greek debt negotiations that inauspiciously had reached a crisis phase at exactly the same time.

But to anyone familiar with Merkel's distinctively uncharismatic governing style, her behavior was not a surprise. Perhaps it's too much to speculate that the chancellor had this episode in mind when, two months later, she spontaneously decided to reverse her position on migration, and that her exchange of a coolly deliberate (if occasionally tone-deaf) pragmatism for sentimental heedlessness was inspired by the withering reaction to her having made a 14-year-old girl cry before an international audience. Regardless of the reason, not even the coldest Teutonic heart could avoid being lifted when, at the end of 2015, after some 1.5 million migrants had entered Europe, the German government extended the Sahwil family's residency permit. Less noticed was the newspaper interview published with Sahwil just a few days after her televised breakdown, in which she expressed the hope of returning home when Israel "is no longer there, rather only Palestine."[54]

5

France without Jews

Let's say it directly to the world: without France's Jews, France would no longer be France! It's up to us to proclaim this message loud and clear. We haven't said it; we're not outraged enough.

Manuel Valls, president of the Republic of France, speech before the National Assembly, January 13, 2015

THE ARRIVAL INTO EUROPE OF MILLIONS of people from Islamic countries over the past two decades has occurred alongside a preexistent exodus of the continent's dwindling Jewish population, a rate of emigration that has spiked in recent years. Of course, correlation does not prove causation, and the flight of Jews from Europe was apparent long before the migration crisis of 2015 began. But it's foolish to think that a massive influx of people raised on a steady diet of government-sponsored anti-Semitic ideology does not imperil an already beleaguered Jewish population.

In the fall of 2014—several months before terrorists loyal to the Islamic State carried out murderous assaults on the French satirical newspaper *Charlie Hebdo* and the Hyper Cacher kosher supermarket—I walked the winding, narrow streets of Paris's Marais neighborhood, dotted with cafés, *boulangeries,* and specialty food shops. By chance, I came across the Notre Dame de Nazareth Synagogue, a grand nineteenth-century house of prayer constructed in the Moorish revival style that serves a congregation of Sephardic Jews from the former French colonies of North Africa. After enduring a quick pat down at the entrance by a security guard (every Jewish institution in Europe has at least one), I entered the synagogue as the rabbi and his wife were departing. After some pleasantries, I asked him, "What's the situation?" There was no need for further elaboration; he understood exactly what I was getting at. "There is no future for Jews in France," he answered.

Anti-Semitism is a problem across Europe, but it is most visible in France, home to both the largest Jewish population and the largest Muslim population on the continent. In a speech to the National Assembly after the terrorist attacks of January 9, 2015, which took the lives of seventeen people, French prime minister Manuel Valls, the son of Spanish immigrants, declared, "If 100,000 French people of Spanish origin were to leave, I would never say that France is not France anymore. But if 100,000 Jews leave, France will no longer be France. The French Republic will be a failure." Unconvinced by the prime minister's appeal, about 8,000 French Jews moved to Israel over the following year, part of the largest migration of Western European Jews to Israel since the state's founding in 1948. (This was in addition to an unknown number of French Jews who left for other countries.) Taking the prime minister at his word, if this rate of Jewish emigration from France continues, then the "failure" of the French Republic will be upon us in little more than a decade.

French government officials, Prime Minister Valls foremost among them, repeatedly denounce anti-Semitism and have taken active measures to combat it. Recognition of the problem and efforts to alleviate it have progressed a great deal since 1980, when Prime Minister Raymond Barre infamously described a 1980 bombing as "aimed at Jews worshiping in synagogue and striking down four innocent Frenchmen." When more than a million Parisians poured into the streets to declare solidarity with the murdered cartoonists of *Charlie Hebdo,* many held up "Je suis Juif" placards alongside those proclaiming "Je suis Charlie." As encouraging as this sign of ecumenical camaraderie was, given the numbing regularity of anti-Semitic slayings across Europe over the past ten years—the 2006 kidnapping, three-week-long torture, and murderous dismemberment of twenty-one-year-old Ilan Halimi in Paris; the 2012 assassination of a rabbi and three children, including an 8-year-old girl shot at point-blank range, at a Jewish school in

Toulouse; the 2014 murder of four people at the Jewish Museum of Belgium: all committed by Muslims—one could not help but wonder if, had there been an attack on just a kosher supermarket and not a satirical newspaper, more than a million French men and women would have taken to the streets of Paris in protest of four more dead Jews.

It's not outright indifference that characterizes the feelings of Europeans when their Jewish countrymen are attacked or killed, but nor is it the unadulterated sympathy most felt for the casualties of *Charlie Hebdo*. All too often, prominent political, media, and religious figures excuse anti-Jewish sentiment in a way they never would any other kind of hatred. For instance, after the January 2015 attacks, a BBC reporter interviewed a Jewish Parisian woman about the anti-Semitic climate in her country. When she told him that the problem was bad and getting worse, the journalist responded, "Many critics, though, of Israel's policy would suggest that the Palestinians suffer hugely at Jewish hands as well," as if the Jews of Paris must answer for the human rights abuses of the Israeli government.[1] Ilmar Reepalu, the former Social Democratic mayor of Malmö, Sweden's third largest city, embodies the de facto "red-green" alliance between secular left and Islamist right that has emerged in several Western European countries over the past few decades. As Muslims have gradually come to comprise one-third of the city's total population, the size of its Jewish community has decreased by half. A Malmö rabbi has resorted to Internet crowdfunding to pay for enhanced security for his family and institutions (in 2010, the Simon Wiesenthal Center issued a travel advisory warning Jews to take "extreme precaution" when visiting Malmö). During the 2008–2009 Gaza War, when a group of Muslim immigrants shouting "damn Jews" and "Hitler, Hitler, Hitler" violently attacked a demonstration organized by the city's Jewish community, Reepalu blamed the Jews. Rather than condemn Israel, he complained, "instead they choose to have a demonstration at the main square, which can send the wrong signals."[2] Swedish Muslims, it would appear, can only be expected to react violently when confronted by an Israeli flag. When you combine this guilt by association with the view, embraced by 59 percent of Europeans, that Israel is the greatest threat to world peace, then European Jews become implicated for every sin, real or imagined, committed by that much-loathed state.[3]

One can liken the moral equivocations inevitably spun in some left-wing precincts following anti-Semitic attacks to the ambiguous response registered by many liberal intellectuals in the aftermath of the *Hebdo* killings: Similarly to how illustrators of Mohammed bring violence upon themselves by "insulting" downtrodden Muslims, Jews invariably become targets by dint of their association with the Zionist enterprise in the Middle East. In early 2016, for instance, a Marseilles Jewish community leader urged members of his flock to stop wearing skullcaps (*kippot*) in public for fear that they mark individuals as targets for anti-Semitic violence. While the prospect of Jews once again feeling unsafe to walk the streets ought to be a source of great shame for any European, not all Frenchmen thought so: The former president of Doctors without Borders, himself a Jew, approved the self-imposed ban as wearing the skullcaps is "an affirmation of loyalty to the State of Israel."

It only takes an analogy to American racism to see the intellectual shallowness of this logic. Were a group of skinheads to burn down a black church in the American South, citing the theft of white-owned Zimbabwean farmland by the Mugabe regime as pretext, no decent person would accept such an argument as offering even the slightest exculpation for what is plainly a racist act. Yet that is precisely the rationale that a German court validated in sentencing two Palestinian men who attempted arson against a synagogue in the city of Wuppertal following the 2014 Gaza War. The attack, the jurists argued, was not a crime of anti-Semitism per se, but a politically motivated one, meant to "bring attention to the Gaza conflict."[4] By this reckoning, the last arson of the Wuppertal synagogue—when Nazi thugs burned it to the ground during the 1938 *Kristallnacht*—could also be interpreted as a political act, meant to "bring attention" to Jewish control over Germany.

To be sure, the court's stance does not represent the official position of the German government, which, under the leadership of Angela Merkel especially, condemns anti-Semitism in all forms. And though Berlin's Syrian migrant policy has opened the doors to a potentially limitless number of people from a country still officially at war with the Jewish state, Germany's interior minister Thomas de Maizière defied those who would say that the country's Jews had nothing to worry about when he issued this statement: "Everyone who comes here must know what we stand for: This country has a special commitment to the Jews and to the state of Israel. This country has a very good reason to protect Jewish life and encourage its free expression. This country is a place where Jews should never again have to live in fear of persecution."[5] While it was reassuring to see such sentiment expressed by a high-ranking German government official, that he felt the need to do so was worrying.

For Europeans, Jews are not just fellow citizens: They are also painful, living reminders of their nations' and ancestors' historic criminality, the remnant of the people an earlier generation of Europeans tried to murderously expunge from the human race. Responses to the societal trauma engendered by this memory generally take three forms. A plurality of Europeans are apathetic, wholly ignorant of Jews on an individual or historical level, but vaguely aware that something bad happened to them many years ago. A conscientious minority commit themselves to dutiful commemoration of the Holocaust as a unique and unprecedented evil, to preservation and enrichment of contemporary Jewish life, and to political affinity with Israel as the democratic homeland of the Jewish people. Another minority, more prevalent today on the left than the right, engage in overwrought and highly disproportionate condemnation of Israel, sometimes via comparisons to the Third Reich, renderng Jews the new Nazis. In this reductionist reading, European Jews are extensions of the Israeli state, and crude anti-Semitism, when expressed by Muslims or their sympathizers, is for the most part an ill-mannered venting of an otherwise legitimate anti-imperialism.

Nowhere in Europe has the elite mainstreaming of anti-Semitism been more successful than in Great Britain. In 2016, the British Labor Party was racked by a series of scandals involving members making anti-Semitic statements on social media and other public fora. Some claimed the State of Israel had created ISIS.[6] Others asserted that a Jewish banking conspiracy controlled the country.[7] A co-chair of Oxford University's Labor Club quit in disgust, accusing his former comrades of having "some kind of problem with Jews"; student leaders, he said, used the epithet "Zio" with "casual abandon." Many described the presence of so much anti-Jewish bigotry, and the party's seeming tolerance of it, as a result of nothing more sinister than the bumbling and ineffectual management style of Jeremy Corbyn, the Trotskyist backbencher who won his underdog bid for the party leadership in September 2015.

Few bothered to ask whether Labor's anti-Semitic infestation had anything to do with the leader himself—whether he and his associates had created an environment in which such bigotry could openly fester. For hidden behind the comely exterior of the disheveled, jam-making lefty who takes photographs of manhole covers as a hobby lay a sinister figure, a man who had repeatedly shared the stage with Islamic extremists, donated to the charity of a Holocaust denier, and referred to members of Hamas and Hezbollah as "friends."[8] Between 2009 and 2012, Corbyn made five paid appearances on PressTV, the English-language propaganda channel of the Islamic Republic of Iran, where all manner of fringe views including Holocaust denial are regularly aired. None of this bothered Corbyn; he even appeared on PressTV after a British government regulatory agency suspended the network's broadcast license for airing a forced confession made by a tortured *Newsweek* journalist.[9]

Were any other minority group the repeated target of such prejudice and conspiratorial insinuation, there can be no doubt that Labor would have dealt with the problem in a swift and decisive manner—putting aside the fact that no left-wing European political party would ever elevate to leadership someone who shared such warm relations with anti-black or anti-gay bigots as Corbyn has with anti-Semitic ones. Eventually, Labor commissioned an inquiry into anti-Semitism "and other forms of racism," a deliberate attempt to obfuscate the matter by diluting the specifically anti-Jewish nature of the controversy.

Presented with the opportunity to identify and root out anti-Jewish prejudice within its own ranks, however, Corbyn's Labor Party wallowed deeper into the anti-Semitic sewer. To begin with, the inquiry did not address Corbyn's leadership, thereby absolving him and his team of any direct responsibility for engendering a climate in which so many Labor members felt comfortable expressing anti-Semitic invective. At the inquiry's launch event, attempting to rebut the pernicious logic advanced by so many of his followers that Jews must be made to answer for Israeli misdeeds, Corbyn proclaimed, "Our Jewish friends are no more responsible for the actions of Israel or the Netanyahu government than our Muslim friends are for those of various self-styled Islamic states or organizations."[10] Thus, even when attempting to denounce anti-Semitism, Corbyn could not help but engage in a classic bit of anti-Semitic formulation himself: demonizing the Jewish State. In this case, the demonization came through likening Israel to the most savage band of sadistic murderers on the planet, the Islamic State. Indeed, this invidious comparison is precisely the slander that had led to the suspension of several Labor members and prompted the inquiry in the first place. Regardless of whether or not he believed himself to be defending his Jewish comrades, Corbyn impugned the vast majority of them when he likened support for Israel to support for ISIS, because most Jews support the former, certainly a far higher percentage than those of Muslims who support the latter. According to Mark Gardner, director of communications for the Community Security Trust, a Jewish communal organization that works to protect Jews and the physical security of their institutions, the event was then "hijacked" by a Corbynite "rent a mob," one of whose members verbally attacked a Jewish female MP in the audience for working "hand-in-hand" with a conservative newspaper against the party.[11] As the woman left the room in tears, Corbyn looked on in silence. Afterward, the shaken MP wrote that the Labor Party, under Corbyn's leadership, "cannot be a safe space for British Jews."[12] Adding insult to injury, just weeks after submitting her report effectively clearing Corbyn and his leadership team of charges that they had created an atmosphere in which anti-Semitism could fester, Shami Chakrabarti, the civil liberties activist tasked with leading the inquiry, was awarded a seat in the House of Lords by the very same Labor Party she had been asked to investigate.[13] Indeed, to the extent that it is mainstreaming and normalizing anti-Jewish prejudice, the British Labor Party—and not some obscure far-right organization or underground Islamist terror outfit—is today the most influential anti-Semitic institution in the Western world.

Jewish life in much of Europe, and France in particular, is becoming intolerable. The number of anti-Semitic attacks in France doubled to more than 850 in 2014, and the effect they have had on Jews can be seen at both the communal and individual level. The weekend of the *Charlie Hebdo* attack, Paris's Grand Synagogue closed for Sabbath services due to security concerns, the first time it had done so since World War II. (After the manhunt for the perpetrators of the November 13, 2015, Islamist massacre at Paris's Bataclan Theater led authorities to Brussels, synagogues there were also forced to close for the first time since the war.) When a Jewish man walking in Marseilles was forced to use a Torah to defend himself from a 15-year-old, machete-wielding ISIS supporter in January 2015, it was the third such anti-Semitic attack in the port city in as many months.[14] Regular disruptions in French classrooms over teaching the Holocaust, along with more physical forms of anti-Semitic abuse, have led to an exodus of Jewish students from state schools. According to Shimon Samuels, director of international relations at the Simon Wiesenthal Center's Paris office, 40 percent of France's Jewish students are enrolled in Jewish schools and 35 percent are in Catholic schools, largely to avoid bullying by Muslim peers.[15] A 2004 report prepared by then-French education minister Jean-Pierre Obin on the state of religion in French schools, quietly suppressed by the government and eventually leaked, commented that "Jewish children, and Jewish children alone, cannot be educated in all of our schools."[16]

For those Jews who have decided to remain in the country of their birth, safety has become such a concern that a process of re-ghettoization is underway. The Socialist mayor of Sarcelles, a suburb north of Paris, reports "a phenomenon of internal migration" among his Jewish constituents that began around 2010. Although "achiev[ing] social and ethnic integration" with Jews and Muslims is the ideal, he says, "France has been trying to achieve this for the past 30 years and it still hasn't happened."[17] A 2015 survey found 63 percent of French Jews reporting they had been publicly insulted and more than half threatened due to their religious identification; three-quarters of Jews say they simply avoid identifying as Jewish in public.[18] It's not hard to understand why. After the *Charlie Hebdo* attacks, journalists in various European cities carried out an experiment: Donning a traditional Jewish skullcap, they walked about for hours with a hidden camera to record the response of pedestrians to an identifiable Jew in their midst. In some cities, like Berlin, the journalist walked about without incident or, encouragingly, received expressions of support from passersby. In most places, however, the response was far different. "Kippah walks" in the largely Muslim neighborhoods of Manchester, Bradford, and outside Paris elicited cries of "fight the Jewish scum," "fuck off Jew," and "homo." A yarmulke-wearing Swedish journalist who walked through Malmö was shouted at by dozens of people, pelted with eggs, and physically attacked. Asked about the perpetrators of anti-Semitic attacks in Stockholm, a Jewish leader said, "Almost exclusively, they have some sort of background in the Middle East."[19] Such was the context in which the aforementioned Marseille Jewish community leader advised his co-religionists to avoid publicly identifying themselves as Jews.

In this environment, an increasing number of Jews—fed up with having to worry about their families' safety—are uprooting their lives and moving abroad. Citing "historical processes" at work, Natan Sharansky—the one-time Soviet refusenik and present chairman of the Israeli government agency responsible for handling Jewish emigration to Israel—concludes, "There is no future for the Jews in France because of the Arabs, and because of a very anti-Israel position in society, where new anti-Semitism and ancient anti-Semitism converge."[20] To place the current exodus into perspective, only 1,900 French Jews (of an estimated population of about 475,000) emigrated to Israel in 2011. Four years later, that figure quadrupled to 8,000.

Two weeks after the January 9, 2015, attacks, the municipality of Paris announced it would sue the Fox News Channel. Discussing events in France, two guests on the network had spoken separately of so-called no-go zones in the French capital and other European cities, where, they said, Islamic Sharia law is applied and non-Muslims are prohibited from entering. One guest, former U.S. Air Force officer Nolan Peterson, claimed there were more than 700 such "no-go zones," some of them as "scary" as places he encountered in Afghanistan and Iraq; the other, terrorism analyst Steven Emerson, reported that entire cities such as Birmingham, England, are "totally Muslim." An indignant Paris mayor Anne Hidalgo responded, "The image of Paris has been prejudiced, and the honor of Paris has been prejudiced."[21] A French comedy show launched a massive social media campaign mocking Fox, and after a week of enduring widespread derision, the network apologized, stating that "there is no formal designation of these zones . . . and no credible information to support the assertion that there are specific areas in these countries that exclude individuals based solely on their religion."

That carefully worded correction was accurate, as far as it went. Although it's true that the sprawling public housing projects on the outskirts of Paris almost exclusively inhabited by people of North African Muslim extraction are not "formally designated" as "no-go zones" for non-Muslims, and that their residents do not bar entrance to private individuals based on their religion, they are nonetheless places where the authority of the French government has little sway. As early as 2002, a writer filed a Paris-datelined story for the *International Herald Tribune* reporting that "Arab gangs regularly vandalize synagogues here, the North African suburbs have become no-go zones at night, and the French continue to shrug their shoulders."[22] Unfortunately, the subtleties of a very serious problem—the presence within European societies of an increasingly alienated and ghettoized Muslim underclass—were lost amid the sensationalist and inaccurate commentaries by the guests of an American cable news network and the self-righteous retorts by various French public figures.

Before launching her lawsuit, Hidalgo might have consulted with Malek Boutih, the son of Algerian immigrants, a deputy in the National Assembly, and a fellow member of Hidalgo's Socialist Party. "One has to get into them, hit hard, vanquish them, retake control of territories that have been abandoned to them by local officials out for their own peace and quiet," Boutih, then president of the antiracist organization SOS Racisme, told *Le Monde* in 2002. He was speaking about "barbarians of the cités,"[23] the colloquial French term for public housing projects, and their de facto control by what he has since called "Islamo-Nazis."[24] To distinguish these *"zones de non-droit,"* or "lawless areas," a term commonly used by the very same French media and political class that would later assail Fox News, from "no-go zones," is splitting hairs. Ultimately the existence of such areas—constituting swaths of the Parisian slums, the Molenbeek neighborhood of Brussels, Rinkeby in Stockholm, and other districts across Europe—is not in doubt.

"If we're in pursuit of a vehicle, it can evade us by driving to certain neighborhoods where a lone patrol car simply cannot follow because we'll get pelted by rocks and even face riots. These are no-go zones. We simply can't go there."[25] So testifies a policeman patrolling the suburbs of Stockholm, engulfed in riots ignited by Muslim immigrants in the spring of 2013 after police shot a knife-wielding crime suspect. "We don't officially have no-go zones in Brussels, but in reality, there are, and they are [found] in Molenbeek," says the former security advisor to the Belgium prime minister.[26] Molenbeek, a Brussels district, was home to the man charged with shooting up that city's Jewish Museum and was searched as part of investigations into the *Charlie Hebdo* attacks and an Islamist terrorist rampage on a Brussels-to-Paris train in August 2015. "Nobody wanted to know because this did not fit their political agenda," Dutch writer Arthur van Amerongen, who lived in Molenbeek while researching a book on Islamic extremism, observed after the Bataclan massacre.[27] Two of the perpetrators, along with the attacks' architect, resided in Molenbeek.

While large swathes of Muslim habitation are patrolled by vigilantes, those places where Jews live are the complete opposite. Visit a synagogue, day school, or any other Jewish institution anywhere in Europe, and you will see a heavily fortified edifice that might often look more like a military base than a spiritual community. Armed guards, high walls topped with barbed wire, security cameras everywhere: This is the reality of Jewish life in twenty-first-century Europe. By contrast, mosques, madrassas, and other Islamic facilities don't feel the need to take similar precautions.

This contrast between Jewish communities, which resemble besieged encampments, and some Muslim ones, where police, firemen, and social workers fear to tread, is conspicuous across the continent. It is hard to find a more apt illustration of Europe's state of social discord. The incongruity of safety measures undertaken by Jews and Muslims in Europe belies the ethical fog that clouds most discussions about anti-Semitism and Islamophobia, in which too many are hesitant to identify victims and perpetrators—when they even concede that such categories exist. While the French government doesn't hesitate to express "solidarity" with its Jewish citizens, it refuses, in the name of civic republican values, to classify the race, religion, or ethnic identity of those who commit crimes against them. Such obstinacy makes the formation of a coherent and effective policy response all but impossible. Part of a broader "terrible fear of naming Islamism as such," according to the spokesman for Hamburg's Jewish community, it has ineluctably led to an ever more dangerous situation for Europe's Jews.[28]

The sad fact is that, in Europe today, there's only one group of people who are regularly killed on the basis of their identity. Yet every time Jews (or gentiles) are attacked or slain in the name of Islam, right-thinking Europeans immediately warn against "Islamophobic backlash." In an early report on the 2015 shootings at a Copenhagen synagogue and a café that hosted a discussion by a Swedish cartoonist who had drawn images of Mohammed, the *New York Times,* while not using the word "anti-Semitism" once, noted the following: "Anti-immigrant and anti-Muslim sentiment is rising in Europe, and although there was no indication who was responsible for the shootings in Copenhagen, Twitter was ablaze with anti-Muslim indictments."[29] A follow-up story, after the gunman was identified as a Palestinian Arab who had sworn fidelity to ISIS and shouted "Allahu Akbar" while spraying his targets with bullets, carried the headline, "Anger of Suspect in Danish Killings Is Seen as Only Loosely Tied to Islam."[30] As for the much-feared "backlash" against Muslims that is always inevitable, it rarely if ever actually occurs. Indeed, Jews are far more likely to be victims of bias-motivated violence in Europe than Muslims. Anti-Semitic attacks in France comprise 51 percent of all hate crimes even though Jews represent less than 1 percent of the population; Muslims account for just under 10 percent of the population and are the targets of still less than 7 percent of hate crimes.[31] The "backlash" European societies should be primarily worried about isn't Islamphobia but further Jewish emigration in the face of an increasingly hostile, anti-Semitic climate.

One reason they don't worry about Jewish emigration, however, is that, for a large swathe of the European left, the Muslim *ummah* (global faith community) has become the new proletariat. Hearing self-proclaimed Muslim "community leaders" express grievances about Western racism and imperialism, a left that once saw religion as the opiate of the masses now considers it, at least in the case of Islam, to be a revolutionary and emancipatory force. "Many leftists are so irrationally afraid of an irrational fear of Islam that they haven't been able to consider the very good reasons for fearing Islamist zealots—and so they have difficulty explaining what's going on in the world," the philosopher Michael Walzer writes of his comrades.[32]

Correlating Muslim authenticity with revulsion toward the West, this "regressive left" politics (a term coined by the British ex-Islamist Maajid Nawaz to describe liberals who "ignorantly pander" to Muslim extremists) emboldens the most reactionary voices in Muslim communities, in effect rewarding those who drown out more moderate voices.[33]

Sammy Ghozlan, a French ex-policeman who started a civic patrol organization to protect Jewish institutions, says that French Muslims would not be so bold in their defiance of the Republic and its values "if they didn't have the sense that they were encouraged by political movements and opinions in France that incited them to behave in this way."[34] On July 13, 2014, at the height of the Gaza War, what can only be described as a pogrom descended on the Don Isaac Abravanel synagogue in the Marais, Paris's best-known Jewish neighborhood. A crowd of several hundred people, chanting "Death to the Jews" and wielding iron bars and axes, tried to break into the building where about 200 worshipers were caught inside. Shimon Samuels, of the Simon Wiesenthal Center, reported seeing Socialist Party politicians in the crowd (in addition to a hotel concierge and a bank teller, a depressing indication that, in some communities, hunting Jews has become a bourgeois affair).[35] Though French police rushed to the scene, one eyewitness reported that, had it not been for members of the vigilante Jewish Defense League, "the synagogue would have been destroyed, with all the people trapped inside."[36] In retrospect, the 2002 murder of the Dutch gay liberal sociologist and politician Pim Fortuyn, just days before his party was bound to win national elections, was a harbinger of the red-green political coalition. Many forget it was a left-wing environmental activist, Volkert van der Graaf, who committed Holland's first political assassination in four centuries, citing as his motive the defense of Muslims. The "internal migration" of French Jews has seen them move away not only from neighborhoods with large Muslim populations to more homogenous areas, but also from communist- or socialist-run neighborhoods to those governed by right-wing or center-right mayors.[37]

It's not only a mendacious ideology positing Muslims as the new wretched of the earth that has persuaded a vocal segment of the European left to prioritize parochial Muslim interests while forsaking Jews; the rude facts of demography also matter. About 8 percent of France is Muslim; a full quarter of teenagers identify as such.[38] As a whole, the Muslim community in France is growing more religious; the proportion labeling themselves "observant" increased from 36 percent in 2001 to 42 percent in 2014, whereas those describing themselves as "French citizens of Muslim origin" fell from 25 percent in 2007 to 21 percent in 2014.[39] Disputing the contention that Islamist radicalization is the result of societal dispossession and stigmatization, the French Islam expert Olivier Roy calls it "a youth revolt against society, articulated on an Islamic religious narrative of jihad. It is not the uprising of a Muslim community victim of poverty and racism: only young people join, including converts who did not share the 'sufferings' of Muslims in Europe."[40] As of late 2015, 11,000 names were listed in a database of suspected radical Islamists, far too many for the security services to monitor.[41]

Although you need not spend much time on the Internet before uncovering expressions of genuine Islamophobia, Muslim community leaders, assisted by sympathizers in European media, government, and the nonprofit sector, have used the word to tar any criticism of Islamic theology, practices, or attitudes as the equivalent of racism, sexism, and homophobia. (The prevalence of these very bigotries within Islamic communities themselves, in contrast, is conveniently ignored by many progressives.) To a post-Marxist left that remains incapable of recognizing religion as a powerful motivating force of human behavior, entirely legitimate concerns about political Islam and its ambitions in secular, liberal societies are conflated with bigotry directed at individual Muslims. Terrorism, support for blasphemy laws, oppression of homosexuals, and the subjugation of women through forced veiling are all rationalized to some degree as the cry of the dispossessed standing athwart Western imperialism and racism.

The term "Islamophobia" came into popular use following a 1997 report by the Runnymede Trust, a UK-based think tank.[42] Devoid of any data about actual discrimination, the study sought to stigmatize certain criticisms and judgments of Islam itself as beyond the pale, and its dictates have largely been adopted by European political, media, and academic elites. After devising a tidy summary of "open" and "closed" views of Islam, the report's authors deem as "phobic" the tendency whereby "Muslim criticisms of 'the West' are rejected" rather than "debated," the belief that Islam is "inferior" to Western belief systems rather than "different but equal," and the opinion that Islam is "intolerant of internal pluralism and deliberation." One can avoid the dreaded "Islamophobia" tag by adopting an "open view" of Islam that "does not see it as deficient or as less worthy of esteem" as other faith traditions. The report thus insidiously conflated legitimate concerns about Islamic practices and political aims with far more questionable positions: It became impermissible—Islamophobic—to refuse to "debate," never mind refute, even the most rancid Islamist conspiracy theories or to report factually on intolerance or the stifling of dissent within Muslim communities. Use of the term "phobia" itself is highly problematic. Derived from psychoanalysis, it refers to an irrational fear of a nonexistent threat. "Islamophobia" thus undermines statements of the obvious: Namely, that there is a demonstrable connection between Islamist ideologies and terrorism.

Conflating criticism of Islam with anti-Semitism, misogyny, or ethnic bigotry, some European Muslim leaders and their allies on the regressive left have cynically assumed the mantle of "anti-racists." Dieudonné M'bala M'bala, a French comedian of North African lineage who derides Holocaust remembrance as "memorial pornography" and popularized a neo-Nazi salute known as the *quelnelle,* has developed a massive following in the *banlieues* as a symbol of resistance against the supposedly Jewish-ruled French establishment; in his perverse worldview, anti-Semitism has become a necessary *component* of anti-racism, not its antithesis. Those who support the right of cartoonists to blaspheme, or oppose gender-segregated swimming pools, women wearing a veil in government buildings, and other intrusions of Islamic cultural practices into the public sphere, can be expected to be called not only "Islamophobic" but also "racist." So perverse has this discussion become that many Muslim advocates and their left-wing fellow travelers write of Muslims as "the new Jews." A cover story in the *New Statesman,* Britain's leading left-wing news magazine, warned of "The Next Holocaust," whose victims will be Muslims.[43] Not only is this appropriation of the Shoah morally obtuse but it also tiptoes around the fact that, judging by the level of hate crime, the "new Jews" are the same as the old ones: Jews.

According to a 2013 poll, 50 percent of the French think their country's "decline" is "inevitable."[44] Less than a third believe that France's democracy functions well. A stagnant economy and rising Islamic extremism have created a combustible situation where the dominant sentiment is fear. On such anxieties does a leader like Marine Le Pen thrive. Her National Front is the leading political party among workers, farmers, youth, and the unemployed. Though always categorized as "far right," the National Front is pulling away many traditional Socialist voters. So extensive is its support that it is frankly inaccurate to call the party "far" anything: It can claim to represent as broad a cross-section of the French public as the ruling Socialists or conservative Gaullists. Le Pen's foreign policy is anti-European, anti-American, and pro-Russian; in 2014, her party received an €11 million loan from a Russian bank,[45] and two years later she publicly requested €27 million more to fight in the 2017 presidential election.[46] (Prohibiting foreign funding of political parties is an urgent task that ought to be taken up not just by individual European governments but at the EU level as well.) National Front economic policies are even more statist and protectionist than those of the Socialists; a Le Pen administration would only prolong France's economic misery, if not hasten its further decline. Were she ever to be elected president, it would be a disaster for European unity, transatlanticism, and the assertion of liberal values abroad.

Yet of all French political leaders—with the notable exception of Valls, who pointedly refuses to use the word "Islamophobia," recognizing how Islamists exploit it to stifle legitimate criticism of their practices and beliefs—Le Pen speaks most passionately the language of defending France's republican values from Islamist assault. It is this quality that explains the party's surging popularity. Le Pen has cleverly tried to cleanse the National Front of its racist and anti-Semitic reputation, carrying out a series of high-profile expulsions of less salubrious party members up to and including her father, the avuncular reactionary Jean-Marie. This clever *dédiabolisation* (de-demonization) policy seeks to gain the support of influential Jews as a means of persuading the majority of French citizens, who could not imagine voting for the National Front, that the party has cleansed itself of neo-fascist stigma and is now "kosher." But the strategy of Le Pen *fille* has every indication of being purely opportunistic.[47] Marine, after all, lived with her father until the age of 46 (moving out at the same time as she ousted him from the family business), and reputable polling shows that the party's rank and file continue to harbor anti-Semitic views: 48 percent, for instance, believe "Jews have too much power in the media." Nonetheless, it is to this political faction that so many of France's disillusioned voters are rallying. A feeling that political elites are ignoring or even abetting the slow erosion of the Republic's secular nature feeds Marine Le Pen's rise.

Current trends may convey the impression that the eventual desertion of French Jewry by emigration is inexorable. But permanent Jewish-Muslim discord need not be a foregone conclusion, in France or anywhere else. If there is any silver lining to be found in the Islamist war on European Jews, it is that the enemies of the Jews are also the enemies of European civilization, meaning that Europeans ignore anti-Semitism at their own peril. Islamism strikes at the heart of European societies themselves. In both the Paris and Copenhagen attacks, assailants first struck at symbols of free speech and then at Jews, a bloodily unambiguous signal that the fates of European liberty and Jewry are inextricable. "Things that were previously felt by the Jewish community are now felt by the population at large," says Jérôme Fourquet, a well-known French pollster.[48] Indeed, today's Islamist assault on the French republic can trace its origins back to 2000, when the Second Palestinian Intifada against Israel incited an upsurge in anti-Semitism among French Muslims. That antipathy toward Jews eventually widened into a broader antagonism against the French republic, visible in the 2005 riots that led to thousands of arrests and a state of emergency, and it has continued to inspire murderous attacks like those at the Bataclan nightclub and Nice's Promenade des Anglais. A final factor militating against the end of Jewish life in Europe is that, while state sponsorship made the anti-Semitism of the last century so deadly, today's European governments resolutely oppose anti-Semitism and actively defend Jewish institutions.

What would happen to a continent that, having almost lost its Jewish citizens by mass murder, loses them entirely by attrition? History, especially European history, tells us that anti-Semitism always starts, but never ends, with the Jews. Across time and place, Jewish welfare has been a reliable marker of wider societal health. A country that turns on its Jews is paving the way for greater misfortune. British historian Paul Johnson distinguishes anti-Semitism from other, more everyday forms of bigotry in that it is "an intellectual disease, a disease of the mind, extremely infectious and massively destructive."[49] To return to Prime Minister Valls's point: A France without Jews would not only "no longer be France" in the sense of its losing so many of its artists, writers, philosophers, entrepreneurs, and many other ordinary citizens. A France without Jews would mark its end as a place of *liberté, egalité,* and *fraternité* and the beginning stages of its descent into barbarism.

To Europe's beleaguered Jews, being told that their fate is intertwined with that of the continent itself may sound like cold comfort. For even death offers them no reprieve. Six days after the assault on the Hyper Cacher kosher market, the bodies of the four victims were buried in Jerusalem. Their families feared their relatives' graves would be desecrated in France.

6

Brexit: From Great Britain
to Little England

England . . . will save Europe by her example.

William Pitt the Younger, 1805

We seem, as it were, to have conquered half the world in a fit of absence of mind.

John Robert Seeley, 1883

IF THE ORIGINS OF THE LIBERAL WORLD order can be traced to May 7, 1948, when leaders ranging from Konrad Adenauer to Winston Churchill and a young François Mitterand gathered at The Hague Congress to chart the future of European political and economic cooperation, future historians may pinpoint its unraveling as having begun on June 23, 2016. That was the day Great Britain decided—against the counsel of every major political party, the governor of the Bank of England, nine out of ten economists, the president of the United States, the leaders of every European country, labor union heads, captains of industry, the International Monetary Fund, Stephen Hawking, the secretary general of NATO, the former chiefs of MI5 and MI6, and David Beckham—to leave the European Union by a margin of 52 percent to 48 percent, becoming the first member state to do so. After more than four decades of tempestuous marriage, the relationship between Britain and Europe entered into protracted divorce proceedings.

Approval of "Brexit," the portmanteau adopted to describe this less than amicable separation, immediately plunged the United Kingdom into political, economic, and social crisis. Within hours of the vote result, Prime Minister David Cameron announced his intention to resign, setting off a Conservative Party leadership race to succeed him. Several days later, Labor MPs overwhelmingly passed a vote of no confidence against their leader Jeremy Corbyn, furious that he had barely lifted a finger to assist the "Remain" campaign. Acknowledging that businesses and households would indefinitely delay spending and investment in the face of such profound economic uncertainty, Bank of England governor Mark Carney warned of "economic post-traumatic stress disorder."[1] The Economist Intelligence Unit, meanwhile, warned of a 6 percent contraction in GDP by 2020 and increasing unemployment.[2] Britain's AAA credit rating, which it had enjoyed since 1978, was downgraded to AA. After only a week in post-Brexit Britain, police logged a 500 percent increase in hate crimes, with everyone from long-resident Cypriots to native-born black Britons reporting abuse at the hands of freshly emboldened English nationalists.[3] Finally, beyond all these tangible aftershocks, a deep and ineffable sense of unease set in among many Britons, particularly younger ones, who had voted overwhelmingly to stay within the EU. At risk was their future conception of themselves as Europeans, along with the benefits that identity accrues, not least of which are the "four freedoms" they had long taken for granted: the free movement of goods, services, persons, and capital across the union.

Brexit has many fathers, none so telegenic and omnipresent as Nigel Farage. A perpetually tanned and pinstriped, chain-smoking former London City banker, Farage was until July 2016 the longtime leader of the United Kingdom Independence Party (UKIP), whose raison d'être for the past quarter-century has been Britain's withdrawal from the EU. Farage believes British employers should have the right to discriminate based upon race, gender, and national origin,[4] and is the sort of chap who blames foreigners for the most quotidian of problems, like missing a party meeting due to traffic on roads supposedly clogged with immigrants.[5] Once dismissed as a fringe dispenser of pub wisdom whose party was little more than a passing fad, Farage, who has been a member of the European Parliament for nearly two decades, is perhaps the most consequential British political figure of the past quarter-century second only to former prime minister Tony Blair. In the 2014 European Parliament elections, UKIP— scorned by Prime Minister David Cameron eight years earlier as "a bunch of fruitcakes and loonies and closet racists"[6]—earned more seats than any other British party, the first time that neither Labor nor the Conservatives won a national election. In the following year's general election, UKIP earned 12 percent of the popular vote, making it the third most popular party in the country. (Because of Britain's first-past-the-post electoral system for parliamentary constituencies, however, this impressive result translated into just one seat in the House of Commons at Westminster.) UKIP's influence is best measured not by parliamentary representation, however, but by its effect on British political debate.

UKIP's threat to steal Euroskeptic Tory voters emboldened the Conservative Party's anti-European wing and pushed Cameron to adopt a more anti-EU stance. In 2009, a year before he became prime minister and as a sop to his party's right wing, Cameron withdrew the Tories from the European Peoples' Party (EPP), the center right (and largest) grouping in the European Parliament, home also to the French Républicans, German CDU/CSU, and Spanish Popular Party. Abandoning the Conservatives' traditional allies on the continent, the Tories then affiliated with the Alliance of European Conservatives and Reformists (AECR), a Euroskeptic faction one-third the size of the EPP. Through this act of self-marginalization, Cameron diminished the ability of British Conservatives to influence politics on the pan-European level. But his most drastic concession to the Euroskeptics was to promise, in the 2015 Conservative Party election manifesto, a nationwide referendum on Britain's EU membership. So improbable did Brexit actually seem that, as late as weeks before the referendum, few people seriously believed that Britain would ever vote to leave the Union.

Four days after the Brexit plebiscite, Farage could be found delivering one of his infamous tirades from the well of the European Parliament in Brussels. "Virtually none of you have ever done a proper job in your lives!" he bellowed as a Lithuanian MEP, a former cardiac surgeon born in an Arctic gulag, sat behind him with his head in his hands, in an image captured by a photographer. It is the EU's legislative body to which Farage owes his considerable fame and political success, which is ironic considering how much he expresses his distaste for the institution and its occupants. Try to imagine a Christian being fed to a Coliseum full of lions (but make the Christian a fusion of John Cleese and Colonel Blimp and the lions all herbivores), and you begin to capture the essence of Farage's regular performances before the European Parliament. Over his long career as an MEP, Farage's brisk anti-EU diatribes have racked millions of views on YouTube, earning him a Europe-wide—indeed worldwide—following. Most memorable was a 2010 rant in which he accused the then-president of the European Council, former Belgian prime minister Herman von Rompuy, of possessing the "charisma of a damp rag and the appearance of a low-grade bank clerk."

Farage's routines struck continental Europeans as, at best, the mildly amusing blathering of a British eccentric or, at worst, as the rancid xenophobia of a Little Englander. Back home, they caused no end of embarrassment to many of his countrymen. But Farage's impassioned briefs advocating UK "sovereignty" and "democracy" against the EU "dictatorship" became a source of pride for a growing audience back home. Great Britain had never been an enthusiastic participant in the European project, viewing it mostly as a vehicle to break down trade barriers. Brits, by and large, were never convinced by the body's broader, supranational political agenda. For decades, an obsessively anti-EU tabloid media exploited this natural suspicion of Europe, embellishing each and every arcane regulation promulgated by Brussels as an act of imperialist subjugation. In his 2011 testimony to the Leveson Inquiry, a judicial proceeding into British media ethics and standards, former Blair aide Alastair Campbell reflected that

> If the Eurosceptic press is to be believed, Britain is going to be forced to unite as a single country with France, Church schools are being forced to hire atheist teachers, Scotch whisky is being classified as inflammable liquid, British soldiers must take orders in French, the price of chips is being raised by Brussels, Europe is insisting on one size fits all condoms, new laws are being proposed on how to climb a ladder, it will be a criminal offense to criticize Europe, Number 10 [Downing Street] must fly the European flag, and finally, Europe is brainwashing our children with pro-European propaganda![7]

Perhaps the most notorious progenitor of this irresponsible style of British journalism was Boris Johnson, former Conservative mayor of London and once-and-future favorite for prime minister. A cunning politician and prose stylist who cultivates an air of shambolic charm, the Eton-educated, tow-headed Johnson started to earn a national profile in 1989 when the *Daily Telegraph,* the broadsheet bible of the Tory elite, hired him as its Brussels correspondent. Johnson had been fired from his first job in journalism, reporting for the London *Times,* after being caught in the act of perpetrating the tried-and-true British newspaper practice of inventing a quotation, in this case, one he attributed to his own godfather. In Brussels, however, the threshold for what constitutes truthful reporting was substantially lower than that applied to most other matters, particularly in the case of the reliably Euroskeptic *Telegraph.* If his colorful dispatches exposing absurd EU minutiae, such as disputes over condom sizes, won him admiration from the Tories' Middle England base, they also earned the contempt of his journalistic colleagues. "Boris told such dreadful lies/it made one gasp and stretch one's eyes," an erstwhile colleague wrote.[8]

Reflecting on his Brussels stint years later, Johnson—under whose Falstaffian veneer lies a political guile comparable to that of Francis Urquhart, (sly protagonist of the original BBC *House of Cards* series)—essentially admitted that his reportorial embellishments had less to do with conveying accurate information than advancing his career prospects back home. "I was just chucking these rocks over the garden wall and listening to this amazing crash from the greenhouse next door over in England," he reminisced to the BBC in a 2005 interview. "Everything I wrote from Brussels was having this amazing explosive effect on the Tory Party and it really gave me this, I suppose, rather weird sense of power."[9]

Though he started his career as a Brussels basher, Johnson never fit comfortably into the traditional Tory Euroskeptic camp, much less the nativist one embodied by Farage. As mayor of multiethnic London, Johnson enthusiastically advertised the city as a global, cosmopolitan entrepôt, celebrated its rich immigrant communities, and successfully hosted the 2012 Olympics. Following Johnson around for a week during the 2008 mayoral campaign, I witnessed him boast to a live television debate audience that "my own genetic diversity is pretty great and my children resemble a kind of UN Peacekeeping force."[10] As a parliamentarian, his record was mildly pro-European. It was something of a surprise, therefore, when Johnson chose rather late in the game to announce his support for the "Leave" campaign. Cameron, who had agreed to a referendum with great reluctance, saw his fellow Old Etonian's positioning as betrayal. Many British political observers similarly viewed it as an act of pure political opportunism given Johnson's at best mild Euroskepticism and the gravity of an actual Brexit victory. When the referendum was announced in February 2016, the possibility that British voters would actually vote to leave the EU was considered highly unlikely, and so Johnson's joining the Leave side was interpreted as a way for him to shore up support with the party's vocal anti-EU bloc while inflicting minimal real-world damage. In this scenario, Cameron would emerge victorious but weakened after a closer-than-expected Remain victory, and Johnson would have positioned himself for the job he had always coveted: prime minister.

There was only one problem in this clever plot: Britons voted Leave, not least because the charismatic Johnson told them to. Until he joined the "Outers," Vote Leave lacked a credible mainstream spokesman, and it's not an exaggeration to say that Johnson, one of the most recognizable and popular politicians in Britain, tipped the balance. Yet his insincerity about the whole affair was exposed the Monday following the shocking result. Under Brexit, Johnson assured readers of his weekly *Daily Telegraph* column that Britain would be able to retain its access to the European single market while opting out of the EU's freedom-of-movement requirement, the "only change" being "that the UK will extricate itself from the EU's extraordinary and opaque system of legislation."[11] This was disingenuous at best, because even those European countries that have chosen to remain outside the EU—such as Norway and Switzerland—must accept the full raft of EU regulations (including the right of European citizens to travel and work within their countries) in exchange for right of entry to the common market. Asked about precisely this trade-off during the campaign, Johnson often joked that "my policy on cake is pro having it and pro eating it," as if the EU would easily grant London free trading rights with the bloc while letting it waive entirely the freedom of movement clause. Now that Brexit was reality, Johnson's quips weren't so funny. It was allegedly this column, revealing as it did his rank dishonesty and rather less than full-throated Brexit sympathies, that convinced his former friend and ally, Justice Secretary Michael Gove, to withdraw his support for Johnson's nascent prime ministerial bid and declare himself a candidate in one of the most dramatic betrayals in recent British political history.

While the Tory Party found itself in disarray because of Brexit, it was UKIP—and, in particular, Nigel Farage—that emerged as the undisputed victor of Britain's political chaos. From the start, Vote Leave was a collection of constituencies with occasionally conflicting, if not outright contradictory, aims. A coalition of libertarian capitalists hoping to turn the UK into a North Atlantic Singapore, old-fashioned sovereigntists disdainful of supranational governance, and white working-class Labor voters opposed to mass immigration would have great difficulty agreeing to a unifying political vision for post-Brexit Britain. While cosmopolitan Brexit campaigners like Johnson tried to push a more optimistic message, stressing the importance of Britain's relationship with non-EU rising powers such as China and India as a reason to vote Leave and downplaying reservations about immigration, others, like Farage, focused almost exclusively on the threat posed by foreigners and promised to take the country back to a simpler, whiter past. In one of the campaign's more dishonorable episodes, Farage unveiled a poster depicting a long stream of swarthy migrants under the banner "Breaking Point," the explicit message being that Britain would be overrun by hordes of Middle Eastern and North African migrants, a dubious claim because Britain is not even in the Schengen Area, the passport-free zone within the European Union, and therefore not obligated to take in any of the migrants recently welcomed by the EU.

Regardless, it was UKIP's vision of Little England that won the day for Leave. Campaigning for Brexit often brought out the worst in its proponents, not least Johnson, who, in a column criticizing Barack Obama's intervention into the debate, attributed the president's support for Britain remaining within the EU to an "ancestral dislike for the British empire" and "part-Kenyan" heritage.[12] On the campaign trail, Johnson reverted to his old, hyperbolically Europhobic ways, comparing the EU to Hitler in an interview with the *Sunday Telegraph*.[13] Deceiving British voters with the claim that they could enjoy all the fruits of the EU while abnegating any and all of its perceived downsides—that they could have their European single market, immigration restrictionist cake *and* eat it—was itself a concession to UKIP.

I had caught a glimpse of the barnstorming Farage "show" myself one summer afternoon in 2015. Addressing a half-empty lecture hall at the conservative Heritage Foundation in Washington, D.C., Farage opined on the evils of the European project and sounded not at all unlike one of the open-collared, Mediterranean socialist radicals of Greece's ruling Syriza party. Railing against international finance capital in one breath and dispensing populist *bon mots* ("I had a proper job before getting into politics") to his Tea Party audience with the next, Farage shifted between ostensible "left" and "right" positions with aplomb.

"Everything in Europe is going wonderfully well," he began sarcastically, to laughs from the audience.[14] Two weeks earlier, Greeks had voted to reject the terms of the latest bailout from their country's international creditors, and the number of migrants reaching Europe had hit the highest point on record. Disagreements among EU members over the euro, migration, and Russia were escalating to the point that they threatened "the return of old enmities that have done Europe so much harm," Farage declared. Given that his entire political platform rests on stoking fear of foreigners swindling decent, hard-working British people, Farage might not seem like the most credible critic of resurgent nationalism. But he assured his audience that dismantling the EU did not mean a return to 1930s-style balance-of-power politics. The initial impulse for European integration, he allowed with barely concealed insincerity, was a "sensible idea." The problem is that it "has gone too far."

The latest victims of EU machinations, Farage told his mesmerized audience, were the poor Greeks. He fired off a raft of statistics illustrating the country's dire circumstances, though precisely how the catastrophic situation in Greece was the fault of Brussels was left unsaid. Whereas the U.S. economy had contracted by 16 percent during the Great Depression, Farage stated, Greece's had shrunk by 26 percent between 2010 and 2015, the implication being that the severity of the recession was exacerbated by Athens being in the Eurozone. To those who might say that the Greeks themselves bore some of the blame, Farage had a rejoinder: "They never voted to join the Euro; they were taken into it by Goldman Sachs and their own greedy politicians."

In reality, Greece joined the Eurozone in 2001 through a vote of its democratically elected parliament; polls at the time showed 72 percent in favor of the single currency, and support for maintaining Eurozone membership has remained high throughout even the worst points of the crisis.[15] (It would hardly be the first, or last, time that Farage put loathing of the European project before accuracy: Just an hour after the Brexit referendum result was confirmed, he told an interviewer that it had been a "mistake" to promise, as he repeatedly did on the campaign hustings, that leaving the EU would result in the British government spending £350 million more per week on the National Health Service.)[16] At the end of his speech, I rose to ask the uncrowned king of British Euroskepticism what he made of the ongoing crisis in Ukraine. Although I was prepared for something unconventional, I did not expect what came out of Farage's mouth.

War in Ukraine, he said, was the result of a "democratically elected leader brought down by a street-staged coup d'état by people waving EU flags." Russian president Vladimir Putin could hardly be blamed for thinking that the "message" behind the Maidan protests was "we want Ukraine to join NATO." Invading and annexing Crimea were perfectly understandable reactions to European imperialism. Ukraine's dismemberment, the thousands of deaths in its eastern provinces, more than a million displaced people, and heightened tensions between Russia and the West—all of it, Farage told me, was "something we have provoked." A Kremlin spokesperson could not have scripted the response better himself.

In reality, what ultimately "brought down" Viktor Yanukovych, the former president of Ukraine, was his decision to flee Ukraine for Russia after ordering snipers to murder his own citizens. As for Farage's assertion that NATO "wanted" Ukraine to join the alliance, that claim would come as a surprise to, well, NATO. At its 2008 summit in Bucharest, the alliance declined to offer either Georgia or Ukraine a Membership Action Plan. One does not have to be a Russophobic conspiracy theorist to speculate that Putin saw NATO's rejection of these two countries as a green light for aggression against them. Today, Georgia and Ukraine are home to Russian occupation troops and "frozen conflicts," their chances of becoming NATO members slimmer than they had been before. Farage's sympathy for the Kremlin view of the world is long-standing, and comes naturally to a "Little Englander" who seeks a diminished place for his country in global affairs. Asked in 2014 which world leader he most admired, Farage replied, "As an operator, but not as a human being, I would say Putin. The way he played the whole Syria thing. Brilliant."[17]

Farage's laudatory views of the Russian leadership are an extreme manifestation of a country increasingly disengaged from its traditional role of helping uphold the liberal world order. It is incredible to watch Great Britain, which once occupied more than 20 percent of the earth's landmass, moving ever closer to the brink of its own disintegration. In the span of less than two years, Britain held two existential referenda. Though Scotland came short of declaring independence in a 2014 vote, a near-sweep in the following year's general election by the pro-independence Scottish Nationalist Party (SNP), as well as Britain's decision to leave the EU (membership in which Scots overwhelmingly favor), signals that the United Kingdom itself could very well split in the near future. Even though Farage took a swipe at the SNP during his Heritage Foundation address, quipping that it's "a party who are nationalists and socialists at the same time," UKIP actually has more in common with the "Scots Nats" than he might care to admit. Ironically for a party that has "UK" in its acronym, the fulfillment of UKIP's single-issue policy agenda—British departure from the EU—will do more to dismantle the United Kingdom than any other political development. Farage's UKIP is an essentially English nationalist party that, like the SNP, seeks to diminish British influence in the world.

In his address to the Heritage Foundation, Farage spoke animatedly about what a "No" vote would mean not only for Britain's relationship with the EU but also for the entire European project. Brexit would send ripples across the continent, encouraging other nationalist parties to emulate the British example. "If we win this referendum," Farage declared to his American audience, "we can kill off the whole project." And that project, he intoned, in what has become a trite (not to mention morally spurious) analogy, poses no less a menace to human freedom than did the late, unlamented Soviet Union. A year later, in his valedictory address to the European Parliament, Farage triumphantly predicted, "The United Kingdom will not be the last member state to leave the European Union."

It should be said that British skepticism of Europe, often derided as blimpish provincialism, is not without foundation. Britain's Anglo-Saxon heritage, history as a global trading power, geographic position on an island, and the fact that it never experienced a foreign occupation have fostered attitudes that differ substantively from what might simplistically be termed "continental" perspectives on subjects ranging from the role of the state in the economy to immigration to individual liberty and military intervention abroad. Britons are, in general, more sympathetic to free markets, individual rights, national sovereignty, and the use of military force than their continental neighbors. Views of the European project are also shaped by a state's historical experience. For a country like Germany, such memories are heavily influenced by its having started two world wars, which helps explain why the EU is relatively popular among Germans for its role as a damper on nationalism. For the French, whose statehood was repeatedly threatened (and once destroyed) in the twentieth century, the allure of European integration is much the same as for Germans: The EU tames national rivalries and mediates the quest for political and economic supremacy on the continent. In postcommunist countries like Poland and the Baltic States, meanwhile, European integration—along with the tangible economic benefits it has bestowed—denotes membership in the West and rejection of Russian dominance. Embedding their nations deeper within the European project, even when the advantages might not be immediately clear, is for the Eastern EU members a decisive expression of civilizational preference for a Western future over Moscow's neo-imperial domination. None of these impulses for European integration have much resonance for the British, understandably so.

For unlike almost every other country on the continent, Great Britain has a positive experience of national independence, rendering appeals to Europe's dark past less persuasive. Unlike Germans and the Third Reich, the post-revolutionary French, or Eastern Europeans subjugated by the Soviet Empire, the British have not endured totalitarianism or occupation by a foreign power. The last time a foreign army invaded Britain was in the eleventh century. The British are thus far more inclined to view any sort of rule from afar with heightened suspicion and with good reason: They trust themselves with self-government. Nor today do they fear the territorial predations of a large and aggressive neighbor. A "special relationship" with the United States and the worldwide network of cultural and economic exchange sustained through the British Commonwealth contribute to a global outlook and sense of identity distinctly less "European" than that of continentals.

In voting to leave the EU, however, Great Britain demonstrated that it had learned the wrong lessons from its history and experiences. For that history shows Britain cannot be a passive observer to events on the continent. Remaining aloof from European affairs has always been a temptation for the British, who are generally content to mind their own business and let France and Germany sort out the details of European integration. But while the prospect of another European war may lie beyond our imaginations, that does not mean Britain can simply sit on the sidelines. On the contrary, it has always had an interest in maintaining a balance of power on the continent, something that will be more difficult, if not impossible, to achieve absent active British involvement. On all manner of issues, from the single market to border security and relations with Russia, Great Britain's voice has been essential in providing an Atlanticist, liberal, free market perspective to a European debate that tends toward the inward looking, statist, and conciliatory toward Moscow. If Russia's 2014 invasion of Crimea was the first external assault on the post–Cold War European political order, Britain's rash decision to depart the EU the first self-inflicted wound, one that, despite the assurances of its advocates, will have consequences for British security. Brexit's tacit endorsement of the idea that what happens in Europe is not Britain's business fractures the Western alliance and weakens NATO solidarity and resolve.

Britain's shrinking presence in European affairs is symptomatic of a more profound, narrow-minded, isolationist condition. The Royal Navy, once the envy of the world, now calls in U.S. warships to protect British commercial vessels.[18] One of the few NATO members to spend the recommended 2 percent of its GDP on defense, Britain comes perilously close to dipping below it. London has played next to no role in the diplomatic negotiations over Ukraine, leaving the West represented only by Germany and France, even though Britain was one of three signatories to the 1994 Budapest Memorandum guaranteeing Ukraine's territorial integrity in exchange for its giving up what was then the world's third-largest nuclear arsenal. Indeed, the real sign of British impotence was not its absence from the quadripartite Normandy Format on Ukraine, but that London's lack of interest was so widely assumed that no one even thought of asking it to participate. Retreat from the world overseas is mirrored by a retreat from reality at home, as the Labor Party, a once-great institution that secured political representation for the British working class and created the modern welfare state, has been captured by Jeremy Corbyn, an unreconstructed Trotskyist, Putin apologist, and anti-Western firebrand.

Advocates of the EU typically portray it as a soft and gentle multilateral organization formed in reaction to the horrors of World War II. As a way of managing interstate relations, they claim, it is the apotheosis of collective human achievement, the greatest experiment in political cooperation mankind has ever attempted. Amid such grandiose talk, the practical benefits of the EU almost always come across as an afterthought. Yet the EU is, at heart, a utilitarian project: Countries ultimately join not out of a sense of war guilt or a belief that they "owe" something to poorer Europeans, but because membership brings quantifiable material benefits. For generations of Europeans who never experienced the armed conflict and privation that formed the daily experience of their ancestors, or for young people living in Mediterranean countries with 50 percent youth unemployment rates, it is incredibly difficult to explain the enduring relevance of the EU. But Euroskeptics like Farage and Johnson who claim that the EU has "failed" must answer the following question: In comparison to what? The Europe of the Thirty Years War? The Napoleonic Empire? The Third Reich? To paraphrase Winston Churchill, the EU may be the worst system of governing Europe, but it is better than any of the alternatives. If the European political order disintegrates, it may fall apart first in the British Isles.

On September 21, 2012, then-Polish foreign minister Radoslaw Sikorski entered the stately library at Blenheim Palace outside Oxford to deliver a blunt message. Sikorski, who studied at Oxford as a political exile in the 1980s while his country endured communist martial law, began by asserting his conservative bona fides. He had once been a scholar at "the right-wing American Enterprise Institute," reported on anticommunist insurgencies from Afghanistan to Angola for the *National Review,* and counted himself an admirer of Margaret Thatcher. "I tick every box required to be a lifelong member of London's most powerful Eurosceptics' club," he boasted.[19]

Sikorski's message, however, differed greatly from the one I would hear three years later from the most visible leader of that club, Nigel Farage, or even from its titular spokesman Boris Johnson, a friend of Sikorski's from Oxford days. Unlike many of his ideological confrères on the British right, Sikorski is not a Euroskeptic, but rather a committed believer in the "logic and justice of the modern European project." He implored his hosts not to hold a referendum on Britain's continued membership in the EU, which Cameron was considering at the time. "Britain today is living with false consciousness," he said, playfully deploying the Marxist phrase denoting how capitalist superstructures prevent the proletariat from developing class consciousness. "Your interests are in Europe. It's high time for your sentiments to follow."

A compendium of studies completed by the British Foreign Ministry validate Sikorski's assertion. In December 2014, the ministry released the last of thirty-two reports on Britain and the EU. Drawing on some 2,300 articles written by experts, NGOs, businesses, and members of Parliament and covering everything from monetary policy to vocational training to policing, the overall inquiry found substantial benefit, and no significant drawbacks, to Britain's remaining within the EU.[20] The clearest rationale is economic. Forty-five percent of British exports are sold to fellow members of the EU, supporting some three million British jobs.[21] Once outside the EU, Britain would lose preferential access to the common market and be forced to write trade agreements with each of the bloc's twenty-seven members, many of which would be tempted to erect trade barriers. Though Brexit advocates often point out that Britain's trade with non-EU countries is slowly increasing while European economies stagnate, consider that the volume of UK trade with Ireland alone is roughly equal to that of its trade with all of the BRIC countries—Brazil, Russia, India, and

China—combined. Moreover, many foreign multinational corporations locate their European headquarters in the United Kingdom to reach the European market. If Britain leaves the EU, and thus loses the privileged access it currently enjoys to the world's largest free trading area, many of those businesses would presumably relocate their factories, supply chains, and other components of industrial production to the continent, along with their capital. "There is simply no business case for leaving Europe," wrote the chairman of British Telecom. "It would be a leap in the dark we cannot afford to make."[22] Mark Carney, governor of the Bank of England, said that EU "membership reinforces the dynamism of the UK economy," making it "more resilient to shocks, [able to] grow more rapidly without generating inflationary pressure or creating risks to financial stability" and is "associated with more effective competition."[23]

Nonetheless, there is a widely held perception that the EU is an overall drag—imposing onerous regulations, flooding the country with unwanted immigrants, and diminishing the United Kingdom's position on the global stage. All three claims are based on exaggerations and outright deceptions. Though only 8 to 14 percent of British laws originate in Brussels, according to a 2012 House of Commons study, a myth persists that the British Parliament has been subordinated to the EU's supranational institutions.[24] Throughout the Brexit debate, Leave advocates claimed that as much as 60 percent of British laws are written in Brussels, a figure that slyly makes no distinction between hundred-page health care acts passed by Westminster and three-page, EU-wide regulations on tax harmonization devised at the European Parliament (where Britain nonetheless has representation). Misleading statistics such as these fueled what exit polls showed to be the most popular motivation for Leave voters: "the principle that decisions about the UK should be taken in the UK."[25] Emphasizing buzzwords like "sovereignty" and "democracy," both of which are supposedly traduced by membership in the EU to such a grievous degree that the only solution is to leave it, Brexit campaigners promised Britons a return to a sort of prelapsarian England, assuring them that their country would somehow revert to its Victorian-era glories. It is, of course, natural for conservatives to revere the past. What made their support for abandoning the EU—and the more than four decades of accumulated practices, arrangements, and relationships entailed by membership therein—so strange was the utterly flippant and unfounded confidence they projected in urging their country to walk off a cliff.

A more compelling Euroskeptic argument is that Britain's EU membership has allowed for untrammeled immigration onto an already overcrowded island, a sentiment that grew following the EU's 2004 "big bang" enlargement with the addition of eight postcommunist countries. Since then, more than a million Poles, Romanians, Bulgarians, and other Central and Eastern Europeans have relocated to the United Kingdom, where they have proved willing to work at lower wages and for longer hours than their British counterparts. Although there are legitimate concerns to be raised about this sort of immigration (in particular its effect on public services and housing), the popularity of UKIP, and of Euroskeptic arguments more generally, rests on a double conflation: of EU and non-EU immigration, and of the issue of immigration itself with Britain's entire EU membership. The problems associated with immigration are so great, Euroskeptics claim, that the troublesome immigration baby must be thrown out with the institutional bathwater. A 2012 poll found that even among UKIP members, ostensibly obsessed with the EU, only 27 percent said membership in the bloc is one of their top three most important issues, far behind the 52 percent who listed immigration.[26] Even the post-referendum finding that "sovereignty" was the primary concern of Leave voters should be read as a euphemism for immigration, because it was that issue over which Brexit campaigners claimed their country had lost "control" to Brussels. In short, the Leave campaign won because it amalgamated, within the minds of the British public, the single issue of immigration and the entirety of Britain's membership in the EU. Exit the latter, they essentially implied with their ubiquitous mantra of "Take Back Control," and you solve the former.

Yet a closer look at the statistics indicates that immigration from Europe to the United Kingdom is not the problem Brexit campaigners make it out to be, nor that leaving the Union will be the tonic they promised. Over the past fifteen years, 70 percent of immigrants to the United Kingdom have come from non-EU countries, namely Africa, the Middle East, and South Asia.[27] A British government could have decided a long time ago to reduce those numbers, if it so chose, without any interference from the EU. None ever did. Had they done so, it's likely that the issue of immigration would not nearly have been as potent a political topic. As for the remaining 30 percent of immigrants, mostly low-wage workers from Central and Eastern Europe who eagerly traveled to Britain shortly after their nations joined the EU in 2004, like immigrants to the United States they have a higher employment rate than native Britons. A 2014 study found that European migrants to the United Kingdom make an annual net fiscal contribution of £20 billion and that more than 60 percent of the migrants from Western and Southern Europe are university graduates (compared to only 24 percent of UK-born workers). To replace this level of imported "human capital," the United Kingdom would have to spend £6.8 billion on education annually. As for the impression that migrants are scrounging off the dole, they are in fact 43 percent less likely than natives to receive public assistance and 7 percent less likely to live in subsidized housing.[28] Migrants from Central and Eastern Europe contribute 12 percent more to the economy than what they receive in public funds. Intra-European versus non-European immigration is an elementary distinction that Brexit advocates purposefully avoid in their crusade against the EU. Leavers also have little to say about the flip side of EU immigration: the fate of the more than two million British citizens who live, work, and retire without hindrance across Europe and whose ability to do so will be hampered if Britain leaves the union.

Notwithstanding the debate over the relative costs and benefits of internal European migration, it should be noted that, under EU rules, Britain had the opportunity to impose temporary labor market restrictions on workers from the new members after those nations joined the bloc in 2004. Vastly underestimating the numbers that would arrive, Britain was one of just three member countries that chose to forgo the grace period and welcome these immigrants immediately. That Britain accepted far more European immigrants than it had expected was not a structural flaw with the EU's freedom of movement policy but the result of poor planning on the part of British authorities, who chose not to avail themselves of an EU mechanism specifically designed to alleviate the effects of large influxes of cheap labor. This was a "well-intentioned policy we messed up," Jack Straw, foreign secretary under Blair, confessed in 2013. "Thorough research by the Home Office suggested that the impact of this benevolence would in any event be 'relatively small, at between 5,000 and 13,000 immigrants per year up to 2010.' Events proved these forecasts worthless." Indeed, the number of migrants from the new EU members outpaced government projections by a factor of four, with some 420,000 people coming between 2004 and 2012; over the course of the Labor Party's entire thirteen-year run in government, total net annual immigration quadrupled.[29] Labor supporters who voiced concerns about the influx of low-wage workers and the stresses they brought to bear on public services and local communities were usually written off by party leaders and metropolitan elites as nativists. This condescension was epitomized during the 2010 general election campaign when Blair's successor as prime minister, Gordon Brown, was overheard calling a lifelong Labor voter a "bigoted woman" after she challenged him about Eastern European immigration.[30] "The salt of the earth were treated as the scum of the earth and, unsurprisingly, they wouldn't stand for it," James Bloodworth, a Labor-supporting journalist, observed in the aftermath of the Brexit referendum, which more than one-third of Labor voters backed.[31] According to Straw, Labor's utter failure to deal honestly with immigration led to "lots of red faces, mine included."[32]

Had Straw and his colleagues adopted a more prudent position and listened sympathetically to the Labor base instead of reflexively scorning its apprehensions as inherently racist, they could have avoided more than merely red faces. They might very well have defused the salience of immigration as a hot-button issue in British politics and possibly averted the whole Brexit disaster a decade before it erupted. That Britain reached the point where fears over immigration could precipitate so immense and unprecedented a development as leaving the EU was due to failures in national policy making on the part of British politicians and an hysterically Europhobic popular press, not structural problems intrinsic to the EU.

Believing the party's leadership to be out of touch, much of Labor's traditional base of support in the white working class, particularly in the north of England, flocked to UKIP. Though commonly characterized as a "far-right" party, UKIP defies easy categorization. A comprehensive 2014 study found 71 percent of UKIP voters expressing agreement with five tradition-ally left-wing statements such as "big business takes advantage of ordinary people," "ordinary working people do not get their fair share of the nation's wealth," and "there is one law for the rich and one for the poor."[33] Accord-ing to researchers Matthew Goodwin and Robert Ford, UKIP voters can be characterized as losers in the new economy, "left behind" by automation and the export of manufacturing jobs overseas. They support UKIP not for any particular economic policies it espouses, but because it promises to revivify a lost Britain in which they were more valued, one that would in-clude drastically less immigration. "That UKIP's core voters are middle-class Tories animated by the single issue of Europe is the biggest myth in West-minster," they claim. Indeed, eight of the ten "most UKIP-friendly seats" in the UK are in constituencies traditionally held by Labor.

According to Labor's former policy chief, MP John Cruddas, the party risks becoming "irrelevant to the majority of working people" by refusing to rep-resent its views on a host of issues, not only immigration but also crime and welfare. In a 2016 report examining the party's massive general election defeat the previous year, Cruddas and his co-authors concluded that Labor is "becoming a toxic brand. It is perceived by voters as a party that supports an 'open door' approach to immigration, lacks credibility on the economy, and is a 'soft touch' on welfare spending."[34] In exchange for the support of a relatively small number of middle-class, university-educated, metropoli-tan liberals—who are unbothered by mass immigration and treat working-class concerns about crime and welfare with patronizing disdain—Labor has sacrificed its roots. And those socially conservative voters it abandoned fled to UKIP in large numbers. Ceding this terrain not only alienated its base; it also left the party listless and vulnerable to infiltration by a sect of hard-core leftists with a very different agenda from that of previous party leaders and the broad majority of Labor-supporting Britons. If Labor's drift into "irrelevance" that Cruddas warned about had a harbinger, it was the election of Jeremy Corbyn as leader.

Corbyn is a literal blast from the past, a man who has not changed his opinions about anything since his election to parliament in 1983. That Cor-byn was one of a handful of new Labor MPs elected that year is noteworthy, because it was when the party lost in a massive landslide to Margaret Thatcher's Conservatives after having stubbornly run on a manifesto so hopelessly left wing that one of its own MPs immortally described it as "the longest suicide-note in history." As party leader, Corbyn has tried to resurrect that note—which called for everything from unilateral nuclear disarmament to the nationalization of industry—and make it official party policy. Since Tony Blair stepped down from the premiership in 2007, Labor has gradually ditched his center-left, "New Labor" ideas and chosen successively more left-wing leaders, losing by successively greater margins at the polls. By electing Corbyn in the fall of 2015, the party base only reconfirmed its commitment to the illogical notion that a country that decisively rejects Labor in favor of the Tories does so because Labor is *not left-wing enough.*

In addition to entertaining the reinstatement of a clause to the party constitution calling for the "common ownership of the means of production, distribution and exchange" (scrapped by Tony Blair in 1994, three years before he won the biggest election victory in party history), Corbyn has advocated abolishing the British Army, endorsed "dialogue" with the Islamic State, and proposed tens of billions of pounds in new, unfunded government social spending.[35] His shadow chancellor John McDonnell once said he wished he could have gone back in time to kill Thatcher;[36] he has since signed a document calling for the dissolution of the MI5 internal security service (which would have certainly made his hypothetical retroactive assassination easier to pull off).[37] Corbyn is a longtime patron of the misnamed Stop the War Coalition, a protest outfit whose curiously selective "anti-imperialism" mandates it keep quiet about the Iranian- and Russian-assisted Assadist genocide in Syria.[38] This strand of sectarian, radical left politics has been as consistent in ideological rigidity as it has been at losing elections. "There are people in my party who I think regard the achievement of government and winning elections as, indeed, *prima facie* evidence of betrayal," Blair told an American audience in 2015, to much amusement. "Which you cannot rebut if you go and win again. That is the final proof of iniquity and treachery."[39] (Corbyn, who has applauded the "massive contributions" made by the late Venezuelan strongman Hugo Chavez,[40] believes that his former prime minister, the most successful Labor leader in history, should be tried for war crimes.)[41]

While Corbyn's surprise victory in the 2015 leadership election owes much to a change in party rules extending the franchise to anyone willing to pay a mere £3 (thereby opening the process to hard-left activists), it would be wrong to conclude that the reasons for his rise are purely procedural— that if Labor simply reverts to a system in which MPs enjoy more power in choosing their leader the party will protect itself from infiltration by Trotskyists and subsequent electoral oblivion. "The average Briton is 40 years old, with 1997 the first general election in which they voted," writes Mike Harris, a former Labor councilor in the London borough of Lewisham.[42] Their earliest knowledge of the Labor Party was Tony Blair, whose reputation, whatever his achievements and success in leading Labor to an unprecedented three general election victories, remains tarnished in many people's minds by the Iraq War and "spin" associated with the New Labor era. "They simply do not remember or care about the Militant Tendency or the Bennites," hard-left factions that came close to taking over the party, as Corbyn and his acolytes essentially did in the fall of 2015. "They do remember Iraq and the MPs expenses scandal, the shadows of which loom large over the parliamentary Labor party."

Corbyn, despite representing the tony London borough of Islington North, fashions himself the tribune of the working class. But he has proven himself utterly incapable at addressing their anxieties regarding the cultural and economic effects of globalization and immigration. In his victory speech accepting the party leadership mantle, Corbyn did not mention immigration once and has elsewhere insisted that "the amount of net immigration is actually very small." McDonnell, his closest ally, further demonstrates the disconnect between the leadership and its voters by saying that Britain needs "open borders" and that national boundaries will become "irrelevant" by the close of the century.[43] Corbyn was nominally pro-Remain and ambivalent about his party's official commitment to EU membership. Like other social democrats across Europe, most Laborites see the EU as a means of protecting workers' rights that would otherwise be scrapped by national governments (indeed, many Conservatives supported Brexit for precisely this reason). Corbyn, who in 1975 voted against Britain's membership in the common market and later opposed the Maastricht and Lisbon treaties, which effected further integration, belongs to an atavistic Labor faction that sees the EU as a neoliberal project, and he shares as least as much of the blame for Brexit as any of its proponents. After missing the Labor Remain campaign's kick-off event so he could instead attend an anti-nuclear rally, Corbyn barely showed up on the hustings and, when he did, refused to appear at cross-party, pro-Remain events with the prime minister (a revealing decision considering the wide variety of Islamists with whom Corbyn *has* shared platforms). The ambiguity about Europe from the Labor leadership clearly had an effect on the party's supporters, slightly over half of whom could correctly identify its position prior to the referendum.[44] Indeed, Labor's failure to turn out the vote in favor of Remain may have been the decisive factor in guaranteeing Brexit's success. On referendum day, more than a third of Labor voters chose to leave the EU.[45] Corbyn himself may have been one of them: Asked afterward by one of his own shell-shocked MPs how he voted, Corbyn refused to answer.[46] Amid the ruins, Labor sources accused him of "deliberate sabotage."[47]

Corbyn's political priorities, whether dismantling the independent UK nuclear arsenal or expressing solidarity with various and sundry left-wing authoritarian regimes abroad, are not those of the vast majority of British citizens or even of Labor voters: They are the obsessions of the sort of fringe Trotskyite movements with which Corbyn has long associated. Even on seemingly superficial issues such as the monarchy, Corbyn is hopelessly out of touch, a republican in a land where 85 percent or so of his country-men consider themselves loyal subjects of Elizabeth II. (At a ceremony commemorating the Battle of Britain, Corbyn pointedly refused to sing "God Save the Queen.")[48] It is hard to exaggerate the damage Corbyn and his acolytes have done to the British social democratic tradition, transform-ing one of its great achievements—the institutional manifestation of the belief that the redistribution of wealth and power is better garnered through democratic politics than revolution—into a personality cult.

None of this ought to come as a surprise given Corbyn's history. As a young MP in the early 1980s, Corbyn was an outspoken defender of a small, Leninist organization that tried to infiltrate the Labor Party. Known as the Militant Tendency, or Militant, its members were grouped around a news-paper of that name and managed to secure control over the Liverpool City Council. When Labor Party leaders tried to expel Militant, accusing it of operating as "a party within a party," Corbyn opposed their efforts. Eventually, Labor leader Neil Kinnock succeeded in ousting the entryist group, which he referred to as "this maggot in the body of the Labor Party." Thirty-five years later and Corbyn is more solicitous of the hard-left group Momentum—self-described "successor" to his leadership campaign—than his own parliamentary caucus (which overwhelmingly passed a no confidence measure in his leadership) or the broader Labor electorate. Members of this parallel organization have repeatedly harassed and intimidated Corbyn's critics within the parliamentary party, sending threatening messages to those Labor MPs who rebelled against their pacifist leader and voted their conscience in favor of airstrikes against ISIS.[49] Over forty female Labor MPs wrote to Corbyn about an "extremely worrying trend of escalating abuse and hostility" from his supporters toward them, abuse that included "rape threats, death threats, smashed cars and bricks through windows."[50] Momentum inspires comparisons to the German "extra-parliamentary opposition" of the late 1960s and 1970s, elements of which eventually turned to violence.

Until very recently, the British did not vote in appreciable numbers for fringe parties. But with the rise of UKIP and the gradual takeover of the Labor Party by the hard left—both the consequence of an elite failure to address immigration—what was once a continental phenomenon to which the British had proudly considered themselves immune now afflicts a substantial portion of their electorate. This is a trend being replicated across Europe, as social democratic parties hemorrhage support to populists. In Germany, where a taboo on the far right has prevented it from ever achieving parliamentary representation, the era of the *Volksparteien,* or "people's parties," is coming to a close as the Social Democratic Party (SPD) bleeds support to the right-populist Alternative for Germany. Two decades ago, the SPD won more than 40 percent of the national vote; today, it garners half that in opinion polls. For the first time in Germany's postwar history, combined support for the CDU and SPD has fallen below 50 percent.[51] Echoing Labor's John Cruddas, the Austrian Social Democratic (SPÖ) MEP Josef Weidenholzer calls his party, whose membership has declined from 730,000 in 1980 to around 200,000 today,[52] "the politburo" for its condescension toward working-class voters. Reacting to the SPÖ's historic defeat in the 2016 presidential elections, when its candidate earned a measly 11 percent and, for the first time in postwar history, did not advance to the second round, Weidenholzer wrote that "the greatest enemy of the Left is widespread self-righteousness."[53] After decades running the country mostly in grand coalitions with the mainstream center-right People's Party, the Social Democrats, says Vienna mayor Michael Häupl, cannot "understand the language of the suburbs."[54] And in France, many erstwhile Socialist Party supporters are flocking to the National Front,[55] which, despite its reputation as a force of the hard right, participates in the grand French socialist tradition of the May Day rally and whose leader inveighs against a "draconian policy of austerity" that privileges "globalized elites at the expense of the people."[56]

Britain's recoil from Europe has occurred alongside a diminution of its role in world affairs. From 2010, when the Conservative Party came to power in coalition with the Liberal Democrats, to 2014, funding for the Foreign and Commonwealth Office shrank from £2.4 billion to £1.7 billion. Defense expenditures have also been drastically slashed; an army that comprised slightly over 100,000 soldiers six years ago is expected to shrink to 82,000 by 2020. General Sir Richard Shirreff, former deputy supreme allied commander of NATO, says that Britain has "shrunk in on itself" and carries an "increasingly impotent stick."[57] The only serious European military power alongside France, it has become "little different from any other semi-pacifist, European social democracy, more interested in protecting welfare and benefits than maintaining adequate defenses." Lest one consider this to be little more than the predictably belligerent musings of a former man in uniform pining for the days of lost empire, consider the perspective of Richard Norton-Taylor, security editor of *The Guardian*, not a paper known for its militarism, who described the coalition government's first Strategic Defense Review as "an embarrassing and unseemly shambles."[58] It has only gone downhill from there. So debilitated is the current state of British military readiness and so timid its foreign policy that the former head of the Royal Navy was recently moved to write of the "uncomfortable similarities" and "disquieting parallels between the situation that confronted our country some 90 years ago," on the eve of World War II, "and that which now prevails."[59]

Drifting away from Europe, Britain has begun looking eastward, an inclination that will only grow stronger in Brexit's aftermath. A 2015 visit to China by Chancellor of the Exchequer George Osborne was a folderol of obsequiousness. Britain, Osborne pledged, hoped to become "China's best partner in the West." Chinese state media praised the chancellor's "pragmatic" decision "not to stress human rights," part of a years-long overcompensation for Cameron's meeting with the Dalai Lama in 2012. (So cowed was Cameron by Chinese displeasure that he refused to meet again with the exiled Tibetan leader and declined to register a public complaint when a group of British MPs were prevented from visiting Hong Kong—a former British colony—during pro-democracy protests in November 2014.) "At times he seemed to be auditioning for the role of the Chinese Communist Party's new best friend," Fraser Nelson of the conservative *Spectator* magazine wrote of Osborne.[60] Beijing's deplorable human rights abuses, increasing cyberattacks on Western targets, naval aggression in the South China Sea, unfair competition policies that have weakened the once-mighty British steel industry, rampant intellectual property rights violations—none of these hostile acts against the liberal international order, of which Britain was once a steady pillar, has dissuaded London from cozying up to Beijing. "We are wary of a trend toward constant accommodation of China, which is not the best way to engage a rising power," a senior U.S. administration official told the *Financial Times*.[61]

In fall 2015, London awarded the Chinese a $9 billion contract to help construct the first British nuclear power plant in a generation. The United Kingdom also supports China's attempt to convert its renminbi into a global reserve currency. And it was the first member of the G7—the group of leading, advanced industrial democracies—to join the $50 billion Asia Infrastructure Investment Bank (AIIB). An institution that excludes democratic Japan, South Korea, and Australia, the AIIB was created to rival the Washington-based World Bank. It is an explicit tool of Chinese foreign policy designed to be the centerpiece of a potential Sinocentric financial system that would parallel, and eventually transcend, the Bretton Woods apparatus of international finance. With the AIIB, the New Development Bank (also known as the "BRICS Bank"), and a proposed Development Bank of the Shanghai Cooperation Organization (a multilateral economic and security grouping founded by China and Russia), Beijing is slowly building the institutional architecture of a new world order that would challenge Western dominance. In a symbolic move two days after Britain voted to leave the EU, China convened its first meeting of the AIIB in Beijing, where President Xi Jingping met with Vladimir Putin. Against this backdrop of authoritarian cooperation and simultaneous fracturing within the democratic ranks, London is straying from its once firmly Atlanticist, Western orientation and careening toward a heretofore unexplored and unpredictable strategic gray zone.

If the UK follows through with Brexit, the domino effect of its departure will exacerbate the emergent balkanization of Europe—beginning with Britain itself. In the 2014 Scottish independence referendum, many Scots voted to remain within the United Kingdom precisely because they feared the prospect of a newly independent Scotland *outside* the EU. Two years later, Scots voted overwhelmingly to maintain Britain's EU membership while most English voters chose to sever it. Now, with Scotland being taken out of the EU against its wishes, the chance that another independence referendum would pass is significantly higher than it was in 2014. Similarly in Northern Ireland, most citizens voted Remain. By potentially resurrecting a hard border between Ulster province and the Republic of Ireland, therefore undermining a key provision of the 1998 Good Friday Agreement eliminating that border, Brexit, writes Irish journalist Fintan O'Toole, has "placed a bomb under the Irish peace process."[62]

On the continent, Britain's withdrawal will bolster anti-EU sentiments precisely when grave economic and security threats require unity and cooperation. If one of Europe's largest economies and military powers leaves the body, we can expect other Atlanticist trading nations such as Holland, Denmark, and possibly even Sweden to follow, leading to the unraveling of the union itself. Britain has long served as an important counterweight to German dominance of Europe; without London's voice and vote, German power—and the inevitable resentment it breeds—is bound to grow. With a right-wing nationalist, anti-German government now ruling in Warsaw,

Britain's decision to abandon the EU will mean the loss of an important mediating force and the worsening of a German-Polish relationship that took decades to rebuild. Not for nothing has Marine Le Pen, an ardent opponent of European unity and an open admirer of Vladimir Putin, giddily declared that Britain's leaving the bloc would be "like the fall of the Berlin Wall" in its geopolitical impact. As was once said about the conquest of its erstwhile empire, Britain may bring about the collapse of Europe in a fit of absence of mind.

7

Greece: From *Polis* to Populists

Empty the coffers!

> Andreas Papandreou, 1989

The money exists.

> George Papandreou, 2009

IT WAS A WARM SUMMER NIGHT IN ATHENS, and along with the folk-infused melodies of a Greek stoner band and the wafting aroma of kebabs, a spirit of revolution filled the air. Thousands of people milled about the lighted courtyard of the city's Agricultural University, gathered under the banner of the "Anti-Capitalist Left Cooperation for the Overthrow," whose acronym in Greek, ANTARSYA, means "mutiny." It was less than two weeks before Greece's second financial bailout was set to expire, and the country was on tenterhooks waiting to hear if another package would win approval. The stubborn negotiating tactics of the radical left Syriza party, which had come to power earlier that year promising an end to austerity measures mandated by international creditors in exchange for bailout funds, were bringing the country closer to the point where it might have to drop the euro, adopted to great fanfare in 2001.

Stalls promoting every conceivable cause of the third-worldist left, from "Free Mumia" (as in Mumia Abu-Jamal, the Philadelphia black nationalist and convicted cop killer) to "Free Palestine," lined the campus's perimeter.

The people whose struggle most captured the moral imagination of the festivalgoers, however, were not the victims of American police brutality or Israeli military occupation, but rather the serfs laboring under the rapacious triumvirate of financial overlords dubbed the "Troika": the European Commission, European Central Bank, and the International Monetary Fund. The world's most unjustly persecuted and pitiable victims that evening were the Greeks themselves.

Later that week, I would hear that a group of anarchist youths attacked the headquarters of ANTARSYA, furious that it had imposed a €5 entrance fee for the "Resistance Festival." It was, in microcosm, an entirely fitting reaction in a country whose citizens have grown accustomed to receiving the benefits of living in a modern, industrialized state without having to pay the costs required to fund them. If one wanted to pinpoint a cause for Greece's six-year agony, and of the crisis confronting the European social welfare state more generally, it would be this fundamental incompatibility between expectations and commitments.

For decades, Greece has employed a massive public sector workforce and sustained a generous entitlement system while posting some of the highest tax evasion rates in the developed world. Greeks have also professed an overwhelming desire to stay within the Eurozone while refusing to accept the budgetary measures contingent on using the common currency. These paradoxical impulses—high government expenditures without raising the revenues needed to fund them and preserving membership in a currency union while repeatedly refusing to abide by its obligations—manifested themselves most clearly in Syriza's elevation to power in early 2015.

Syriza's rise ended the duopoly on political power long maintained by the center-right New Democracy and center-left Panhellenic Socialist Movement (PASOK), which alternately ruled Greece for four decades. It also signified the broader decline of traditional European social democracy, as mainstream, center-left establishment parties have been overtaken by radical populist insurgent forces (like Podemos in Spain or the hijacking of British Labor by the far left). From the downfall of military dictatorship in 1974 to the legislative elections of 2012, New Democracy and PASOK dominated Greek politics. But the European financial crisis upended this system of alternating majoritarian power. In May of that year, Syriza replaced

PASOK as the country's second largest party, and the right-wing national-ist Independent Greeks (ANEL) and neo-Nazi Golden Dawn (GD) entered parliament for the first time.

The reasons for this reordering of the Greek political landscape are not hard to decipher. In 2010, when Athens announced it would go bankrupt unless given an emergency infusion of funds, both the then-ruling New Democracy and opposition PASOK parties agreed to the terms of an inter-national bailout agreement (known as the "First Memorandum") that pro-vided Greece with €110 billion in exchange for implementing a combination of budget-cutting and tax-generating measures that would collectively become known as "austerity." But just two years of living under even a perfunctory enactment of these policies led many Greeks to conclude both that the effort wasn't worth it and that the parties that had voted for the Memorandum should be punished for having agreed to its execution. Syriza promised the best of both worlds: an end to austerity while keeping Greece in the Eurozone. Alexis Tsipras, a young, ex-communist student activist who pledged that all would be better if only Greece had a leader brave enough to tell international creditors to stuff it, led Syriza into govern-ment. A party that had won less than 5 percent of the vote in 2009 cata-pulted to 27 percent in 2012 and 36 percent by 2015, becoming the largest party in the Hellenic parliament.

If there was a silver lining to be found in Syriza's victory, so the conven-tional wisdom went, it was that Greeks had finally rejected the corrupt patronage mills that New Democracy and PASOK embodied. These politi-cal clubhouses, alternating the reins of power every few years, had brought Greece to the precipice of economic disaster. That they were hoisted on their own petards, therefore, was taken as a sign of democratic health. Out-side of Greece, this was the near-universal interpretation of Syriza's ascent, but it did not fully capture the mood within the country. Greeks didn't turn out New Democracy and PASOK because they were corrupt (which they were) or had acted irresponsibly with the public purse (which they had). Greeks rejected the establishment parties because both had consented to taper, at least in theory, the "spend and don't tax" policies to which their constituents had become accustomed. By promising to maintain the clien-telist apparatuses that New Democracy and PASOK had cultivated so diligently over their four-decade dominance of Greek politics, Syriza would only compound—not alleviate—Greece's problems.

Syriza's victory (along with the rise of ANEL and Golden Dawn) attests to more than just a collapse of the political center, a phenomenon mirrored across Europe as voters express frustration with establishment institutions and political elites. It signifies a society's preference for the short-term preservation of the spoils it has acquired over a long-term outlook acknowledging painful reforms as the cost of maintaining its quality of life. This was further reflected in Syriza's choice of coalition partner, ANEL, a nationalist, far-right faction inimical to Syriza in nearly every way, except for its antipathy to the bailout agreement and hostility toward the country's creditors. Where the Syriza foreign minister Nikos Kotzias has called the EU an "empire" seeking to make Greece a "debt colony,"[1] ANEL party leader Panos Kammenos declares that "German neo-Nazis" rule the continent.[2]

Europe's debt crisis has led many to conclude that the creation of the euro, and Greece's adoption of it, was a curse. It wasn't one, nor need it be a perpetual strain. Though most analysts claim today that the common currency's purpose was political—a means of forging cooperation among countries that had fought devastating wars against each other—there is a strong economic rationale for the euro. Particularly as the economy becomes more and more globalized, with multiple firms in different European countries contributing to the assembly of various products, a single currency facilitates the production process by reducing the risks associated with currency fluctuations. The negative consequences of individual Eurozone nations' inability to control their own exchange and interest rates, a foregone tool that critics of the common currency claim Greece could have used to devalue its way out of the crisis, is exaggerated considering how no country can exert total control over these things. Countries outside the Eurozone like the United Kingdom and Switzerland, for instance, must take global trends into account when setting their exchange and interest rates.

For the Greeks, entering the currency union could have accelerated their country's modernization—had they the discipline to put their economic house in order. In the 1990s, the aspiration to join the European Economic

and Monetary Union (EMU), a precursor to formal Eurozone membership, incentivized important reforms in Greece that led to unprecedented
budget surpluses. Adopting the euro, if all went according to plan, would
dramatically increase trade by ending competitive currency devaluations
and the unpredictability attendant in exchange-rate fluctuations. Productivity increases and long-term growth would follow, and inflation, a perpetual problem in Europe's spendthrift south, would come under control.
After Greece adopted the euro in 2001, many of these external forces did
indeed benefit the country's economy, which posted an average growth
rate of 4.2 percent over the next six years, compared to a Eurozone average
of just 1.9 percent.[3]

A closer look, however, revealed an ominous picture. The 1990s and
early 2000s should have been the time to trim the bloated state bureaucracy, improve a backward education system, eliminate Byzantine regulations protecting favored professions, and boost competition in the private
sector. Instead, the low interest rates suddenly available to Greece encouraged an irresponsible level of borrowing, a mistake for which the Greeks
are at fault at least as much as the European banks that lent to them. Not
until three years after Greece joined the Eurozone did its leaders admit
having fudged the figures they presented to gain entry to the common
currency: The ratio of Greece's annual deficit to GDP was far above the
3 percent required by the 1992 Maastricht Treaty. (This falsification of statistics would be repeated later.) But the statistical deceit exercised to join a
currency union for which it wasn't fully prepared did not necessarily presage economic oblivion. Many Eurozone countries have run deficits over the
Maastricht ceiling (even Germany) without requiring massive, external financial assistance. Greece's problems were structural, and its fiscal woes
stem from these structural weaknesses, not any inherent flaws within the
idea of the euro.

For Greeks, joining and keeping the Euro have long been more points of
national pride than economic logic. How else to explain polls simultaneously
demonstrating 70 percent support for Eurozone membership alongside refusal of the terms necessary to stay in the currency union, as expressed by
the overwhelming approval for the "No" side in a 2015 referendum rejecting

creditor demands, as well as repeated electoral victories for a party that runs on an explicitly anti-austerity platform? Perhaps not unreasonably, given their location on the edge of Europe, their 400-year history of Ottoman rule, and later subjugation by a military dictatorship, Greeks see the euro as the most tangible marker of their country's place in Western civilization. Letting go of the currency means far more than a redenomination of assets to drachma. To many Greeks, it would mark nothing less than a civilizational rupture with Europe and everything it represents.

This tendency to view the country's euro membership in symbolic terms has encouraged irresponsible behavior on both the macro and micro levels, with both regular Greeks and their leaders continually insisting that Europe must bend to Greece, not the other way around. In Greece, reforms that would be uncontroversial in comparable economies are decried as inhumane. Over the ten years leading up to the crisis, unit labor costs in Greece increased by more than 35 percent, compared to the Eurozone average of 20 percent.[4] Before the crisis, only 43 percent of Greeks aged 55 to 64 worked, compared to 51 percent of Germans and 62 percent of Americans. Most absurdly, on retirement, Greek public employees received an average 96 percent of their salary in pension payments, versus an average of 59 percent in developed Western democracies.[5] Asked why significantly poorer Eastern Europeans should be expected to subsidize Greek pensions that are in some cases twice or even three times larger than their own, a Greek economist told the Czech journalist Martin Ehl, "They are post-communists. They are used to living in poverty."[6]

A conviction that they had no less a right to use the euro than any other European country, regardless of the state of their economy or the exactitude of their bookkeeping, bred a collective sense of entitlement leading Greeks to blame anyone for their country's dire state—foreign investors, the Germans, banks—but themselves. Emblematic of this refusal to accept responsibility was former Syriza finance minister Yanis Varoufakis's assertion that Greece is no more culpable for the mess it is in than Ohio was for the Great Depression, thus absolving Greece for decades of economic mismanagement. Greeks have been indulged in this self-aggrandizing habit by a succession of foreigners seduced by the ancient splendor of what former

French president Valéry Giscard d'Estaing once called "the mother of all democracies," as well as a bevy of radical left political tourists raring to exploit Greeks as lab rats in "resistance" to "neoliberalism." Much as concerns about Greece's suitability for joining the Euro were breezily dismissed at the time, earlier doubts that the country was prepared to join the European Economic Community (EEC) in 1981 were swept aside largely out of gauzy nostalgia. Becoming an official member of the European club, a British foreign office minister remarked at the time, would be "a fitting repayment by the Europe of today of the cultural and political debt that we all owe to a Greek heritage almost three thousand years old." Not until thirty years later did Giscard declare Greece's hasty EEC admission "a mistake."[7]

The mistake was not inevitable. At the heart of Greece's crisis is the failure—at all levels of society—to embrace modernization. "We did not fulfill the requirements, but the bad thing is not that we entered [the euro]," Pantelis Sklias, professor of International Political Economy at the University of the Peloponnese, told me.[8] "The bad thing is that we did not work over the years to come in order to fill the gap and finally be able to play the game on equal terms." Nor can the infusion of cheap credit by European banks be faulted as the prime cause of Greece's latter-day travails; no one forced the Greeks to accept loans they could not reasonably pay back. Regarding the flow of easy credit during the heady days of high growth, Stefanos Manos, who served as finance minister and national economic minister in the early 1990s, commented that "the U.S. was using some of that money to produce stuff, to innovate. In Greece we produce practically nothing, and we were taking on massive debts just to live lavishly."[9] The numbers bear this out: In 2009, the year before it approached the Troika for a bailout, Greek households were consuming 12 percent above the EU average, while their incomes and labor productivity were, respectively, 5 percent and 20 percent below average.[10]

As much as they may curse the euro now (while saying that they would do anything to keep it), Greeks may one day look back on its adoption as a blessing in disguise. When 2010 arrived and Greece finally acknowledged the unsustainability of its debt, the option of private financing had long passed. Had Greece not been in the Eurozone at that time, it could have devalued its currency and thus boosted exports and tourism, a remedy that many critics of the euro project insist would have saved the country. But even those steps might not have been enough to forestall an IMF bailout, as Argentina's perpetual cycle of devaluation and IMF rescue packages has shown, and it is that scenario that suggests Greece's Eurozone membership has actually helped it. Sharing a currency with nearly twenty other countries almost certainly ensured Greece better bailout terms than what it would have been offered in a package presented solely by the IMF. The risk of continent-wide financial contagion due to the number of countries holding Greek debt, the use of a shared currency, and a political commitment to keep the Eurozone intact all gave Athens the sort of leverage it would not have had were Greece just another insolvent country prostrating itself before the IMF. In this sense, Eurozone membership and solidarity (however stingy and conditional Greeks may find it) helped prevent Greece from becoming Venezuela on the Med.

Moreover, were it not for the exogenous factors holding Greece in line, a variety of indigenous ones—most notably a populist political culture that has bred a parasitic relationship between special interests and the state—might have led the nation into a calamity far worse than the one its people currently endure. The collapse of the Greek economy and resultant political instability are attributable to deep institutional problems that long predate Greece's entry into the Eurozone. To learn how Greece can get out of this mess, it's first necessary to understand how it got into it.

The Greek crisis is fundamentally political, not economic. The Western liberal conception of the state as an impartial arbiter, fairly distributing public resources through consensus and implementing policies with an eye toward the long-term generation of the greatest good for the greatest number of people, is alien to Greece. The prevailing view, accepted by those on both the ostensible "right" and "left" of the political spectrum, considers the state a public trough to be seized by one's political clan for the doling out of privileges exclusively to their clients.

Andreas Papandreou, the fiery, third-worldist founder of PASOK, perfected this rent-seeking system of patronage when he came to power in 1981. The son of a former socialist prime minister and father to another, his family represented, in the words of the late Lebanese scholar Fouad Ajami, "a dynasticism that Arab officeholders would envy."[11] It was more than just the practice of hereditary rule that Papandreou borrowed from the Middle East; he also adopted its culture of *baksheesh* (bribery) and populism. Early in his tenure, Papandreou merged party and state by replacing civil servants with political appointees as ministry general directors and eliminating performance-based pay. A mere two years after taking power, PASOK's membership rolls doubled, as many Greeks saw the party card as a job opportunity. They were right to do so: By 1984 an estimated 89 percent of PASOK members had a state job or contract.[12] Though PASOK was wary about joining the EEC, Papandreou was more than happy to receive its development aid, money he used to fund a massive government expansion. State sector employment grew at four times the rate of the private sector, increasing more than 50 percent by the end of PASOK's decade in power. By that point the Greeks had been transformed, in relation to their state, from citizens to clients.

Papandreou also intensified a populist and polarizing style of Greek politics. The Greek political scientist Takis S. Pappas identifies three core components of populism, all of them driven by antagonism and embraced by Papandreou: suspicion of markets, hostility to foreigners, and a lack of respect for institutions. Purporting to speak for that nebulous entity beloved by populists of all stripes and known only as "the people" (his campaign slogan was "PASOK in office—the people in power"), Papandreou, who imitated De Gaulle in his strong-arm tactics, *dirigiste* preference for state-controlled economic policy, and quasi-monarchical governing style, divided the country into "the forces of light" (his followers) and "the forces of darkness" (anyone who opposed him). In this, Papandreou was drawing on the legacy of the Greek Civil War, fought between communists and the Western-backed Greek government. In a largely agrarian society without substantial class differences, postwar Greek political identification depended heavily on historically informed identities—which side of the war one fought on or sympathized with—rather than substantive ideological beliefs. Polarization nurtured an emotive, resentment-based politics with little room for compromise, and the "pervasive politicization of the public space,"[13] in the words of Greek political scientist Stathis Kalyvas, ran so deep that even the coffee shop one patronized became a sign of political affiliation.

In his rhetoric, Papandreou cast Greek history as an eternal battle between these two forces, conflating opponents with all manner of reactionaries from monarchists to collaborators with the military junta. He derided Konstantinos Karamanlis, Greece's first post-coup prime minister, as "he who reorganizes the established oligarchic forces" to "found a far-right rule in order to face the rising popular movement while fastening the country to the US chariot." New Democracy, in turn, referred to Papandreou's government as the "junta of PASOK." The writer Petros Markaris, explaining his country's politics to the bewildered readers of the *Frankfurter Allgemeine Zeitung,* commented, "Greek society does not know what consensus means. She knows neither consensus nor compromise. She knows only the camp, standing hostile to each other."[14]

Papandreou's Manichean view of the world profoundly shaped the Greek left. Internationally, he was antagonistic to the United States and cool to NATO, membership in which, he said, "conceded our national sovereignty." In the same manner as he divided Greeks into good and evil camps, he spoke of countries as belonging to one of two blocs: the "establishment" vs. the "non-privileged."[15] With the nationalistic rallying cry "Greece for the Greeks," he cultivated a conviction among his people that they were eternal victims of Western machinations. "Greece is a dependent country," he declared; "we are a colony. Our metropolis is the US and its branches in Western Europe"—precisely the sort of divisive language later adopted by his political heirs in Syriza. (Varoufakis, improbable head of the black students union while a student at Essex University, explained to *Zeit Magazine* that "we Greeks are the blacks of Europe.")

But it was in his approach to the state that Papandreou's legacy has been most toxic. One could not find a more paradigmatic expression of the populist mindset than his declaration: "There are no institutions— only the people rule in this country." The winner-take-all, zero-sum approach to politics established a cyclical pattern in which the two major parties attempted to outbid each other for votes, promising vaster and vaster outlays in order to buy and maintain support. Polarization bred a lack of "social trust," the belief that most other citizens are honest and will not abuse the social welfare system. A 2013 study by Denmark's Aarhaus University suggests a link between high levels of social trust and both the size and sustainability of publicly funded welfare, health, and education programs. This link goes a long way in explaining the connection between the ethnically homogeneous, stable, consensus-seeking political cultures of Scandinavia and the generous benefits provided by their governments.[16] Even though Greece is also ethnically homogeneous, widespread social distrust and corruption encouraged an atmosphere where, in the words of one of the study's authors, citizens felt it permissible "to take as much as you can if you feel that others are doing the same."[17] A study by the University of Chicago's Booth School of Business found that, among Greece's exceptionally high number of self-employed workers (which, at 35 percent of the working population, is more than double the OECD average), €28 billion of income went unreported in 2009, enough to cover 32 percent of that year's deficit.[18] Although much of the criticism directed at Greece has focused on the size of the state, it is not so much the number of employees that is the problem but rather the lack of revenue to fund their salaries. Athens could better afford its large and bountiful state sector if Greeks did their taxes as honestly as Finns.

A problem with populist democracies is that, by gaining votes through promising inducements to voting blocs, parties establish a vicious cycle. Public policy is determined not by the long-term effect on society but by the short-term interests of favored groups. "An increase in the payoffs from lobbying and cartel activity, as compared with the payoffs from production, means more resources are devoted to politics and cartel activity and fewer resources are devoted to production," the economist Mancur Olson wrote in his 1982 book, *The Rise and Decline of Nations*. "This in turn influences [a society's] attitudes and culture."[19] Associations representing groups ranging from lawyers to electricians to pharmacists lobbied the Greek government to gain privileges protecting their professions from competition, driving up costs for everyone else. Entering the pharmacy business, for instance, requires a license that costs an average of $400,000. A vicious cycle is thus created as parties accumulate support by offering more and more privileges to certain groups at the expense of the country's overall economic health. Needless to say, it does not take long for the consequences of such policies to be felt. For the decade Papandreou was in power, GDP increased at an annual rate of less than 2 percent while public spending grew by 40 percent a year and deficits nearly quadrupled from 3.6 percent to 11 percent of GDP.[20] Public debt, as a percentage of GDP, skyrocketed from 39.4 percent to 109.2 percent. By 1991, the Organization for Economic Co-operation and Development concluded that Greece had "probably the largest imbalances of all OECD countries."[21]

The purpose of sharing this history is to demonstrate that Greece's distress is not, mainly, the result of institutional failures intrinsic to the European Union or the common currency, but of the structural problems of the Greek state and economy. For instance, Greece spends significantly more on public sector employee compensation than other European countries, posting the highest public expenditures as a share of GDP in Europe in 2013, higher even than perennial big spenders like France and Sweden.[22] That Spain and Italy face similar difficulties as Greece is a testament mainly to their own particular budgeting practices and political dysfunction, not the Eurozone or austerity (a loaded word, considering that from 2010–2013, Greece ran an average budget deficit of 10.5 percent of GDP, hardly a belt-tightening figure). France, another country beset by economic difficulties, is a place that can effectively be shut down by public employee unions to which less than 700,000 citizens belong.[23] That is not a fault of the euro, German bankers, or "neoliberal" economics: It is the fault of France.

A system such as Greece's could not last forever, and it finally came crashing down in 2010. Looking back on the way the Troika dealt with Greece at the time, there is plenty of room for criticism, but the package given to Athens was hardly an echo of the punishing terms meted out after World War I to Germany at Versailles, as some have alleged. Greece was bestowed the largest IMF loan in history, for a term of thirty years at an effective interest rate of only 1.7 percent, as well as the largest debt write-down in history, with private sector creditors eventually forgiving nearly half of what they were owed.[24] This relief was appropriate, because just as no one had forced the Greeks to borrow so much money, no one had forced the banks to lend it. In exchange for EU funds, the Greek government was tasked with implementing a difficult but necessary set of reforms—boosting private sector competition (in which Greece was ranked twenty-sixth of then twenty-seven member states), increasing the ease of doing business, alleviating a regulatory environment in which it took 230 days to award a public contract (more than twice the EU average),[25] improving an educational sector that drove many motivated Greeks out of the country, and reducing corruption.

Athens approached the reforms halfheartedly. From 2010 to 2013, its average budget deficit was 10.5 percent, significantly larger than what it and the EU had agreed. By 2014, it had shed 150,000 public employees—most of whom, however, left through attrition and retirement. According to a 2013 IMF report, "ownership of the program did not extend far and little progress was made with politically difficult measures such as privatization, downsizing the public sector, and labor market reforms. There was also limited bipartisan support in parliament for the program, while relations with unions were adversarial."[26]

Not long after the First Memorandum was adopted, it became clear that any attempt to adopt its measures would be met with fierce resistance. Greece has a lively culture of protest, dating back to the student occupations that helped bring down the military junta in the 1970s. Takis Pappas observes that the style and demographics of protests have corresponded closely to evolutions in the citizenry's clientelist relationship to the state. In the 1980s, demonstrations were large and peaceful, aimed at obtaining benefits from a government more than happy to provide them. In the 1990s, once those benefits were acquired, protests were small and sporadic. In 2010, when jealously guarded subsidies were threatened, demonstrations grew massive—at their height attracting 30 percent of the country's entire population—and often violent. Originally a tactic to overturn the status quo, protests became a means of maintaining it.

Such massive and threatening demonstrations confronted the Greek government with a real crisis of legitimacy. Fortunately for Athens, the existence of external creditors provided a scapegoat. By the middle of 2014, Greece's economy was the fastest growing in the Eurozone, albeit not a high hurdle. But such figures are by their nature relative, and it is just as much a gamble to believe that throwing more money at the problem and increasing Greece's already unsustainable debt burden even further would have put the country on the road to recovery. Actually balancing the budget while doing more to make Greece an attractive investment opportunity for foreign capital would have, given a few more years, boosted employment and lessened the pain of social spending cuts. Rather than assume responsibility for the reforms they had agreed to implement and to explain to their people the necessity of temporary hardship in the pursuit of long-term and sustainable gains, Greek leaders directed anger toward their European partners. This strategy, meant to save face, backfired.

It turned out that fobbing off responsibility onto foreigners did not appease Greek voters. "All the ideological discussion was somehow evaporated in the Greek political dialogue," Professor Sklias says. "Why? Because it was replaced by a bipolar discourse in which from the one side you have those who were for the MOUs [the creditor bailout packages known as Memorandums of Understanding] and on the other hand you had those who are against the MOUs. But those who were against the MOUs, it was easy to present and sustain their arguments because they had, let's say, the moral stance to do so. Why? Because simply you say that 50 percent, 60 percent unemployment, marginalization, people are dying, commit[ing] suicide, no real economy. And on the other hand you have those who are immoral." Both PASOK and New Democracy, which had supported the austerity packages in order to obtain a lifeline for Greece, irrevocably associating themselves with public sector reform and social spending cuts, were now tarnished as "immoral." Papandreou's polarizing style lived on.

Waiting in the wings were Syriza and its charismatic leader, Alexis Tsipras. Born a few weeks after the restoration of democracy in 1974, Tsipras joined the youth wing of the Communist Party at age 14. He retains something of the romantic revolutionary aura; a poster of Che Guevara hangs in his office. Syriza's affinity for the hard left is more than symbolic. A 2012 party declaration commits it to "organize the democratic overthrow of the political system and its underpinnings, and open the way for a government of the Left" through "strikes, sit-ins, demonstrations, rallies, civil disobedience, and other forms of protest."[27] Its foreign minister, another former Communist Party member and professor of international relations named Nikos Kotzias, wrote a book defending the Polish communist dictatorship and its crackdown on the pro-democracy Solidarity trade union.[28] Like PASOK under Andreas Papandreou, Syriza is more ideologically sympatico with populist Latin American leftist parties than European Social Democratic ones.

As a movement that had never before been in government, Syriza could claim immunity from causing the country's mess. Exploiting Greeks' resentment and wounded pride, Tsipras has called Northern European leaders "gangsters"[29] and promised that "our national humiliation will be over" with his party at the helm, for "we will finish with orders from abroad."[30] But Syriza's diagnosis of the problems facing Greece—that they're ultimately of foreign, not domestic origin—is inherently flawed. Tsipras gave voters the impossible pledge of staying in the Eurozone while abjuring austerity. It's not only critics to Syriza's right who have pointed out the incompatibility of these goals. "Basic intelligence dictates this is impossible," said Alekos Alavanos, a former mentor to Tsipras who left Syrzia to start his own anti-euro party.[31]

By putting Syriza into power, Greeks expressed a sort of fatalism. Incorrectly believing their situation could not get any worse, it seems they figured they might as well go down in a blaze of glory. Mikaelis Alexopoulus, a 45-year-old salesman of household supplies, is like most Syriza supporters in that he used to vote for PASOK. Its support for the Memorandum, however tepid, forever tainted the party in his eyes. "What should have been done five years ago is only happening now," he told me in the summer of 2015, as Syriza's leaders put up a stubborn front before the country's creditors. "We can't be the lab rats for five years." Sitting on a park bench in the port city of Piraeus, outside Athens, he gestured toward a 9-year-old boy playing on the ground in front of him. "I think my son will be 30 before things get better." Yiannis Trantos, a 24-year-old medical student I met at a demonstration outside parliament calling on the government to reject the Troika's terms in the summer of 2015, expressed similar impatience. "Five years ago when the IMF first came we were told if we leave the euro we will have disaster. Five years later we have extremely high unemployment rates concerning youth, my generation has very low wages," he said. "The disaster is already happening . . . leaving the euro is not worse than what we have now."[32] Regardless of the merits of that assessment, the vast majority of Greeks have repeatedly expressed their disagreement by continuing to support their country's membership in the currency union, a membership that, among many other practices, entails responsible budgeting.

Once in power, realizing that the responsibilities of governing are some-what more demanding than delivering xenophobic tirades at political ral-lies, Syriza turned to gestural politics. One of Tsipras's first acts as prime minister was to visit a memorial to resistance fighters killed by the Nazis, an indication of how he viewed German fiscal demands. Many critics of the austerity measures have similarly invoked the past using a less inflam-matory historical analogy, arguing that Greek debt ought to be written off in the same manner as was postwar Germany's. Never mind that the inter-national community slashed German debt by half, about the same amount Greece's creditors have already forgiven; the real glibness of the compari-son lies in the fact that postwar West Germany was a militarily defeated country whose constitution was written by its occupiers and whose govern-ment was largely purged of officials from the previous regime. If the Greeks are willing to surrender a similar degree of sovereignty, then the parallel might stand.

In its first six months in government, Syriza showed a determined resis-tance to confronting reality, going so far as to politicize the gathering of statistics. With the support of its anti-austerity, right-wing coalition part-ner ANEL, Syriza reactivated the legal prosecution of the former head of the Greek statistics agency, an ex-IMF official accused of inflating the country's budget deficit to help justify creditor bailout terms.[33] Rather than accept the need for reform, the Greek government sought to punish the bean-counter, Andreas Georgiou, whose application of honest statistical standards threat-ened further profligacy. Georgiou had taken control of the Greek statistical office three months after the first international bailout in 2010, and his re-vision of the 2009 budget deficit to over 15 percent of GDP—more than the 12 percent estimated by his predecessor, which was itself twice as high as that reported by the previous government—had been verified by Eurostat, the EU statistical agency. At the time, Georgiou faced strong resistance to report this figure from within his own agency (the union representing its employees even went on strike to protest the modernizing of methodolog-ical procedures), and for his scrupulousness, Georgiou became the target of a long-running witch hunt, a convenient scapegoat for a whole slew of ir-responsible and cowardly politicians. Fudging statistics is a tried-and-true

Greek practice, of course—the country was accepted into the Eurozone in 1999 by understating its budget deficit. "It was a smoke-filled-room sort of operation repeated every year," one former government official said of the process by which the finance ministry and Central Bank would meet and agree upon which false numbers to report to Brussels.[34]

Some of Syriza's more intellectually consistent members advocated exiting the Eurozone altogether, a move that would, at least in theory, allow Greece to shed itself of creditor-imposed budgetary demands. (As Greece imports most of its food and energy, however, "Grexit" would also drive up the costs of basic necessities, thus hurting the country's lower-income earners most severely.) Such was the stubborn determination of some ministers to accomplish this feat, in blatant opposition to their own government's stated policy, that they hatched clandestine plans to drop the common currency unilaterally. Finance Minister Yanis Varoufakis met with a secret committee to devise a shadow currency.[35] Meanwhile, Foreign Minister Kotzias took time away from a summit of EU leaders to hold a press conference decrying the continent's "cultural racism" toward Greece, warning that, if Athens did not get what it demanded in bailout negotiations, it would throw open the doors to its refugee camps and flood "thousands of jihadists" into the continent.[36] Energy Minister Panayotis Lafazanis went further, proposing that the Greek government simply seize the national mint and expropriate €22 billion in reserves to pay pensions and public sector salaries. Pledging to axe reforms, the education minister declared that "excellence is a warped ambition."[37] No words could better encapsulate Syriza's tenure.

In need of a third bailout to keep the money flowing but unwilling to accept the sort of cost-cutting measures that had damaged the reputations of his predecessors, Tsipras unilaterally withdrew from creditor negotiations in the summer of 2015 and announced a nonbinding referendum on the Troika's terms. Had Tsipras accepted the package, it would likely have passed the Greek parliament with the support of other parties; it was the hardline faction within Syriza that he felt the need to appease. And so the young prime minister dug in his heels. Scheduled to take place less than two weeks after it was announced, the referendum violated Council of Europe standards, as well as Greece's own constitution, which prohibits plebiscites on fiscal issues. As was his wont, Tspiras presented the measure as a desperate option foisted on blameless Greeks by greedy foreigners: "Greeks, in response to the blackmail to accept an austere and humiliating austerity program which has no end and no prospect of getting back on our feet, I call upon you to decide patriotically and proudly as dictated by the proud history of Greeks," he said in a televised address.[38] Again demonstrating the national proclivity for holding expectations incompatible with their actual commitments, Greeks voted two to one against the bailout conditions while continuing to express an overwhelming desire to keep the euro.

For Greece to find a way out of its morass, it must look to the example set by others that have found themselves in similar economic straits. The experience of the three Baltic States, Latvia in particular, is instructive. Latvia joined the EU in 2004 and the following year pegged its currency, the Lat, to the euro. (It would not adopt the currency until 2014.) When the economic crash struck in late 2008, Latvia's GDP dropped by 20 percent and unemployment rose to more than 20 percent, around the same levels in Greece at the worst point of its crisis. Latvia's response, however, was different, and its recovery is all the more remarkable considering that, unlike Greece, it had no access to the European Central Bank, and thus less liquidity. Riga implemented a series of painful measures that brought it back to its feet, ready to join the common currency just six years later. Thirty percent of civil servants were fired, and salaries dropped an average of 25 percent. In Greece, by contrast, for every seven private sector employees who lost a job during the implementation of the First Memorandum, only one government employee was laid off.[39]

Poor, small countries with large public sectors tend not to grow much, which helps explain why Greece has remained mired in its economic difficulties, while Latvia, following a different path, has not. In spite of its having received a major private debt write-off, Greece's public debt rose from 146 percent of GDP in 2010 to 174 percent four years later. Latvia cut its public debt from 47 percent of GDP (a number already smaller than Greece's by a massive factor) to 36 percent over the same period.[40] Two years into austerity, the coalition government formed by New Democracy and PASOK announced that "the general aim is no more cuts to salaries and pensions, no more taxes," and declared it would stop downsizing public sector employees (doing a better job of actually *collecting* taxes might have made the aforementioned tax increases less severe).[41] Whereas Greeks eventually rejected New Democracy and PASOK for being too miserly, Latvia reelected its pro-austerity government in 2010. After two years of austerity, Latvia accomplished a fiscal adjustment—reducing its governmental primary budget deficit—of 14.7 percent and today boasts a growing economy.[42] Quite an impressive achievement for the country that anti-austerity champion Paul Krugman mocked, in 2008, as "the new Argentina."[43]

Even though the Baltic States were not in the Eurozone at the time, and therefore had the capacity to devalue their currencies as many Euroskeptics insist Greece could have done were it not shackled to the common currency, their experiences impart lessons for Greece all the same. When the IMF suggested that the Baltic governments unpeg their currencies from the euro and devalue—a tool presently unavailable to Athens—the Balts refused, fearful that such a move might delay their joining the currency union. Instead, the Baltic States did what Greece could have done: they regained economic competitiveness through decreasing wages and government expenditures. "Export growth is a reflection of structural reforms and other efforts enhancing supply, which Latvia pursued far earlier than Greece," writes Anders Aslund, an expert on European and post-Soviet economies.[44] Whereas Greek exports grew 45 percent from 2009 to 2013, Latvia's exports increased by almost double that figure.[45] In light of the measures the Baltic States took to recover, it is not hard to understand their frustration at being told that their populations should subsidize the improvident decisions of far wealthier Southern Europeans.

A common stereotype throughout Europe is that Greeks are lazy; a Pew study recently found that, among eight European countries, a median of 48 percent believe Greeks to be the "least hardworking" Europeans. A 2015 Polish political campaign advertisement, featuring images of people sunbathing and long lines forming at ATM machines set to the stringed sounds of a bouzouki, warned voters, "Do not pretend to be Greeks." OECD figures, however, consistently show that Greeks work longer hours than nearly any other people on the continent. What explains this discrepancy between the perception of Greek indolence and the actual number of hours worked is low productivity—structural deficiencies that render Greek work less efficient than it should be. Extensive corruption, outdated technologies, lack of financing opportunities, inept supply chain management, and redundant labor—all of these problems put much of the work accomplished by the individual Greek worker to waste. Greek labor productivity, for instance, is about half that of Germany.[46] Unless entrepreneurship and innovation are encouraged and unleashed, Greek industriousness will continue to be stymied by an oppressive regulatory environment.

The creation of the Eurozone and the subsequent flood of capital into its peripheral economies, where there were not enough productive investment opportunities, meant that funds were heavily directed toward speculative sectors like home building or else went straight into government coffers. Had structural change of the public sector been pursued earlier and more vigorously—had Greece continued along the path it started in 2010—revenue could have been redirected to ease cuts in pensions and salaries. Now, after the Greek disaster, Southern European countries will have to compete properly, which means adopting serious economic reforms, liberalizing labor markets, modernizing bureaucracies and the judiciary, lowering taxes, and improving workers' skills. Such change cannot be imposed from the outside; society must embrace it. Foreigners cannot be blamed for the Greek inability to pay and collect taxes, cut a bloated defense budget, or reduce unit labor costs. "Deficits and debts of this magnitude are not a matter of Keynesian fine-tuning or counter-cyclical balancing," writes British Labor MEP Richard Corbett.[47] They are the result of reckless budgets and a lack of revenue to fund them. Syriza has promised only more of the same.

Greece can, if it wishes, continue to resist reform. In exchange for keeping their clientelist political networks, bloated state sector, protections for favored industries, burdensome regulation, corruption, and lackluster education system, Greeks will have to accept economic stagnation and reduced living standards. Or, they can make the hard but necessary decisions to reform their sclerotic system and set the course for sustainable economic vitality. Stubbornly remaining in the limbo it has occupied for the past several years hurts Greeks most.

But given the treatment regularly meted out by Greeks to those rare politicians attempting reform, it's hard to be optimistic that change will come. "We can take on the task to truly lead the country to a European direction, on condition that the Greeks—those who are living well, not those who are suffering—will make the necessary sacrifices," former PASOK finance minister Alekos Papadopoulos wrote to his prime minister in 1996. When his warnings of pending insolvency threatened to shatter the rosy picture Athens was offering to its people, Papadopoulos was forced to resign. He now heads a marginal liberal party. "I was attacked in brutal ways even by my comrades inside PASOK whose constituents were upset because of the reforms I was passing," he told the *Wall Street Journal*. "It came at an enormous personal cost."[48] Tassos Giannitsis, a former labor minister, tempted the political fates when he tried to reform an unsustainable pension system. "From the fridge to the bin!" screamed a newspaper headline when his plan was inevitably scrapped. His colleagues, Giannitsis said, "were, like, 'everything is going great right now, why are you bothering us with a problem that may implode in a decade?' " Stefanos Manos, the former finance minister, was expelled from New Democracy after his plans to privatize certain industries and break up monopolies threatened some of the party's donors. Like many failed Greek reformers, he has since been involved with various miniscule political groupings that rarely make it into parliament. Surveying the career trajectories of Greece's infinitesimal reformist political class, one cannot help but invoke a figure from Greek mythology: Cassandra, the princess who warned about the dangers hidden within the Trojan Horse.

Syriza's victory, the first for a far-left party in postwar Europe, has several important implications. First and foremost, Syriza's stubbornness in working with Greece's creditors compounded the country's problems. Having won power by promising an impossible end to austerity, the party actually brought about harsher austerity through a negotiating strategy that wasted precious months and alienated creditors. Countries sympathetic to Greece's position, such as France, were turned off by the aggrieved rhetoric and immature behavior of its leaders. Second, and more worrying, Syriza portends the rise of a European hard left exuding the same authoritarian populism of the extreme right. From French Poujadism, the rural movement of farmers and shopkeepers that arose in early opposition to European integration, to today's National Front, Law & Justice, and Fidesz, postwar European nationalism has typically been a right-wing phenomenon. But in the form of Syriza, the reigning Corbynite wing of British Labor, and Spanish PODEMOS, illiberal populism is becoming a bipartisan affair— no less reactionary than its right-wing variety. All three of these parties advocate greater state control over the economy, are deeply suspicious of markets, and seek greater ties with Russia at the expense of the Atlantic alliance. Like other populist forces across the continent, Tsipras casts his country's struggle as a battle between the virtuously downtrodden and the plutocratic elites, a pitched battle between good and evil that reverberates across the continent. "The issue of Greece does not only concern Greece," he wrote in *Le Monde*. "Rather, it is the very epicenter of conflict between two diametrically opposing strategies concerning the future of European unification."[49]

Syriza has found admirers in unlikely places. "It's fantastic to see the courage of the Greek people in the face of political and economic bullying from Brussels," says United Kingdom Independence Party leader Nigel Farage.[50] Similarly enthused by its effrontery toward the EU, leaders of the French National Front and the Hungarian Jobbik have also lavished praise on Syriza, accolades one hopes the proudly antifascist Greeks find at least slightly worrying. When Tsipras addressed the European Parliament, his most enthusiastic fans were located not only on the extreme left but also on the extreme right of the chamber. At the same time, Greek dependence on its European creditors exists in a vicious feedback loop with resentful European populists; bailouts for Greece stoke bitterness in other countries that is in turn exploited by anti-EU parties. "I am really afraid of this ideological or political contagion, not financial contagion, of this Greek crisis," says European Council president and former Polish prime minister Donald Tusk.[51] For everybody, "Brussels" is a convenient scapegoat, blamed equally for Hungary's problems by Hungarian neo-fascists and for Greece's problems by Greek neo-Marxists. Neither is willing to consider the possibility that the roots of their nation's difficulties lie primarily with antiquated and inefficient institutions and outmoded economic arrangements they refuse to adapt.

The solution for Greece is private sector growth. Only a growing economy will slash the country's perpetually high unemployment and sustain a viable tax base to fund the generous social welfare system to which Greeks have become acclimated. But growth takes time, and to see it through, Greeks will have to shed many habits. Otherwise, the result could be disastrous. "When impatience becomes not an individual but a social experience of feeling," Tusk says, "this is the introduction for revolutions."

8

Ukraine: The New West Berlin

Ukraine has not yet perished!
Ukrainian national anthem

Violence finds its only refuge in falsehood, falsehood its only support
in violence.
Alexander Solzhenitsyn, Nobel Prize lecture, 1970

REVOLUTION IN THIS FORMER SOVIET republic began peacefully when thousands of people gathered in the capital calling for the corrupt president to resign. When the crowd refused an order to disperse, security forces loyal to the embattled leader opened fire with live ammunition, killing dozens. That evening the president, accompanied by a coterie of loyalists, absconded to his home region, a temporary stop on the road to exile. As the leader of neighboring Russia warned of looming "civil war," the president fled with the assistance of Russian *spetsnaz* (special forces). After a few days of silence during which no one knew of his whereabouts, the deposed president resurfaced outside the country to decry the politicians who had replaced him, vowing a triumphant return.

Ukraine's Viktor Yanukovych in 2014? No, Kyrgyzstan's Kurmanbeck Bakiyev in 2010. Whereas events in Ukraine gripped the world and sparked the worst East-West confrontation since the end of the Cold War, those in Kyrgyzstan barely registered. Yet the two revolutions bear remarkable similarities and demand careful comparison, because the Kremlin's reaction to the events in Kyrgyzstan directly informed its understanding of, and reaction to, the occurrences in Ukraine four years later.

Small, poor, and landlocked Kyrgyzstan has long been coveted by outside powers for its strategic position in the heart of Central Asia. After the collapse of the USSR, Kyrgyz politicians realized they could leverage their newfound independence as a bargaining chip in the region's broader geopolitical competition, a contest for influence and resources once called "the Great Game." When America launched its war against the Taliban in nearby Afghanistan, Kyrgyz leaders seized the opportunity by offering themselves as partners in NATO's incipient "northern distribution network," the logistical supply chain assisting the coalition forces in theater. By December 2001, three months after the terrorist attacks on the United States, Manas International Airport on the outskirts of the Kyrgyz capital, Bishkek, had been transformed from a sleepy and dilapidated third world airstrip into a major military installation, assisting in what a U.S. government report later called "one of the most complex and challenging logistical operations in U.S. military history."[1] At the time, Kyrgyzstan was the only country in the world hosting both American and Russian military bases, the latter a legacy of Soviet rule.

To Vladimir Putin, the presence of U.S. forces in the former USSR was unacceptable. That he would hold this view confounded a certain superficial reading of Russian foreign policy holding that Russia welcomed Western assistance in the fight against Islamic extremism in its neighborhood. Given its own, decades-long battle against an Islamic separatist insurgency in the North Caucasus, this thinking goes, the last thing Moscow wants in its Central Asian underbelly is a powerful Taliban regime, and in this limited sense, Russian and American interests in Afghanistan converge. But wanting America and its Western allies to fight the Taliban is decidedly not the same as wanting them to defeat it. For Moscow has been more than happy to watch NATO spill blood and treasure battling some of the same Islamist forces the Soviet Union fought unsuccessfully in the 1980s. Perfunctory professions of support for the NATO mission, then, were not mutually exclusive with playing the spoiler, and so Putin extracted a promise in February 2009 from Kyrgyz president Bakiyev to expel the

Americans from Manas Airport in exchange for a $2.15 billion aid package. Lest there be any doubt that this was an explicit quid pro quo, Bakiyev announced his acceptance of the agreement the very same day he met with Putin, then serving as Russia's prime minister.

Putin's jockeying to dismantle the most strategically vital American base supplying the war effort in Afghanistan ought to have signaled that Russia was not particularly interested in improving relations with the United States. But officials in Washington preferred to pretend otherwise. Just a month after the Putin-Bakiyev handshake, then-secretary of state Hillary Clinton traveled to Geneva, where she initiated a policy of "reset" with her counterpart Sergei Lavrov. Washington offered to triple the annual lease it paid to Bishkek for use of the facility and to change its name from the martial-sounding "Manas Air Base" to the more anodyne "Transit Center at Manas." Four months after promising Putin he would evict the Americans, Bakiyev reneged and announced they could stay.[2]

This betrayal set in motion a chain of events leading to Bakiyev's ouster less than a year later. Soon after he agreed to let the Americans maintain their base, Kyrgyz opposition figures began making a series of highly publicized visits to Moscow, where senior Russian officials conspicuously gave them warm welcomes. That November, Putin assailed Bakiyev, accusing him and his family of stealing Russian aid money. "Talk is reaching me of family business in Kyrgyzstan at state level," Putin allegedly said to the Kyrgyz prime minister. In February 2010, the one-year anniversary of Bakiyev's pledge to Putin, Moscow postponed the remaining $1.7 billion of its original $2.15 billion package. Weeks later, Russian-language media, widely watched in Kyrgyzstan, launched a campaign to discredit Bakiyev, airing multiple stories accusing him of corruption and other misdeeds; one report even compared him to Genghis Khan.[3] At this point, Moscow hardly needed to mention how Bakiyev's insolence might affect the fate of the one million Kyrgyz guest workers in Russia, whose remittances comprise nearly one-third of Kyrgyzstan's annual GDP.[4]

The final straw was Putin's March 29, 2010, signing of a decree canceling subsidies on gas exports to Kyrgyzstan. Energy prices spiked, Russia suspended fuel shipments, and antigovernment demonstrations erupted in the eastern Kyrgyz city of Talas before quickly spreading to the capital.

Bakiyev's forces fired on demonstrators, and he eventually fled Bishkek and then the country. Within a day of his leaving the capital, the government collapsed, aided by defections from officials who, thanks to Moscow's skillful brewing of the pot, read the tea leaves. Russia became the first country to grant the new government diplomatic recognition. "Russia played its role in ousting Bakiyev," former Kyrgyz opposition leader Omurbek Tekebayev said at the time. "You've seen the level of Russia's joy when they saw Bakiyev gone."[5] On arriving in Bishkek to cover the revolution, I found that most Kyrgyz thought Moscow had played a critical—and positive—role in Bakiyev's ouster.

Events in Kyrgyzstan halted the momentum of the "color revolutions" that had brought pro-Western, opposition movements to power in Georgia, Ukraine, and (once before) Kyrgyzstan in 2003, 2004, and 2005, respectively. They also complicated the conventional narrative of democracy promotion in the post-Soviet space, which holds that the West is a force for liberalism and good government, and Russia the patron of ossified dictatorships and corruption. Now the roles were reversed, with Moscow viewed as liberation's midwife and America the handmaiden of authoritarianism. Visiting an abandoned government office one evening a few days after Bakiyev fled the capital, I encountered a group of young Kyrgyz men who told me that, while exploring the grounds outside the burned-out presidential administration building, they had come across empty artillery boxes marked "Made in America." Although likely apocryphal, the sentiment expressed through this anecdote was clear: Bakiyev was an American stooge. A man in a Bishkek bar, after learning I was American, wagged his finger at me while repeating, "Money doesn't buy relationships."

To be sure, Moscow's support for the new regime didn't emanate from sympathy for the democratic aspirations of the Kyrgyz people. That would have contradicted the entire history of Russian foreign policy and its longstanding behavior elsewhere in the former Soviet space, Central Asia in particular, where it has consistently supported repressive regimes headed by Soviet-bred autocrats. It was Bakiyev's daring to buck Putin, not his corruption, that estranged him from the Kremlin. There's little doubt that had he simply kept his initial promise to the Russians and evicted the Americans, Moscow would have lauded him as an independent and brave leader. Though it took four years, Russia finally got what it wanted when the post-Bakiyev government shuttered Manas Air Base in 2014.

Moscow's policies toward the regimes in Bishkek and Kyiv were determined solely by those governments' respective willingness to obey Russian diktats. Bakiyev's corruption, the ostensible reason for Russian displeasure, was insignificant compared to that of Yanukovych, whom Moscow supported to the hilt. Whereas Russia offered safe haven to Yanukovych and his lackeys after he abandoned the presidency, it refused to offer it to Bakiyev, who to this day remains exiled in Belarus. Other parallels between the Kyrgyz and Ukrainian events are arresting, right down to the way in which each ex-president's downfall was sparked by their reversal on an agreement with the West. In Bakiyev's case, it was his decision to let the Americans remain at Manas; for Yanukovych, it was the abandonment of a trade and aid agreement with the EU that motivated hundreds of thousands of Ukrainians to brave the bitter cold and protest. Although both regimes collapsed and were replaced by new ones, the crucial difference is that the fall of Yanukovych was the result of indigenous forces, not Russian connivance. Hours after signing an agreement with opposition leaders that ceded some of his authority but allowed him to remain president until the end of 2014, when fresh elections would take place, Yanukovych fled first Kyiv and then the country. No such agreement was ever reached in Bishkek between Bakiyev and the people who overthrew him. The term "coup" does not accurately portray what took place in Ukraine; it is a more fitting description for what transpired in Kyrgyzstan.

This distinction eluded the Russians, however, who cannot make sense of political developments beyond their borders outside the rubric of great power politics. Anything significant that happens in a post-Soviet country like Kyrgyzstan or Ukraine—permanent vassal states, in the Kremlin view—must be connected to outside maneuverings: Russia overthrew Bakiyev for his betrayal, and the Americans, with their European poodles in tow, backed a coup against Yanukovych for a similar fit of disobedience. When Putin saw the protests in Kyiv's Maidan, he didn't see a homegrown movement against corruption and in favor of European integration. He saw a CIA plot, an American version of what he had pulled off in Kyrgyzstan.

That Russia regarded the Maidan revolution as America's belated re-sponse to its loss of face in Kyrgyzstan is apparent in the Kremlin's opposite reactions to similar developments in both countries. In Kyrgyzstan, Rus-sian leaders stressed that the overthrow of a sitting president was a purely domestic matter (Medvedev called it an "internal affair"), brought about by the "extreme degree of discontent that the government's actions had pro-duced among the general public." Such deference to public attitudes con-trasted starkly with Moscow's reaction to events in Ukraine, where claims of pending "genocide" at the hands of "fascists" precipitated an annexation of the Crimean Peninsula and instigation of a bloody war in the country's east. Like Ukraine, Kyrgyzstan also has a large ethnic Russian population, which had at least as much reason to clamor for "protection" as did Russian speakers in Ukraine after Yanukovych's ouster. Yet when actual ethnic cleansing (albeit against Uzbeks) erupted in southern Kyrgyzstan just months after the coup, killing some 2,000 people and causing more than 100,000 refugees, Moscow refused to send peacekeeping troops despite the interim Kyrgyz president's direct appeal for assistance.

Of course, hypocrisy is not unique to Russian statecraft, and so it shouldn't surprise us that the Kremlin would ruthlessly calibrate its policy according to its interests. More significant than the hypocrisy, however, were the lessons Russia gleaned from events in these two former Soviet states. Russia's campaign against Bakiyev—a combination of economic pressure, political subterfuge, and information warfare—contained precisely the ele-ments it would later accuse the West of employing in its "coup" against Ya-nukovych. According to this narrative, the CIA, in cahoots with Ukrainian neo-Nazis, Western intelligence agents fronting as "democracy-promotion" activists, and EU bureaucrats, masterminded a violent takeover. In the Kremlin's eyes, the only difference between Kyrgyzstan and Ukraine was which superpower pulled the strings.

A series of events in the years leading up to Maidan convinced Putin it was a Western-backed uprising and that Russia would be the next domino to fall. First were the "color revolutions" that overturned Moscow-friendly governments and replaced them with Westward-looking ones. Then in 2011, when a vote authorizing NATO military intervention against Libyan dictator Muammar Qaddafi reached the UN Security Council, Medvedev, then president, instructed the Russian ambassador to abstain. Outraged that his country would effectively assent (by not invoking its veto power) to Western military action against a man he viewed as the legitimate leader of a sovereign country, Putin issued a rare public rebuke of his hand-picked successor: The NATO mission, Putin said, "reminds me of a medieval call to crusade." He saw NATO's action as nothing but regime change in the guise of humanitarian intervention, and his suspicion was confirmed when the aerial bombardment eventually led to Qaddafi's gory execution by rebel forces months later. "According to several officials close to the Kremlin," writes Steven Lee Myers of the *New York Times*, "Mr. Medvedev's dangerous irresolution was a decisive factor in Mr. Putin's decision to return to the presidency, which he announced six months later."[6]

Though the prospect of a NATO-backed "Russian spring" seemed highly unlikely, the UN's giving its blessing to a dictator's overthrow was a precedent Putin found abhorrent. For the Russian leader, there exists no higher principle of international relations, at least in theory, than state sovereignty. Putin is careful to present Russian interventions in its near abroad as responses to chaotic political situations that require Moscow to act on humanitarian grounds. The crises requiring Russian intervention, however, are always facilitated by Russia: The respect for sovereignty is only for show. When tens of thousands of Russians took to the streets of Moscow to protest a fraudulent legislative election just two months after Qaddafi's execution in December 2011, Putin's paranoia deepened. He claimed that the demonstrations, the largest in Russia since *perestroika*, had been orchestrated by the State Department, with none other than Hillary Clinton delivering "the signal" for them to begin.[7]

And so it is that Russia, once the headquarters of global revolution, has now emerged as the world's leading counterrevolutionary force. Social movements, Putin and his circle believe, cannot authentically be popular or "grassroots"; there must always be a hidden hand. "The Ukraine crisis was not caused by the Russian Federation," Putin told the Egyptian daily *Al-Ahram* in February 2015. "Last February the USA and a number of EU member states supported the coup d'état in Kiev. The ultranationalists who seized the power using military force put the country on the edge of disruption and started the fratricidal war."[8] This belief that Western plotting determines the course of world events is the ideological mirror image of Cold War anticommunist paranoia that saw a Soviet hand pulling the strings of every left-wing organization. It's a failure of imagination instilled by a KGB education that everywhere suspects CIA skullduggery. If the KGB at one point dreamed up or did similar things, then everyone else must have as well. "Moscow views world affairs as a system of special operations, and very sincerely believes that it itself is an object of Western special operations," says Gleb Pavlovsky, a former advisor to Putin.[9]

Try as they might, however, Western political leaders don't possess the omnipotence attributed to them by the Kremlin. No one remotely familiar with the bureaucratic intricacies of the State Department or the German Foreign Ministry, never mind the EU, could seriously claim that "the West" pulled off a "coup" against Viktor Yanukovych in the way that Russia helped topple Bakiyev.[10] Speaking of the United States and its European allies as a single-minded, well-oiled political bloc elides their significant disagreements on a vast array of issues, not least of which is policy toward Ukraine and the wider post-Soviet space. The combination of economic blackmail, bribery, subtle threats of violent retribution, and denunciatory media campaigns against a foreign leader, all coalescing into a highly combustible situation that ultimately leads to violent revolution, is really only possible for a hardened authoritarian regime working in its own post-imperial backyard to pull off. Even had Western governments wanted to replace Yanukoych, a questionable assumption at best, they lacked the wherewithal to do so. Power in liberal democratic political systems is too diffuse, and the national interests among any collection of democratic states are too varied, for a multilateral grouping of nearly thirty countries to accomplish anything close to what the Kremlin imagines the West did so effortlessly in Ukraine.

Putin is right, though, about one fundamental thing: However it came about, a successful Ukrainian democracy would present a critical threat to the Russian system of personalized power. An ex-Soviet, multiethnic, Russian-speaking country of forty-six million people with an honest, decent, and well-functioning government is historically unprecedented. Putin has convinced Russians that liberal democracy inevitably leads to chaos and that the best they can hope for is "stability." He's expending a great deal of blood and treasure to demonstrate the validity of this claim in a neighboring country.

Russia's war in Ukraine, repression of domestic dissent, and political subversion in the West are all elements of a broader plan to ensure that the post-
Maidan Ukraine becomes a failed state on Europe's door. Putin cannot give
up his imperial project abroad because the demands it makes of his subjects
at home—unstinting loyalty to the president, acquiescence to further consoli-
dation of state power, mass mobilization to defend the Motherland against the
"fascist" West, personal endurance of economic hardship on behalf of the
greater good—validate the repressive apparatus that preserves his regime.

   War in Ukraine is the result of Russia's misunderstanding of the world
and of our misunderstanding of Russia. Moscow's belief that it was next on
the list of "color revolutions" led it to overreact in Ukraine, while the West's
desire to believe it had a potential partner in Moscow led it to overlook the
degree to which the differences between East and West were irreconcili-
able. Ukraine's fate is about far more than the destiny of one former Soviet
republic; it concerns the destiny of Russia, Europe, and the universal right
of national self-determination. This is why Russia will risk so much—
enduring sanctions, economic privation, and diplomatic isolation—to keep
Ukraine under its control.

At 8:00 p.m. on the evening of November 21, 2013, a 32-year-old Afghan
Ukrainian journalist named Mustafa Nayyem posted a short note on his
Facebook page that would alter the course of European history. "Come on,
let's get serious. Who is ready to go out to the Maidan by midnight tonight?"
Earlier that day, President Viktor Yanukovych had announced his rejection
of a trade and aid treaty (known as an Association Agreement) that would
draw Ukraine closer to the EU in exchange for economic and political reforms, opting instead to accept a $15 billion loan from Russia. Yanukovych
had spent years balancing the demands of the many Ukrainians wanting
European integration against a comfortable arrangement with Russia that
allowed him and his cronies in the Party of Regions to maintain a lavishly
corrupt existence. In the end, the old ways of doing business—and not a
little Kremlin bullying—prevailed when Yanukovych announced his surprise decision not to sign the agreement at a European summit in Vilnius.

   Protests, small at first, gained steam as hundreds of thousands of people
gathered in the Maidan, the bricked plaza at the heart of Kyiv. Their

demonstration eventually grew into the largest pro-European rally in history, forming a parallel society with its own self-sustaining organizational structures on the vast expanse of the square. Dubbed "EuroMaidan" for its advocacy of European integration, the protest movement brought together people from all walks of life, ages, regions, religions, and ethno-linguistic identities. Participants slept in tents, endured subfreezing temperatures, and withstood repeated assaults by police. Political leaders from around the world descended on Kyiv to express support for Euro-Maidan's professed aim of a European future for Ukraine, and soon, pro-Maidan rallies spread to cities across the country.

A key turning point occurred on February 18, 2014, when sporadic violence between police and protestors escalated into a bloodbath after government forces unleashed a torrent of gunfire into the crowd. Over the next 48 hours—the bloodiest in Ukraine's history since World War II—nearly 100 demonstrators ranging in ages from 19 to 73 were killed, many of them by Yanukovych's *Berkut* security team. On the morning of February 21, after late-night negotiations, an agreement mediated by Russia, France, Germany, and Poland brought an end to the killing. Signed by Yanukovych and opposition leaders, it called for a redistribution of powers from the presidency to the parliament in accordance with the country's 2004 constitution, the withdrawal of security forces from downtown Kyiv, and the holding of presidential elections no later than December. Hours after signing the settlement, Yanukovych and his entourage fled to his home region in the east and from there to Russia, where he remains to this day.

By running away from his country, Yanukovych legally abandoned the presidency. Pro-European forces in parliament, now a decisive majority because of the steady stream of defections from the Party of Regions, quickly installed an interim government that appointed a new president and prime minister. Russia has since claimed that the chaotic events of February 18–21 amounted to a "coup" carried out by "fascists" and "Nazis," epithets that the Kremlin and its sympathizers consistently use to describe any Ukrainian who opposes Moscow's influence in his or her country. At least initially, they got away with this slander because of the presence of some genuinely far-right organizations on the Maidan that had provided muscle during battles against the regime's security forces. Yet as repeated, internationally certified democratic elections since Yanukovych's departure demonstrate, actual support for the far right in Ukraine is insignificant. Indeed, it stands much lower than in many Western European countries, where far-right parties routinely gain 20 percent or more of the vote. (In April 2016, with barely any controversy, the allegedly "fascist" Ukrainian Parliament overwhelmingly elected a Jewish prime minister.) As to the legality of the process by which the interim government came to power, "virtually everything was according to the constitution," says former Swedish foreign minister Carl Bildt, who played a central role in developing the EU's Eastern Partnership policy and helped resolve the Maidan crisis diplomatically. "It was not foreseen that the president would flee. I'm not sure what we would do in Sweden if the King suddenly disappeared."[11]

Moscow did not anticipate that Yanukovych's rejection of the Association Agreement would ultimately lead to his fleeing the country in the wake of a popular revolution. The Kremlin's plan to keep Ukraine within its "sphere of privileged interests" backfired; with Yanukovych gone, Russia was now in a worse position than it would have been had it just permitted Yanukovych to sign the Association Agreement back in November 2013. Moscow had bitten off more than it could chew, but in Putin's eyes, the only way to avert "losing" Ukraine entirely was to bite off even more. As Yanukovych was fleeing Ukraine, Putin ordered his security officials to begin work on "returning Crimea" to Russia.[12] Five days later, Russian forces wearing unmarked uniforms—"little green men"—seized government buildings on the peninsula, including the regional parliament, and raised Russian flags over their roofs. With their aid, an illegally installed Russian puppet government headed by a local crime boss promptly announced a "referendum" to decide Crimea's future status. When the sham vote took place two weeks later under entirely illegitimate conditions—tanks patrolling the streets and armed men standing next to ballot boxes—a comically high 97 percent of voters, from a turnout of 83 percent, chose to join the Russian Federation.

But annexing Crimea was not enough. To quash any hope of another "color revolution," Putin had to topple the new Ukrainian government in

Kyiv and thus eradicate the contagion before it spread to other parts of the former Soviet empire. A gutter of conspiracy mongering and nationalistic incitement ("Zombie television" in the words of Russian democracy activist Ilya Yashin), Kremlin-controlled media intensified the already alarmist nature of its programming with increasingly feverish exposés of Western plots to destroy Russia.[13] Soon the official Russian narrative moved beyond allegations of a Western-backed "coup" to claims that the new "fascist" government in Kyiv was planning a "genocide" of ethnic Russians in Ukraine. Lurid stories of Ukrainian speakers murdering their Russian-speaking neighbors and crucifying children spread rapidly. (Most Ukrainians speak Russian, this pseudo-ethnic dichotomy being a cynical contrivance that Moscow exploited to murderous effect.) "A crooked mirror of Maidan, a monkey-style imitation of Maidan" developed in Eastern Ukraine, according to Donetsk University history professor Elena Styazhkina, where the onslaught of paranoia and propaganda from Moscow triggered a revival of Soviet-era fears about the West. As to the rallying cry that Russian speakers needed to take up arms against those who would slaughter them over use of their native tongue, "The Russian language is not in need of blood," Styazhkina said. "She needs critics, publishers, writers, teachers, and children."[14]

What had started out as the "Anti-Maidan," a series of pro-Yanuovych demonstrations, eventually spawned ragtag "separatist" militias armed and logistically supported by the Russians. Attempting to mimic the Crimean annexation, they seized government buildings and established self-proclaimed "People's Republics" in the regions of Donetsk and Lugansk. When it became clear that the Ukrainian military might defeat the rebels and regain control of Ukraine's sovereign territory, the Kremlin increased its involvement. Even the downing of a Malaysian Airlines jetliner over the skies of Ukraine by a Russian-supplied anti-aircraft missile did not temper Russian military intervention. Most Western analysts and political leaders predicted that the disaster would finally persuade Putin to pull onto the diplomatic "off-ramp" provided by the Obama administration and EU. On the contrary, Western indecisiveness in the wake of the crash persuaded Putin to transfer even more sophisticated weaponry to Russian proxies and dispatch regular Russian army units over the border into

Ukraine, transforming what had been a barely concealed stealth invasion carried out by special forces into a conventional (if still unacknowledged) war. Russia quickly reversed the course of the ongoing conflict, which has caused upward of 10,000 civilian and 15,000 combatant casualties and created nearly two million refugees.

In both strategy and tactics, Russia's seizure of Crimea and its not-so-secret war in Eastern Ukraine are not without precedent. When Soviet soldiers marched into Poland in 1940, Hungary in 1956, and Czechoslovakia in 1968, and Russian ones entered Georgia in 2008, they did so under the pretense of aiding embattled local forces that had requested their help. In 2013, a year before the Crimean operation and Donbas war, an article appeared in a Russian military journal under the authorship of Valery Gerasimov, chief of the Army General Staff, presaging the shrewd use of subterfuge and disinformation that Moscow would soon deploy to expert effect. Waging this type of "aysmmetric" campaign, which "in general is not declared," requires the "broad use of political, economic, informational, humanitarian, and other non-military measures—applied in coordination with the protest potential of the population."[15] Since then, this "Gerasimov Doctrine" has upended the way strategists see conflict evolving in the twenty-first century. "A perfectly thriving state can, in a matter of months and even days, be transformed into an arena of fierce armed conflict, become a victim of foreign intervention, and sink into a web of chaos, humanitarian catastrophe, and civil war," Gerasimov wrote in a rather apt description of what has since taken place in Ukraine.

Russia's military intervention—dubbed by analysts a "hybrid," "nonlinear," or "special war"—has involved "humanitarian aid convoys" (containing weapons), "local self-defense units" (led by Russian special forces), and other euphemistic implements designed to confuse and distract adversaries while providing plausible deniability that anything like a war is even taking place. It has also occurred alongside a wave of disinformation intended to divide and subvert the West. Confusing one's adversary forms a crucial component of hybrid war; fittingly, Russian institutions of higher education have elevated the study of informational warfare to an academic discipline.[16] "Today, it is much more costly to kill one enemy soldier than during World War II, World War I or in the Middle Ages," says Dmitri

Kiselyev, Russian state television's leading on-air propagandist. "If you can persuade a person, you don't need to kill him.[17]

In the aftermath of the Ukraine crisis, a great deal has been written about Russian-sponsored media, often given the familiar Cold War–era label "propaganda." That term implies exaltation of a country, its political system, and leadership, and although the domestic Russian audience is certainly inundated with nationalistic cant and veneration of Putin, Russia broadcasts a very different message abroad. During the Cold War, Moscow promoted communism as the pinnacle of human aspiration; today, the objective is no longer to endear Russia or its system to foreign audiences. Unlike in Western countries, which care about how others perceive them, Russia isn't bothered by the low approval ratings registered by the Pew Global Attitudes Project. It would rather be feared than respected, never mind loved, because if foreign publics and governments fear Russia, they will be less inclined to challenge it. One astute observer of Russian disinformation operations describes its information strategy as comprising four "d's"—"dismiss the critic, distort the facts, distract from the main issue, and dismay the audience"—creating "a moral quagmire in which everyone is wrong, and therefore wrong actions become normal."[18]

Moscow's nihilism is in a way more cynical and sinister than its Soviet antecedent, which at least propounded an ideology. Today, Russia aims to sow confusion and defeatism in the West by poking holes in its narratives while ridiculing and upending the very notion of objective truth—a strategy the historian Timothy Snyder calls "applied postmodernism."[19] "There are no such things as objective facts," Ginta Krivma, spokeswoman for a Kremlin-backed, Russian-language Baltic news network, bluntly told the *Wall Street Journal*.[20] Not even the weather escapes Kremlin propagandists. An ex-employee of Russia's main state broadcaster revealed that meteorological reports are adjusted to make the winters colder for Ukraine.[21] "The general trend was to stoke fear," the former editor said, "that they depend on us but we're not going to send [Ukraine] gas and you'll all freeze."[22]

This is the modus operandi of RT, formerly known as "Russia Today," the "counter-hegemonic" television network that pumps out conspiracy theories and anti-Western hysteria 24/7. Wildly popular on the Internet, particularly among young people, it can be viewed in English, French, German, Spanish, and Arabic. It "informs" its viewers that Ukrainians are neo-Nazi fascists and also, paradoxically, gay-loving degenerates; that the CIA shot down Malaysian Airlines Flight 17; and that Germany is a "failed state." These are just a few examples of the sort of discursive pollution emitted into the ether by RT and other Kremlin-backed media organs. Narratives are cleverly tailored for discrete audiences; in Germany, where renascent fascism is an understandably sensitive topic, stories about Kyiv "Nazis" are intended to stoke skepticism about Ukraine's democratic bona fides; tales of well-heeled British bankers run amok, meanwhile, rate highly in the struggling Mediterranean countries. Yet Kremlin narratives often contradict each other, depending on the intended audience: Berlin's neo-imperial economic avarice is hawked to Greek viewers, while its humiliating servility as an American colony is advertised to German ones. The one constant from Soviet-era propaganda is anti-Americanism: Taking a page from Orwell's *1984*, in the Kremlin's dystopian picture of the world, America is war and Russia is peace.

Unfortunately, there is a large audience for this material in the West, where ongoing fallout from the financial crisis, wars in Afghanistan and Iraq, and various political scandals have contributed to growing popular distrust of traditional authority structures and elites. RT's beautifully simple motto, "Question More," even if it applies selectively to Western leaders and institutions (and not, say, those in Moscow or Damascus), appeals especially to the anti-establishment tastes of younger viewers. Russian disinformation has found a receptive audience on the web, which, unable to control, the Kremlin has tried to render a cesspool. In 2015, the *New York Times Magazine* published a fascinating report from within one of Russia's various "troll" factories, where a Stakhanovite "army" of young, well-paid, English-speaking technicians take to Twitter, Facebook, website comment sections, and other Internet forums to dismiss, distort, distract, and dismay critics of the Russian government. While on the surface, these workplaces look like any fashionable Silicon Valley start-up, their function in Internet culture is akin to the role that the political cultist Lyndon LaRouche once played in U.S. public policy debates. In exposing the inner workings of Russian informational warfare, a former troll cited by the *Times* resembled a latter-day Vasili Mitrokhin, the former KGB archivist whose meticulous and secretive transcriptions of the agency's files over a decades-long career exposed a raft of "active measures" against the West going back to the 1930s. "Workers received a constant stream of 'technical tasks,'" the *Times* reported: "point-by-point exegeses of the themes they were to address, all pegged to the latest news."[23] During the most recent American presidential election, many journalists and analysts suspected that at least some of the aggressively lewd Twitter accounts supporting Donald Trump's campaign were operated out of Russian troll farms.

The most important fact about the crisis in Ukraine is that it's about far more than Ukraine. Russia's annexation of a neighbor's sovereign territory, its ongoing war on that neighbor's soil, and its attempts to subvert and overthrow that neighbor's democratically elected and internationally recognized government represents the starkest threat to world order since Saddam Hussein's 1990 invasion and annexation of Kuwait—an invasion repelled by a multilateral coalition that included the Soviet Union. If Russia can succeed in Ukraine—riding out sanctions and continuing its low-level war in the east until the government in Kyiv collapses and is replaced with one more pliable to Moscow—it will have set a disastrous precedent with repercussions for the entire community of nations. Behind the events in Ukraine hangs the specter of a lawless world.

It's not just the fragile global security order at stake. Western failure in Ukraine would signal a decisive blow against the values of liberalism, democracy, and consensus-based interstate relations embodied by the European Union. Ukrainians call their uprising the "Revolution of Dignity" for the humane ethics it articulated. The accumulated legislation, human rights, high democratic standards, and rule of law required of countries wishing to join the EU, known as the *acquis communitaire*, collectively represents the greatest menace to the post-Soviet habits of corruption, arbitrary rule, and violent territorial expansion that sustain the Kremlin's domestic power and influence abroad. When I met Mustafa Nayyem, the young journalist whose Facebook post inadvertently sparked EuroMaidan and who has since been elected to parliament, at the shabby offices of the investigative website he once worked for, he was wearing a t-shirt that said "FUCK CORRUPTION." That's a laudable, if crudely expressed goal, and for a former communist state like Ukraine, wedged between Russia and Europe, it's achievable only through greater integration with the West.

Former Georgian president Mikhail Saakasvhili calls EuroMaidan the "first geopolitical revolution of the 21st century," an acknowledgment that its aspirations go far beyond replacing a president, encompassing nothing less than the fundamental reorientation of the region's civilizational trajectory.[24]

Russia would claim that the Association Agreement between Ukraine and the EU was a tool of Western imperialism, part of a larger plan to absorb Ukraine into not only the EU but NATO as well—and that this in turn was part of an even bigger and more nefarious strategy, going back twenty-five years, to "encircle" and "humiliate" Russia. What these assertions willfully ignore is that the courtship goes entirely in the other direction: Ukraine wants the West far more than the West wants Ukraine. Moreover, the Association Agreement said nothing about its joining the European Union—many member nations are happy to see its membership forestalled indefinitely given the massive amount of money and effort needed for Ukraine's economic and political integration into the bloc. NATO membership, for that matter, is an even more distant prospect.

As to Moscow's complaint that the West had rubbed its nose in its Cold War defeat, a list of Western initiatives aimed at welcoming Russia into its club reads like an unrequited love letter. Russia joined the Council of Europe, an intergovernmental body that administers the European Court on Human Rights (to whose judgments Russia is subject), in 1996, and both Europe and the United States have since sought to draw it closer. The following year, the EU and Russia signed a Partnership and Cooperation Agreement, paving the way for increased collaboration in fields ranging from political dialogue to scientific research and space exploration. The year after that, Russia was invited to join the G7 group of industrialized democracies (from which it was expelled in 2014 for its annexation of Crimea). As late as 2012, four years after its invasion of Georgia and with the full backing of the United States and Europe, Russia was offered membership in the World Trade Organization.

Were these initiatives the mark of a United States and Europe determined to "isolate" and "punish" Russia, as the Kremlin and, indeed, many Western critics contend? On the contrary, the purpose of these Western endeavors was to assist Russia's development into a prosperous, democratic state bound by the rule of law, with the eventual goal of full integration into Western political and security organizations, up to and including the EU and, one day, perhaps even NATO. Unfortunately, the men (and they are all men) who took control of Russia after Boris Yeltsin had no interest in modernization and liberalization; if they had, Russia would be a very different place right now. It's also worth stressing how the entirely voluntary nature of Western policy toward Eastern Europe contrasts with Moscow's preference for economic blackmail and brute force. "While the EU's vision of 'wider Europe' relies on soft power, economic integration, and long-term institution building, Putin's 'wider Russia' policy depends on intimidation and violence," writes Bildt. Unfortunately, an asymmetry persists as "it is easier for Russia to fuel short-term volatility than it is for Europe to help build long-term stability."[25]

Putin has stated quite clearly that he sees the consequences of the war in Ukraine reverberating far beyond that country's borders. The crisis there, he said in 2015, "emerged in response to the attempts of the USA and its Western allies who considered themselves 'winners' of the Cold War to impose their will everywhere."[26] Fighting Western influence has now become Russia's mission in the world. In his 2015 speech before the United Nations General Assembly, Putin scolded the West for forgetting the "principles guiding the cooperation among states" laid out at the 1945 Yalta Conference. Putin's invocation of the Yalta agreement as the basis for international cooperation was highly revealing, and not just because he described that Crimean city as located in "our country." Yalta was where the Western allies essentially surrendered Central and Eastern Europe to Soviet domination after World War II.

Then, as now, the Soviet definition of "security" is notably expansive, encompassing everything up to and including the overthrow of elected governments along Russia's borders (and beyond, as in Czechoslovakia) and the installation of communist puppet regimes in their place. Russia would have moved much deeper into Europe had not the West drawn a line in the sand. That policy, known as "containment," is for Putin more than a historical grievance. "The policy of containment was not invented yesterday," he explained in his 2014 annual state of the union address. "It has been carried out against our country for many years."

Though he complains about illegitimate Western forays into Russia's sphere of interest, Putin is actually implementing a containment policy of his own: what Christopher Walker of the National Endowment for Democracy labels "democracy containment."[27] More than a territorial defense, this struggle is deeply ideological, a sort of counterrevolution to the Enlightenment whose instruments and narratives we are witnessing in the battle for Ukraine.

By punishing Ukrainians for their impotence in rejecting Russia, Putin issues a lesson to his own people: Mobilize against me and snipers will shoot at you too. In January 2016, he signed legislation allowing the FSB to do just that: open fire on crowds without warning to prevent "terrorism." Three months later, Putin formed a new national guard under the auspices of the Interior Ministry, commanded by his own former personal bodyguard. Possibly comprising as many as 400,000 men as well as tanks and attack helicopters, this newfangled Praetorian Guard will be unquestionably loyal to Putin in the event of any sort of civil unrest.[28] Moscow's behavior in Ukraine has had a chilling effect in the post-Soviet space, making painfully clear the costs of choosing a Western path and discouraging former Soviet satrapies from repeating the mistakes Ukrainians made.

But Russia's contestation of democratic norms has also had a baleful effect in the parts of Europe beyond its direct military reach, exposing divisions within the transatlantic community that were largely dormant and unseen before the war in Ukraine exposed them. Across the continent, politicians on both the left and right have emerged as ardent defenders of Russian prerogatives. When Crimea held its sham referendum, "observers" from parties as ideologically diverse as the German postcommunist Die Linke and the Hungarian neofascist Jobbik linked arms to declare the balloting free and fair. Although it was never a secret that these groups were outside the European mainstream, it was a sight to behold the far left and far right join together publicly in effective support for armed aggression against their fellow Europeans. Russia now provides a sort of intellectual (and in some cases, pecuniary) glue to unite disparate illiberal forces across the continent and around the world. Owing to Moscow's leadership, writes Alexander Cooley of Columbia University's Harriman Center, global "norms privileging state security, civilizational diversity, and traditional values over liberal democracy now enjoy significant backing, and they are reshaping the international environment."[29]

Sympathy and occasionally overt support for Russian revisionism are hardly limited to the European political extremes. In July 2015, nine members of *Les Républicains,* the main French center-right party led by former president Nicolas Sarkozy, traveled to Crimea and then Russia in defiance of Western sanctions. (One member of the delegation defiantly tweeted from Moscow that "France has no autonomous diplomacy; we are zealous servers of American Empire and have no autonomous thinking.") Although Sarkozy himself did not join the group, he had already blessed the bogus referendum with the assertion that "Crimea can't be blamed for choosing Russia," a sentiment later echoed by Trump in the United States. To comprehend just how far the French political elite has shifted toward accommodation with Russia, consider that in 2007, when President George W. Bush was at the nadir of his international disapproval, Sarkozy declared that he'd still "rather shake Bush's hand than Putin's."[30]

Unless the West's desire to safeguard the international system on which Europe's existence as a democratic community depends is stronger than Russia's desire to replace that system with one where might makes right, the rules-based liberal order will collapse. Essential to this effort must be a demonstration that Europe's commitment to national self-determination is stronger than Russia's desire to control Ukraine. Ukraine's downfall at the hands of Russian economic strangulation and military aggression would be far more disastrous than another Greek default or even exit from the Eurozone. It would inflict a devastating blow on Western credibility and also spark a refugee crisis to rival the one originating in the Middle East and North Africa. Western governments ought to open their markets fully to Ukraine to alleviate the massive blow the country's economy has suffered from the Russian invasion and supply Kyiv with the defensive lethal weaponry they should have sent long ago.

Not only has the West refused to aid Ukraine in this manner, but it has also carried on as if Russia were not in fact waging war on a fellow European democracy. Western leaders, up to and including the EU High Representative for Foreign Affairs and Security Policy, the German chancellor, and the president of the United States, have all painstakingly avoided using the word "invasion" to describe Russian actions in Ukraine. By refusing to acknowledge reality, Western governments slowly condition themselves to the evasions and rationalizations Russia will pressure them to make should it employ similar tactics against a Baltic or other NATO member in the future. Moscow has keenly watched the West's reaction to its war on Ukraine, and although Western military intervention against Russia was never (and ought never have been) in the cards, the failure to even accurately speak about what is taking place demonstrates a fecklessness that could provoke more hostility.

Russia is content to keep Ukraine teetering indefinitely on the brink of collapse. Sacrificing Ukraine for a temporary alliance with Moscow would have disastrous effects, and not just for the Ukrainians. Such a rash and iniquitous bargain would send the message that Europe is willing to negotiate away the very principles that have blessed it with the longest period of peace and prosperity in history.

From Poland to Hungary, many see the EU flag as a symbol of bureaucratic oppression, a trapping of Brussels' "imperialism" and strangulation of national sovereignty. To Ukrainians, this simple standard of twelve gold stars arranged in a circle, set against a blue background, signifies something else. It is an aspiration, an icon of grand ideals such as individual rights, the rule of law, economic prosperity, and political freedom, as well as more quotidian goals like not having to pay a bribe whenever one interacts with a government official. Whether Europeans appreciate it or not, their flag is the adopted emblem of Ukraine's Revolution of Dignity. Maidan was the first place anyone died under that flag, a point stressed by the young Ukrainian civic activist and parliamentarian Hanna Hopko. "Ukraine," she says, "might be the only nation that has given life for values which Europeans are not even ready to continue sanctions for."

Conclusion: The European Dream

> Democracy may, after all, turn out to be an historical accident, a
> brief parenthesis that is closing before our eyes.
>
> Jean François Revel, *How Democracies Perish*, 1983

AS WORLD LEADERS HUDDLED IN PRAGUE'S glorious St. Vitus Cathedral on a
gray December day in 2011, the casket containing the body of former Czech
president Vaclav Havel made its way from Old Town square, across the
scenic Charles Bridge, and up the sloping hill to the city's castle complex.
Ten thousand mourners joined the funeral cortège, which used the same
horse-drawn gun carriage to carry Havel that once held the casket of
Czechoslovakia's first president, Tomas Masaryk.

The playwright, essayist, moral philosopher, and one-time political prisoner had presided over that rare and remarkable thing: a peaceful and
democratic revolution. Havel devoted his presidency to bringing the Czech
Republic into the EU and NATO, advocating humanitarian intervention in
the Balkans, and championing the rights of imprisoned dissidents in far-
flung places. Through his own experience as a victim of communist oppression, he understood, more than most European statesmen, the important
role that a united Europe, in firm partnership with America, had to play in
the survival of freedom.

Havel's death seemingly marked the passing not only of a great man but
also of a legacy. His vision of an open, pluralistic, and confident Europe

has been neglected, if not outright repudiated, in his own country and elsewhere across the continent. Havel's immediate successor, Vaclav Klaus, a friend and ally of Vladimir Putin, forsook his own nation's history as a target of Warsaw Pact invasion and supported Russia unequivocally when it invaded and annexed Ukrainian territory. The current Czech president, Miloš Zeman, whose campaign was largely funded by the Russian state energy concern Lukoil, is even more slavish in deference to Moscow, expressing approval for the imprisonment of the punk rock protest band Pussy Riot. While readers in many languages found in Havel a humane and humble soul who spoke to our better instincts, a senior official in the Czech Foreign Ministry assailed him for "false universalism" that seeks to "impose on others our idea of the ideal society."[1]

Across Europe, as the generation of leaders who struggled to unite a cruelly and unnaturally divided continent leaves the scene, their places have been overtaken by a crop of shortsighted populists. Where Europe once had men and women like Havel, Kohl, Thatcher, Mitterand, and Walesa, today the likes of Zeman, Corbyn, Orbán, Kaczynski, and Le Pen are ascendant. Belief in joint prosperity and the rejection of zero-sum politics—necessary precursors to Europe's unprecedented peace and prosperity—are losing adherents. To judge from the decreasing voter turnout in European parliamentary elections, Europeans care less and less about how the continent is governed, believing that salvation lies in the renationalization of politics.

Europe's manifold crises collectively represent a crisis of liberalism. As the memory of World War II, the Holocaust, and the gulag fades, so too does antipathy to the illiberal ideologies that spawned Europe's past horrors. This is evident in the rising electoral success of populist authoritarian parties of the extreme left and right, none of which have anything new to say yet claim the mantle of ideological innovation and moral virtue. During the Cold War, Western leaders offered a robust defense of their values in the face of an existential totalitarian challenge. Today, while the threats to freedom may be more diffuse, they are no less potent, and yet moral relativism and self-doubt sap Western will at every turn. The consequences of such abdication are dire: If the values of America and Europe do not continue to shape the future as they have its recent past, then those of authoritarian powers like Russia will.

Although there are many arguments in favor of European integration, perhaps the strongest is that the alternative is so much worse. Europe's best years have come during its (consensual) confederation. Before the establishment of the EU, the continent was plagued with arbitrary rulers who led their peoples into wars of aggression and genocide over matters like religion or family honor. Historically, the alternative to peaceful and democratic European integration is not a collection of sovereign, independent nation-states trading and cooperating together with ease, but violent competition for mastery and imperial expansion. For all of its utopian trappings, the EU is ultimately based on negative lessons. Its creation is meant to be a renunciation of everything Europeans have done wrong. That is not an argument for a European federal superstate, wherein nations would surrender power to Brussels to the same degree that the American states do to Washington. But amid cries that Europeans are losing "sovereignty" to faraway bureaucrats, it's useful to remember that more Europeans have enjoyed far greater rights and freedoms while living under some form of supranational EU authority than they have at any other point in history.

Europe's most pressing problems can only be solved collectively. Better integrated and coordinated fiscal and monetary policies will prevent another Eurozone crisis. A common external border control and continent-wide asylum policy will impose some sort of order on the flow of migrants whose presence is unraveling the Schengen Agreement, driving support for populist parties, and threatening the existence of the union itself. A cohesive and robust foreign policy, as well as more and freer trade with its former colonies in Africa and the Middle East, will alleviate economic and social conditions in failed states along Europe's periphery that drive refugee flows in the first place. Bans on foreign funding of election campaigns would stop the flow of Russian money to extremist parties and defend Europe's hard-won democracies from subversion. Placing stronger political conditions on the payment of EU structural funds to wayward members like Poland and Hungary—both of whose GDPs depend significantly on assistance from Brussels—would help stop democratic backsliding.

Before Europeans proceed further down the path of integration, they must ask themselves what they believe in. For "Europe" itself means different things to different people. To Easterners desperate to crawl out from under the thumb of a four-decade-long communist subjugation, the primary motivation for rejoining Europe was to get rich fast, not to acquire the socially liberal values of the Dutch or transfer sovereignty over traditionally domestic competencies like migration. Seeing Europe as largely transactional, many there are beginning to feel that the project has been a waste of time because their living standards have not risen fast enough to equal those of their Western neighbors. But if Europe is to survive, its people will have to embrace a civic patriotism that venerates more than just pensions and holidays.

"More Europe," the mantra of federalists in response to every setback for their project, need not mean the investiture of more power in Brussels. The paradigm for further European integration should more often than not be greater cooperation along the lines of De Gaulle's "Europe of nation-states," not the strengthening of the Brussels bureaucracy. Practically, this would translate into shifting some powers from the unelected European Commission to the EU Council, composed of the ministers of the national governments. "Ever closer union," a clause in the Preamble to the 1957 treaty establishing the European Community which became a major sticking point in the Brexit debate, need not be a religion. Forging greater consensus on a common external policy is the most important aspect of integration, as it holds the key to Europe's wielding influence alongside the United States as a liberal world power.

As for the values they should consider worth defending, both Europeans and Americans take for granted the peace and integration that allowed them to blossom. Hardly anyone believed the Soviet Union would ever collapse, right up to the moment it did. Just as we were wrong to assume the permanence of Soviet rule, so would we be wrong to assume the permanence of European political and economic stability. It is not the natural state of things. Across the grand sweep of European history, countries and empires disintegrating into smaller governing units or being violently subsumed into larger empires is the norm. For the United Kingdom to wash its hands of the continent and go solo is not out of national character, nor would it be a historical novelty for Germany and Russia to form a strategic axis.

Not long ago, when disagreement over the Iraq War brought transatlantic relations to a nadir, cheering for European disintegration was a fashionable attitude among many American conservatives. Goaded on in their Europhobia by a cohort of like-minded British conservatives for whom the EU represented an intolerable usurpation of national sovereignty, they saw dismantling the European project as a step forward for freedom and a means of weakening a competitor to American global hegemony. In 2001, a prominent right-of-center British American writer ominously foresaw a federal Europe undermining the United States. "By the end of [George W.] Bush's term," he wrote, "the United States could well be the second-largest economic and political power in the world, playing second fiddle to a European behemoth powered by Germany, handled by France, with Britain as a mere province within. The United States will have lost its most critical ally and gained its most formidable competitor since the Soviet Union."[2]

Fifteen years later, that fearsome prediction seems a luxury, born of the hubristic assumption that Americans and Europeans could afford to go their separate ways. While a European superstate—always a chimera despite the wishes of a small European federalist elite—might pose a hypothetical threat to American global preeminence, there is no question that its increasingly conceivable opposite—a weakened, splintered Europe riven by political and economic fractures—would be disastrous. There can be no "pivot" away from Europe, as Europe is inherently the strategic focal point of American foreign policy.

Europe's diminishment on the world stage, never mind collapse, would constitute a tragedy not only for the continent but also for America and the world. A divided, weaker, and less influential Europe means a more dangerous international state of affairs. For as much as it was the invention of great European statesmen such as Jean Monnet and Robert Schumann, the European project of political, military, and economic integration would have been impossible without American foresight, sacrifice, and generosity. Twice, American presidents intervened in the continent's wars. Hundreds of thousands of young men from California to Maine gave their lives to defeat fascism in Europe; millions served under arms to stop the advance of communism. A continent composed of peaceful, economically prosperous democracies—rebuilt by Marshall Plan aid and protected by the U.S.

military—is America's greatest gift to the world. We would be foolish to let it slip away.

If the problems enumerated by this book are not addressed, a nightmare future could unfold. Absent a common energy policy, Europe will continue to be held hostage to Moscow's pipeline politics. Lacking a common defense policy to deter Russian aggression, Europe risks another conventional war. Without a thriving common market fueled by the free flow of labor, goods, and workers, production and trade will fall, leading to increased unemployment and rising social unrest. And without political cohesion, Europe's critical role in maintaining the liberal world order will be severely diminished. All of these problems—fecklessness in the face of Russia, persistent unemployment, slow growth, and uncontrolled migration—have at their root a lack of solidarity. Germany won't arrest its creeping neutralization unless it reaffirms its alliance with America; Hungary's model of "illiberal democracy" will gain advocates across the continent unless the EU intervenes; Greece will become a third-world economy absent EU-imposed structural reforms; the entire Western security order could collapse on the banks of the Narva River if NATO doesn't protect its eastern flank; the war on European Jewry will continue unless Muslim communities adopt Europe's post-Holocaust commitment to sustaining Jewish life and recognizing Israel's legitimacy; and the whole parade of horribles could be set in motion if other European countries take Britain's lead and leave the EU.

Reading the headlines from Europe, it's easy to get depressed. Yet there are glimmers of hope. Polls show younger Europeans identifying more as "European" in addition to their respective nationalities. A rising cohort from Europe's East, who have a more direct knowledge (if not personal experience) of living under dictatorship, possess a greater appreciation for democracy. Some of the most remarkable Europeans I've encountered are young people from the postcommunist world: the upstart Ukrainian twenty-somethings who launched an independent investigative television network in the revolutionary cauldron of the Maidan, the Polish democracy activists imparting the lessons of their nation's struggle to democrats in Burma, the Belarusian actors who illegally stage subversive plays in abandoned houses on the outskirts of Minsk. If Europe is to regain a sense of its purpose, it will be in the example set by the "new" Europeans of the East who cannot afford to take democracy and liberal values for granted in the way their Western brethren so often do. I also acquire optimism from more unexpected places. When a bearded Austrian drag queen named Conchita Wurst won the 2014 Eurovision Song Contest, provoking denunciations of European decadence and depravity from Russia and other predictably reactionary quarters, it was heartening to see a wide-ranging assemblage of European voices rise up in her defense and assert, yes, this is a product of European ingenuity and pluralism and we are proud.

The time for muddling through is over. To ensure that the past seventy years of relative utopia are not the exception to its history but the rule, Europe needs a renewal of the muscular liberal center that is as proud of a hirsute diva as it is willing to use force to defend itself, as welcoming of Muslim refugees as it is unyielding in defense of the values it insists they adopt, and as devoted to the social welfare state as it is committed to private entrepreneurship. Much more is at stake than the continuation of a currency union, the freedom to travel from France to Germany without a passport, or the existence of that massive, much-derided bureaucracy in Brussels. A Europe unmoored from the Enlightenment values it brought to the world, ignorant of and unwilling to protect its civilizational achievements, captive to chauvinist demagogues, indisposed to defend itself, bereft of its Jews, estranged from America, cowed before Russia, and reverted to its traditional state of nature with nations pursuing mercenary self-interest at the expense of unity would not only spell the end of Europe as we know it. Such a collapse would usher in nothing less than a new dark age.

NOTES

Introduction

1. Agnes Heller, remarks at "Unravelling Europe," Free Word and Index on Censorship, London, June 15, 2016.
2. Stefan Zweig, "The Unification of Europe: A Discourse," unfinished manuscript, 1934, translated by Will Stone in *Messages from a Lost World: Europe on the Brink* (London: Pushkin Press, 2016).
3. World Values Survey, Waves 5 and 6 (2005–2014), cited in Roberto Stefan Foa and Yascha Mounk, "The Democratic Disconnect," *Journal of Democracy* 27, no. 3 (July 2016).
4. Andreas Johansson Heinö, "Timbro Authoritarian Populism Index," 2016, Timbro, http://timbro.se/sites/timbro.se/files/files/reports/4_rapport_populismindex_eng_0.pdf.
5. Letter from senators Ron Wyden, Patrick J. Leahy, et al. to the National Commission on Fiscal Responsibility and Reform, October 13, 2010, https://www.wyden.senate.gov/download/?id=6901E1E2-CA23-4835-8041-F57F79873092&download=1.
6. Pew Research Center, *NATO Publics Blame Russia for Ukraine Crisis, but Reluctant to Provide Military Aid* (Washington, DC: Pew Research Center, June 2015).
7. Alexis de Tocqueville, *Democracy in America* (New York: Walker, 1847), 457.

Chapter 1. Russia

1. Address by President of the Russian Federation, March 18, 2014, Kremlin website, http://en.kremlin.ru/events/president/news/20603.
2. Speaking of the Kazakh strongman Nursultan Nazarbayev, Putin credited him for having "created a state on territory where no state had ever existed. The Kazakhs had never had statehood. He created it. In this sense, he is a unique

person for the former Soviet space and for Kazakhstan too." Although Nazarbayev could not be faulted for feeling flattered by such attention, nor could he miss the way in which the Russian president's lauding him as George Washington of the Central Asian steppes was damning with faint, and ominous, praise.

3. Andrius Sytas, "Worried about Russia? Lithuania says 'Keep Calm and Read the War Manual,'" *Reuters,* January 15, 2015.

4. Andrew Higgins, "Increasingly Frequent Call on Baltic Sea: 'The Russian Navy is Back,'" *New York Times,* June 10, 2015.

5. Iulian Fota, comments delivered at "U.S.-Central Europe Strategy Forum," Center for European Policy Analysis, Washington, DC, October 2, 2014.

6. Marius Laurinavičius, "The Russians are Coming to Occupy the Baltic States," *Baltic Times,* April 30, 2015.

7. Speech to the Munich Security Conference, February 10, 2007.

8. Andrew Kramer, "Putin Is Said to Compare U.S. Policies to Third Reich," *New York Times,* May 10, 2007.

9. "The Rewriting of History," *The Economist,* November 8, 2007.

10. Ibid.

11. "Putin Defends Notorious Nazi-Soviet Pact," AFP, May 10, 2015.

12. Mikhail Danilovich and Robert Coalson, "Revamped Perm-36 Museum Emphasizes Gulag's 'Contribution to Victory,'" RFE/RL, July 25, 2015.

13. "Poll: Majority of Russians Say Stalin Played 'Positive Role,'" Voice of America, January 20, 2015, www.voanews.com/content/reu-poll-finds-majority-of-russians-say-stalin-played-positive-role/2606272.html.

14. Maria Lipman, Lev Gudkov, Lasha Bakradze, and Thomas de Waal, *The Stalin Puzzle: Deciphering Post-Soviet Public Opinion* (Washington, DC: Carnegie Endowment for International Peace, 2013).

15. James Kirchick, "Statue of Limitations," *The New Republic,* September 2, 2010, 8.

16. Esther B. Fein, "Soviets Confirm Nazi Pacts Dividing Europe," *New York Times,* August 19, 1989.

17. Press Statement and Responses to Questions following the Russia-European Union Summit, May 10, 2005, President of Russia website, http://archive.kremlin.ru/eng/speeches/2005/05/10/2030_type82914type82915_88025.shtml.

18. Pew Research Center, *NATO Publics Blame Russia for Ukraine Crisis, but Reluctant to Provide Military Aid* (Washington, DC: Pew Research Center, June 2015).

19. Robert Coalson, "Turning back Time: Putting Putin's Molotov-Ribbentrop Defense into Context," RFE/RL, May 15, 2015.

20. Anton Barbashin and Hannah Thoburn, "Putin's Brain," *Foreignaffairs.com,* www.foreignaffairs.com/articles/russia-fsu/2014-03-31/putins-brain, March 31, 2014.

21. Putin's remarks to Valdai International Discussion Club, September 20, 2013.

22. If Russia wants to set a moral example to the world as its preeminent defender of traditional family values, it has a novel way of going about doing it: The coun-

try boasts one of the world's highest rates for abortion, divorce (about which Putin is personally familiar, having left his wife of thirty years allegedly for a rhythmic gymnast), HIV infection, and human trafficking.

23. David Satter, *The Less You Know, The Better You Sleep* (New Haven: Yale University Press, 2016).

24. Agnieszka Łada, *All Quiet in the Baltics? Estonians, Latvians and Their Russian-Speaking Minorities: Different Assessments of Current European Issues* (Warsaw: Bertelsmann Stiftung and Institute of Public Affairs, December 2015).

25. Sanita Jemberga, Mikk Salu, Šarūnas Černiauskas, and Dovidas Pancerovas, "Kremlin's Millions," *ReBaltica.Lv*, August 27, 2105, www.rebaltica.lv/en/investi gations/money_from_russia/a/1257/kremlins_millions.html.

26. Lennart Meri, remarks at Matthae-Supper, Hamburg, February 25, 1994.

27. Natalia Gevorkyan, Natalia Timakova, and Andrei Kolesnikov, *First Person: An Astonishingly Frank Self-Portrait by Russia's President Vladimir Putin* (New York: Public Affairs, 2000).

28. See https://wikileaks.org/plusd/cables/09TALLINN371_a.html.

29. "An Open Letter to the Obama Administration from Central and Eastern Europe," *Gazeta Wyborcza*, July 19, 2009.

30. Alexandr Vondra, "Letter to Obama: Five Years Later," *CEPA Review*, July 10, 2014.

31. "Georgia: Misha Tells ASD Vershbow Georgia Is Committed to Peaceful Integration and a Long-Term Defense," November 2, 2009, U.S. State Department Cable, Wikileaks, https://www.wikileaks.org/plusd/cables/09TBILISI1965_a .html.

32. Michael R. Gordon, "U.S. Says Russia Tested Cruise Missile, Violating Treaty," *New York Times*, July 28, 2014.

33. Damian Paletta and Devlin Barrett, "DNC Hacks Prompt Allegations of Russian Involvement," *Wall Street Journal*, July 25, 2016.

34. Toomas Hendrik Ilves, "25 Years after—Still Not Whole and Free," Oslo, September 2, 2014.

35. John Mearsheimer, "Why the Ukraine Crisis Is the West's Fault: The Liberal Delusions that Provoked Putin," *Foreign Affairs* 93, no. 5 (September/October 2014): 127.

36. Thomas L. Friedman, "Why Putin Doesn't Respect Us," *New York Times*, March 4, 2014.

37. Russian National Security Strategy, available at http://en.kremlin.ru/events /president/news/51129.

38. Vladimir Putin, "Presidential Address to the Federal Assembly," Kremlin, Moscow, December 4, 2014.

39. Sam Jones, "Estonia Ready to Deal with Russia's 'Little Green Men,'" *Financial Times*, May 13, 2015.

40. Interview with Jamie Shea, Brussels, March 19, 2015.

41. Catrin Einhorn, Hannah Fairfield, and Tim Wallace, "Russia Rearms for a New Era," *New York Times*, December 24, 2015.

42. David A. Shlapak and Michael Johnson, *Reinforcing Deterrence on NATO's Eastern Flank: Wargaming the Defense of the Baltics* (Santa Monica, CA: RAND Corporation, 2016).

43. Robin Emmott and Andrius Sytas, "Nervous Baltics on War Footing as NATO Tries to Deter Russia," *Reuters,* June 13, 2016.

44. Philip M. Breedlove, "NATO's Next Act: How to Handle Russia and Other Threats," *Foreign Affairs,* July/August 2016.

45. Nikolai N. Sokov, "Why Russia Calls a Limited Nuclear Strike 'De-Escalation,'" *Bulletin of the Atomic Scientists,* March 13, 2014.

46. Interestingly, a 2015 Gallup poll found most European publics even less willing to fight for *their own* country, with only 15 percent of Dutch, 18 percent of Germans, 19 percent of Belgians, and 20 percent of Italians responding in the affirmative, a drastic contrast to the world average of 60 percent.

47. Ulrike Demmer and Ralf Neukirch, "Fear of Russia: NATO Developed Secret Contingency Plans for Baltic States," *Der Spiegel,* December 7, 2010.

48. Mikhail Gorbachev, "The Common European Home," speech to the Assembly of the Council of Europe, Strasbourg, July 6, 1989.

49. "Speech at Meeting with German Political, Parliamentary and Civic Leaders," June 5, 2008.

50. Fyodor Lukyanov, "From Vancouver to Vladivostock," *Moscow Times,* January 19, 2008.

51. Sergei Lavrov, "The Challenges of 'Hard Security' in the Euro-Atlantic Region: The Role of the OSCE in Establishing a Stable and Effective Security System," presented at the OSCE Annual Security Review Conference, Vienna, June 23, 2009.

52. Jeffrey Tayler, "The World According to Russia," *The Atlantic,* December 30, 2015.

53. NTV interview with President Vladimir Putin, November 8, 2009.

54. Thomas Graham, *Resurgent Russia and U.S. Purposes: A Century Foundation Report* (New York: Century Foundation, 2009), 24.

Chapter 2. Hungary

1. Randolph Braham, "The Assault on the Historical Memory of the Holocaust," *Hungarian Spectrum,* March 22, 2014, http://hungarianspectrum.org/2014/03/22/randolph-l-braham-the-assault-on-the-historical-memory-of-the-holocaust.

2. Although these initiatives strive for a veneer of intellectualism, they sometimes end up resembling the antics of the Keystone Cops. In a particularly outlandish episode from 2012, the speaker of parliament participated in a secretive ceremonial reburial of a long-deceased Hungarian fascist writer, whose remains were smuggled from Spain (where the Franco regime sheltered him after World War II) to Romania, where he was born on what had then been Hungarian-controlled

territory. Mindful of the Romanian government's vow to prevent the burying of a Hungarian Nazi in its soil, Hungary's state secretary for culture waited until several days after the internment to boast that the urn containing the dead writer's ashes had been furtively (and illegally) transported across the border and entombed in an undisclosed location. In 2015, the Hungarian Postal Service issued a commemorative stamp honoring a Hungarian actress known for her roles in fascist wartime propaganda.

3. Letter to Viktor Orbán from Eliot L. Engel et. al, May 21, 2014.

4. Letter to Katalin David from Viktor Orbán, April 30, 2014, http://hungarianglobe .mandiner.hu/cikk/20140430_Viktor_orban_the_german_occupation_is_a _fact.

5. See http://hungarianspectrum.org/2014/01/10/the-hungarian-holocaust-year -and-the-reaction-of-jewish-organizations.

6. Veritas Institute, "About Us," http://veritasintezet.hu/en/main-page.

7. "Nagy-Magyarország matrica díszíti Orbán autóját," February 14, 2005, Origo. hu, http://www.origo.hu/itthon/20050214nagymagyarorszag.html.

8. Paul Lendvai, *Hungary: Between Democracy and Authoritarianism* (London: Hurst & Company), 55.

9. László Csösz, personal interview, February 18, 2015.

10. Pablo Gorondi, "Thousands Gather at Inauguration of Hungary's 'House of Terror,'" Associated Press, February 24, 2002.

11. Mária Schmidt, "'Holocaustok' a huszadik században," *Magyar Hírlap*, November 13, 1999.

12. Mária Schmidt, lecture, Party of Independent Smallholder's Tibor Eckhardt Political Academy, November 11, 1999.

13. Mária Schmidt, personal interview, February 14, 2012.

14. Jerry Z. Muller, "Communism, Anti-Semitism and the Jews," *Commentary*, August 1988.

15. György Schöpflin, personal interview, May 12, 2015.

16. Mária Schmidt, "A múlt fogságában," *Valasz*, June 30, 2014.

17. Mária Schmidt, personal interview, February 14, 2012.

18. Ferenc Gyurcsány, personal interview, February 16, 2012.

19. "Elie Wiesel Renounces Hungarian Award, Claims Nazi Past 'Whitewashed,'" *Reuters*, June 19, 2012.

20. Janos Kornai, "Hungary's U-Turn," *Capitalism and Society* 10, no. 1 (March 2015).

21. Katalin Ertsey, "One Year under Pressure," *Visegradrevue.eu*, July 21, 2015.

22. Zoltan Kovacs, personal interview, February 15, 2015.

23. Orbán made several other statements that territorial revisionists must have welcomed warmly. For instance, the Hungarian "community . . . sometimes coincides with the country's borders and sometimes doesn't." Given the context, this statement could easily be read as a rumination about more than only the historical shifts of European borders but also on their enduring impermanence. In a message for "the Hungarian community of the Carpathian Basin and in

fact for the whole Hungarian community scattered throughout the world," he offered the ambiguous wish that, "since anything can happen, our time will come."

24. Viktor Orbán, speech at the 25th Bálványos Summer Free University and Student Camp, Baile Tusnad, Romania, July 26, 2014.

25. Zoltan Simon, "Hungary on Path to Shed Junk Grade and Shield Forint, Orban Says," *Bloomberg Business,* December 15, 2014.

26. Viktor Orbán, speech at the 26th Bálványos Summer Free University and Student Camp, Baile Tusnad, Romania, July 25, 2015.

27. See www.iwm.at/read-listen-watch/transit-online/really-surprised-Viktor-orbans -hungary-heading.

28. Eva Balogh, "Moderate Fidesz as Bulwark against the Hungarian Extreme Right?" *Hungarian Spectrum,* March 9, 2015, http://hungarianspectrum.org/2015 /03/19/moderate-fidesz-as-a-bulwark-against-the-hungarian-extreme-right.

29. "Kremlin Text of Russian Leader Vladimir Putin's Phone-In," BBC Monitoring, April 18, 2014.

30. Laurence Peter, "New Hungary Citizenship Law Fuels Passport Demand," BBC, January 4, 2011.

31. "Slovaks Retaliate over Hungarian Citizenship Law," BBC. March 12, 2012.

32. "Orban: Economic Sanctions Run Contrary to Hungary's Interest," *MTI Econews,* August 15, 2014.

33. Neil Buckley, "Hungary Halts Flow of Gas to Ukraine," *Financial Times,* September 26, 2014.

34. "Jobbik: NATO Membership Is Rather a Security Risk for Hungary," www.jobbik .com/jobbik_nato_membership_rather_security_risk_hungary.

35. Marton Dunai, "Anger as Hungary Far-Right Leader Demands Lists of Jews," *Reuters,* November 27, 2012.

36. Viktor Orbán, speech to the World Jewish Congress, Budapest. May 5, 2013.

37. "Jobbik's Policy Proposals Realized by Fidesz: A Summary in 10 Points," Political Capital Institute, Budapest.

38. Ivan Krastev, "The Plane Crash Conspiracy Theory that Explains Poland," *Foreignpolicy.com,* December 21, 2015.

39. Marcin Goclowski, "Poland's Walesa Calls for Early Election, Sees Democracy at Risk," *Reuters,* December 23, 2015.

40. Henry Foy and Christian Oliver, "Czech President Milos Zeman in War of Words over Russia Stance," *Financial Times,* February 9, 2015.

41. Dan Bilefsky, "Picture Him in a Mohawk: A Young Prince Seeks Votes," *New York Times,* January 24, 2013.

42. Karel Schwarzenberg, personal interview, May 6, 2015.

43. Peter Schneider, "Hitler's Shadow: On Being a Self-Conscious German," *Harper's,* September 1987.

44. Ernst Nolte, "Vergangenheit, die nicht vergehen will," *Frankfurter Allgemeine Zeitung,* June 6, 1986.

45. Gergely Szakacs, "Illegal Migration Clearly Linked with Terror Threat: Hungary PM," *Reuters*, July 25, 2015.

Chapter 3. Germany

1. Hans Leyendecker and Georg Mascolo, "BND-Mann verriet Spionageabwehr," *Süddeutsche Zeitung*, July 19, 2014.
2. "Embassy Espionage: The NSA's Secret Spy Network," *Der Spiegel*, October 27, 2013.
3. Edward Lucas, *The Snowden Operation: Inside the West's Greatest Intelligence Disaster*, Kindle Single, January 23, 2014.
4. See https://twitter.com/wikileaks/status/461862504243953664?ref_src=twsrc %5Etfw.
5. Damien Gayle, "Julian Assange 'Told Edward Snowden Not to Seek Asylum in Latin America,'" *The Guardian*, August 29, 2015.
6. Lana Lam, "Snowden Sought Booz Allen Job to Gather Evidence on NSA Surveillance," *South China Morning Post*, June 24, 2013.
7. James Risen, "Snowden Says He Took No Secret Files to Russia," *New York Times*, October 17, 2013.
8. "Snowden: I'd Go to Prison to Return to US," Associated Press, October 5, 2015.
9. Gordon Corera, "British Spies 'Moved after Snowden Files Read,'" BBC, June 14, 2015.
10. "Gemeinsames Interview der Präsidenten Gerhard Schindler und Hans-Georg Maaßen," *Focus*, April 16, 2016.
11. Mary Louise Kelly, "During Tenure in Russia, Edward Snowden Has Kept a Low Profile," National Public Radio, June 29, 2016.
12. Martin Dempsey, statement to the House Armed Services Committee, "The FY 2015 National Defense Authorization Budget Request from the Department of Defense," hearing, March 6, 2014.
13. Ewan MacAskill et al., "G-20 Summit: NSA Targeted Russian President Medvedev in London," *The Guardian*, June 17, 2013.
14. Adam Entous et al., "U.S. Scurries to Shore up Spying on Russia," *Wall Street Journal*, March 24, 2014.
15. Michael Morrell, *The Great War of Our Time* (New York: Twelve, 2015), 294.
16. "Gilles de Kerchove: The Terror from Within," *Handeslblatt Global Edition*, December 1, 2015.
17. Dirk Banse, Manuel Bewarder, and Florian Fade, "Die Amerikanische Freund," *Die Welt*, June 20, 2014.
18. Jörg Diehl, Matthias Gebauer, and Fidelius Schmid, "Scherze unter Freunden," *Der Spiegel*, September 8, 2014.
19. Jörg Diehl and Matthias Gebauer, "Der Spion, der keiner war," *Der Spiegel*, January 28, 2015.
20. Ibid.

21. Helmut Schmidt, "Überflüssige Dienste," *Die Zeit,* November 1, 2013.

22. Josef Joffe, "Of Spycraft and Statecraft," *Wall Street Journal,* July 17, 2014.

23. Gerhard Schroeder, remarks, Deutsche Bank Event Hall, Berlin, February 14, 2014.

24. "Targeting Turkey: How Germany Spies on its Friends," *Spiegel International,* August 18, 2014.

25. Michael Sauga et al., " 'Secrets Must Remain Secret': German Intelligence Coordinator on NSA and Media Leaks," *Spiegel International,* August 14, 2015.

26. Melissa Eddy, "Germany Drops Inquiry into Claims U.S. Tapped Angela Merkel's Phone," *New York Times,* June 12, 2015.

27. Pew Research Center, *Global Opposition to U.S. Surveillance and Drones, but Limited Harm to America's Im*age (Washington, DC: Pew Research Center, July 14, 2014); Pew Research Center, *Global Publics Back U.S. on Fighting ISIS, but Are Critical of Post-9/11 Torture* (Washington, DC: Pew Research Center, June 23, 2015).

28. "America's Willing Helper: Intelligence Scandal Puts Merkel in Tight Place," *Der Spiegel,* May 4, 2015.

29. Philip Agee was a former CIA officer whose 1975 book, *Inside the Company: CIA Diary,* exposed the agency's covert operations, as well as the names and addresses of hundreds of undercover agents, at least one of whose murder by left-wing terrorists was attributable to Agee's disclosures.

30. Friedbert Plüger, "Germany—Facing its History, Facing its Future: An Event Honoring Richard von Weizsäcker," presented at German Marshall Fund, May 5, 2015.

31. Andrei S. Markovits and Philip S. Gorski, *The German Left: Red, Green and Beyond* (New York: Oxford University Press, 1993).

32. Matthew Aid, "The CIA in Germany: A Secret History," *Daily Beast,* July 10, 2014.

33. Eli Lake, "One Big Reason the CIA Spied on Germany: Worries about Russian Moles in Berlin," *Daily Beast,* July 12, 2014.

34. Elias Groll, "Laura Poitras: American Spies Have Me 'Lit Up like a Christmas Tree," *foreignpolicy.com,* October 30, 2014, http://foreignpolicy.com/2014/10/30/laura-poitras-american-spies-have-me-lit-up-like-a-christmas-tree.

35. Andrew E. Kramer, "Russia Gas Pipeline Heightens East Europe's Fears," *New York Times,* October 12, 2009.

36. Erik Kirschbaum, "Putin's Apologist? Germany's Schroeder Says They're Just Friends," *Reuters,* March 27, 2014.

37. Foo Yun Chee and Alastair MacDonald, "EU Charges Russia's Gazprom, Alleging Price Gouging," *Reuters,* April 22, 2015.

38. Elizabeth Schumacher, "US Threatened Germany over Possible Snowden Asylum, Greenwald Says," *DeutscheWelle,* March 21, 2015.

39. Noah Barkin, "Russia Serious about Solution in Syria, German Minister Says," *Reuters,* November 22, 2015.

40. "German Minister Warns NATO against 'Warmongering,'" BBC, June 18, 2016.

41. Jeffrey Herf, *War by Other Means: Soviet Power, West German Resistance, and the Battle of the Euromissiles* (New York: Free Press, 1991).

42. Ibid., 271.

43. Timothy Garton Ash, "Europa Über Alles," *Spectator* (London), May 11, 1984.

44. Michael Getler, "Seeking a Balance of Power in Europe; West Germans Press Americans to Protect European Interests in Strategic Arms Talks," *Washington Post*, September 16, 1978.

45. Herf, *War by Other Means*, 118.

46. "Nichts geändert," *Der Spiegel*, no. 1, 1983.

47. Herf, *War by Other Means*, 54

48. John Vinocur, "New German Worry: Nationalism on the Left," *New York Times*, November 12, 1981.

49. Markovits and Gorski, *The German Left*, 170.

50. Ibid., 171.

51. Noel D. Cary, "Reassessing Germany's *Ostpolitik*. Part I: From Détente to Re-freeze," *Central European History* 33, no. 2 (2000): 240.

52. Herf, *War by Other Means*, 41. From his perch at the Institute for Peace Research and Security Studies, one of innumerable such bodies created during Brandt's administration, Bahr vocally opposed reunified Germany's remaining within NATO. Twenty-five years after the collapse of the Soviet Union, the dream of Brandt's "European peace order" devoid of "confrontation" between Russia and the West lives on in calls for "mutual security."

53. Agnes Heller and Ferenc Feher, "Eastern Europe under the Shadow of a New Rapallo," *New German Critique* 37 (1986).

54. John Vinocur, "Germany's Season of Discontent," *New York Times*, August 8, 1982.

55. In a speech before a joint session of the Polish parliament and senate in 2000, none other than Gerhard Schröder acknowledged that "a number of German politicians, including some Social Democrats, prioritized stability at the time of the rise of the Solidarity movement" and thus "failed to do justice to the historic significance of the Polish fight for liberty."

56. Herf, *War by Other Means*, 230.

57. Gordon A. Craig, "Did *Ostpolitik* Work?" *Foreign Affairs*, January/February 1994.

58. Herf, *War by Other Means*, 221.

59. Richard Herzinger, comments at Heinrich Böll Stiftung symposium, "Exposing Russian Disinformation in the 21st Century," Berlin, June 25, 2015.

60. Markovits and Gorski, *The German Left*, 136.

61. "'A Serious Mistake of Historic Dimensions': Libya Crisis Leaves Berlin Isolated," *Spiegel International*, March 28, 2011.

62. Anton Troianovski, "Ukraine Crisis Sparks Debate in Germany over Russia Actions," *Wall Street Journal*, April 15, 2014.

63. In 2013, three German schools won the Aachen Peace Prize for their "Schools without Bundeswehr" campaign, an initiative banning visits by members of the

German military. These appearances are not recruitment drives but rather informational presentations in which members of the armed forces educate students about the Bundeswehr's role in a democratic society, relationship with alliance partners, and work upholding international security and assisting humanitarian missions abroad.

64. Pew Research Center, *Germany and the United States: Reliable Allies* (Washington, DC: Pew Research Center, May 2015).

65. Kirschbaum, "Putin's Apologist?"

66. Frank Walter-Steinmeier, "Brüche und Brücken: Deutsche Aussenpolitik in bewegten Zeiten," GIGA Distinguished Speaker Lecturer Series, Leibniz Institute for Global and Regional Studies, Hamburger Rathaus, June 27, 2016.

67. Interview on German TV Channel ARD, November 17, 2014, http://en.kremlin.ru/events/president/news/47029.

68. Timothy Snyder, "Putin's Project," *Frankfurther Allgemeine Zeitung,* April 16, 2014.

69. "Wieder Krieg in Europa? Nicht in unserem Namen!" *Die Zeit,* December 5, 2014.

70. "Steinmeier mahnt Russland und USA in Syrien-Konflikt," *DeutscheWelle,* October 14, 2015.

71. Marieluise Beck, comments at Heinrich Böll Stiftung symposium, "Exposing Russian Disinformation in the 21st Century," Berlin, June 25, 2015.

72. Interview with Martin Erdmann, *Deutsche Presse-Agentur,* July 31, 2015.

73. "Breedlove's Bellicosity: Berlin Alarmed by Aggressive NATO Stance on Ukraine," *Der Spiegel,* March 6, 2015.

74. "Den Wählen ist ein Bär aufgebunden worden, SPD-Generalsekretärin Yasmin Fahimi über die BND-NSA Affäre, Streit in der Koalition—und Tippfehler bei Twitter," *Der Tagesspiegel,* May 17, 2015.

75. Noah Barkin, "Thousands in Germany Protest against Europe-U.S. Free Trade Deal," *Reuters,* April 18, 2015.

76. Henry Kissinger, *A World Restored: Metternich, Castlereagh, and the Problems of Peace, 1812–1822* (Boston: Houghton Mifflin, 1957), 29.

Chapter 4. The European Union

1. *OECD Migration Outlook* (Paris: OECD, 2014).

2. Heather Saul, "Refugee Crisis: Sweden's Deputy Prime Minister Asa Romson Cries as She Announces Asylum Policy U-Turn," *The Independent,* November 26, 2015.

3. Dan Hyde, "IKEA Running out of Beds due to Migrant Crisis," *Daily Telegraph,* November 6, 2015.

4. Henriette Jacobson, "Sweden Considers Cutting Development Aid Budget by 60% due to Refugee Crisis," *Euractiv.com,* November 5, 2015.

5. "Oh Boy," *The Economist,* January 16, 2016.

6. Barbara D. Miller, "Female-Selective Abortion in Asia: Patterns, Policies, and Debates," *American Anthropologist* 103, no. 4 (December 2001): 1083–1095.

7. Pew Research Center, *The World's Muslims: Religion, Politics and Society* (Washington, DC: Pew Research Center. April 30, 2013).

8. See www.internationalwomenstravelcenter.com/content/2015-list-safest-countries-world-women-travelers.

9. Kamel Daoud, "The Sexual Misery of the Arab World," *New York Times*, February 12, 2016.

10. Jochen Bittner, "Can Germany Be Honest About Its Refugee Problems?" *New York Times*, January 15, 2016.

11. Ibid.

12. Elizabeth Schumacher, "Pubs and Clubs in German Town of Freiburg Forbid Refugees," *Deutsche Welle*, January 23, 2016.

13. Basil El-Dabh, "99.3% of Egyptian Women Experience Sexual Harassment: Report," *Daily News Egypt*, April 28, 2013.

14. Will Worley, "Six out of 10 Migrants to Europe Come for 'Economic Reasons' and Are Not Refugees, EU Vice President Frans Timmermans Says," *The Independent*, January 27, 2016.

15. Anthony Failoa and Souad Mekhennet, "Tracing the Path of Four Terrorists Sent to Europe by the Islamic State," *Washington Post*, April 22, 2016.

16. Christopher Caldwell, *Reflections on the Revolution in Europe: Immigration, Islam and the West* (New York: Doubleday, 2009), 35.

17. Martin Feldstein, "Immigration Is No Way to Fund an Ageing Population," *Financial Times*, December 13, 2006.

18. OECD, "Employment and Unemployment Rates by Gender and Place of Birth," OECD International Migration Statistics (database), 2016, http://dx.doi.org/10.1787/data-00722-en (accessed August 29, 2016).

19. Ibid.

20. Alberto Bisin, Eleonara Patacchini, Thierry Verdier, and Yves Zenou, "Are Muslim Immigrants Different in Terms of Cultural Integration?" Discussion Paper no. 3006, Institute for the Study of Labor, August 2007.

21. See http://jyllands-posten.dk/indland/ECE8070155/Muslimer-fastholder-modstand-mod-Muhammed-tegningerne.

22. Pew Global Attitudes Project, *The Great Divide: How Westerners and Muslims View Each Other* (Washington, DC: Pew Global Attitudes Project, June 22, 2006).

23. ComRes poll for BBC Radio 4 Today, February 25, 2015.

24. Trevor Phillips, "What Do British Muslims Really Think?" *Times of London*, April 10, 2016.

25. Niall Ferguson, "The Degeneration of Europe," *Prospect*, November 2015. To be sure, these figures do not include the 13 million ethnic Germans expelled from Central and Eastern Europe after World War II, the largest population transfer in human history, nor the 16 million East Germans who became citizens of the reunited Federal Republic of Germany overnight on October 3, 1990. Because all of these people were ethnic Germans (and, in the latter case, already living on German territory and employed in preexisting German workplaces, thus not

imposing the sort of economic and infrastructural dislocations that the postwar expellees did), the circumstances of their integration into Germany are not germane to analysis of the current immigration from the nondeveloped, Islamic world.

26. Giulio Meotti, "Manent fotografa il cristianesimo in Europa," *Il Foglio*, July 28, 2016.

27. Markus Feldenkirchen, "A Brutal New Germany: What's Happening to My Country?" *Der Spiegel*, November 12, 2015.

28. Heinrich August Winkler, "Germany's Moral Hubris," *Frankfurter Allgemeine Zeitung*, September 30, 2015.

29. Andrew Higgins, "German Village of 102 Braces for 750 Asylum Seekers," *New York Times*, October 31, 2015.

30. Benjamin R. Teitelbaum, "Sweden's Fraying Tolerance," *New York Times*, September 16, 2014.

31. Pew Research Center, *Number of Refugees to Europe Surges to Record 1.3 Million in 2015* (Washington, DC: Pew Research Center, August 2016).

32. Kate Connolly, " 'Like a Poison: How Anti-Immigrant PEGIDA Is Dividing Dresden,' " *The Guardian*, October 27, 2015.

33. "Deutsche trauen Politik keine Lösung der Flüchtlingskrise zu," *Frankfurter Allgemeine Zeitung*, October 21, 2015.

34. Adam Withnall, "Cologne Police Ordered to Remove Word 'Rape' from Reports into New Year's Eve Sexual Assaults Amid Cover-up Claims," *Independent*, April 7, 2016.

35. "Chaos and Violence: How New Year's Eve in Cologne Has Changed Germany," *Der Spiegel*, January 8, 2016.

36. Justin Huggler, " 'Cover-up' over Cologne Sex Assaults Blamed on Migration Sensitivities," *Daily Telegraph*, January 6, 2016.

37. Georg Mascolo and Britta von der Heide, "1,200 Frauen wurden Opfer von Silvester-Gewalt," *Süddeutsche Zeitung*, July 10, 2016.

38. Riham Alkousaa et al., "Two Weeks in September: The Makings of Merkel's Decision to Accept Refugees," *Spiegel International*, August 24, 2016.

39. James Traub, "The Death of the Most Generous Nation on Earth," *Foreignpolicy.com*, February 10, 2016, http://foreignpolicy.com/2016/02/10/the-death-of-the-most-generous-nation-on-earth-sweden-syria-refugee-europe.

40. Email to author, June 16, 2016.

41. Paulina Neuding, "Europe's Refugee Culture Clash," *Project Syndicate*, June 16, 2016.

42. Anthony Faiola, "Germany Springs to Action over Hate Speech against Migrants," *Washington Post*, January 6, 2016.

43. Pew Research Center, *Faith in European Project Reviving* (Washington, DC: Pew Research Center, June, 2015).

44. James Kirchick, "In Defense of Denmark," *Foreignpolicy.com*, May 20, 2016, http://foreignpolicy.com/2016/05/20/in-defense-of-denmark-immigration-europe-refugee-crisis.

45. Frank Hornig and Barbara Schmid, "An Interview with Cologne's Mayor: 'I Have Been Subjected to a Ton of Ridicule and Criticism,'" *Spiegel International,* January 8, 2016.

46. Claudia Kade, "'Mob ruft zur Jagd auf nicht weiße Menschen auf,'" *Die Welt,* January 8, 2016.

47. Matthew Holehouse, "EU Leaders: 'No Link' between Cologne Sex Attacks and Migrant Crisis," *Daily Telegraph,* January 29, 2016.

48. Dror Mishani and Aurelia Smotriez, "What Sort of Frenchmen Are They?" *Haaretz,* November 17, 2005.

49. Vince Chadwick, "POLITICO Caucus: West Needs to Make up with Putin," *Politico Europe,* December 23, 2015.

50. Justin Huggler, "German Teenager 'Made up' Migrant Rape Claim," *Daily Telegraph,* January 31, 2016.

51. "Russland spioniert mehr in Europa," *Die Zeit,* February 25, 2015.

52. Ruth Bender, "Merkel's Bavarian Critic Meets Putin to Discuss Migrants, Sanctions," *Wall Street Journal,* February 3, 2016.

53. Andrea Franc, "Free Trade in an Era of Mass Migration," *Eurozine,* October 14, 2015, http://www.eurozine.com/articles/2015–10–14-franc-en.html.

54. Per Hinrichs, "So sieht das berühmte Flüchtlingsmädchen die Welt," *Die Welt Am Sonntag,* July 26, 2015.

Chapter 5. France without Jews

1. Hannah Furness, "BBC Presenter Apologizes tor Telling Paris Mourner: 'Palestinians Suffer Hugely at Jewish Hands as Well,'" *Daily Telegraph,* January 12, 2015.

2. Paulina Neuding, "Sweden's 'Damn Jew' Problem," *Tablet,* April 5, 2012.

3. Thomas Fuller, "European Poll Calls Israel a Threat to World Peace," *New York Times,* November 1, 2003.

4. Benjamin Weinthal, "German Judge: Torching of Synagogue Not Motivated by Anti-Semitism," *Jerusalem Post,* February 7, 2015.

5. Thomas de Maizière, "What Will Never Change," *Jüdische Allgemeine,* November 5, 2015.

6. Heather Stewart and Ben Quinn, "Labor Suspends Three Councilors over Alleged Anti-Semitic Remarks," *The Guardian,* May 2, 2016.

7. Ashley Cowburn, "Labor Suspends Two Councilors over Israel Facebook Posts in Latest Anti-Semitism Row," *The Independent,* May 2, 2016.

8. Andrew Gilligan et al., "Pressure Grows on Jeremy Corbyn as Dossier of Anti-Semitism in Labour Party Is Revealed," *Daily Telegraph,* May 1, 2016. Kate McCann, "Jeremy Corbyn Refuses to Denounce Terrorist 'Friends' Hamas and Hizbollah," *Daily Telegraph,* May 2, 2016.

9. Adam Payne, "Jeremy Corbyn Was Paid by an Iranian State TV Station that Was Complicit in the Forced Confession of a Tortured Journalist," *Business Insider,*

July 2, 2016, www.businessinsider.com/jeremy-corbyn-paid-iran-press-tv-tortured-journalist-2016–6?r=UK&IR=T.

10. "Labor's Corbyn: Jews no More Responsible for Israel than Muslims Are for Islamic Organizations," *Haaretz,* June 30, 2016.

11. Mark Gardner, "Corbyn and the Rent-a-Mob: How to Wreck an Anti-Racism Event," *Jewish News,* July 1, 2016, http://blogs.timesofisrael.com/corbyn-and-rent-a-mob-how-to-wreck-an-anti-racism-event.

12. "Statement on Today's Launch of the Chakrabarti Report," June 30, 2016, www.ruthsmeeth.org.uk/statement_on_the_launch_of_the_chakrabarti_report.

13. Christopher Hope and Laura Hughes, "Shami Chakrabarti Handed Peerage Weeks after Suppressing Jeremy Corbyn Interview from 'Whitewash' Anti-Semitism Report," *Daily Telegraph,* August 5, 2016.

14. "French Pro-Palestinian Jewish Activist: Wearing Kippa Signals Allegiance to Israeli Politics," Jewish Telegraph Agency, January 22, 2016.

15. Marie Brenner, "The Troubling Question in the French Jewish Community: Is It Time to Leave?" *Vanity Fair,* August 2015.

16. Mark Lilla, "France on Fire," *New York Review of Books,* March 5, 2015.

17. Pauline Froissart and Benoît Fauchet, "Rising Anti-Semitism Forces Jews out of Paris Suburbs," Agence France-Presse, May 31, 2016.

18. *Enquête auprès des juifs de France* (Paris: Jean Jaurès Foundation, September, 2015).

19. "Sweden's Immigrant Influx Unleashes a Backlash," *All Things Considered,* NPR, February 5, 2015.

20. "Natan Sharansky: There is No Future for Jews in France," Jewish Telegraphic Agency, June 28, 2016.

21. Anne Hidalgo, *Amanpour,* CNN, January 21, 2015.

22. David Ignatius, "Wake up to the Problem: Separate and Unequal in France," *International Herald Tribune,* April 27, 2002.

23. Claude Patrice, "Malek Boutih: Le Desillusionniste," *Le Monde,* June 13, 2002.

24. Emmanuel Berretta, "Malek Boutih: 'Des élus locaux corrompus ont pactisé avec les gangsters et les islamo-nazis," *Le Point,* January 13, 2015.

25. Henrik Hojer, "Därför ökar de kriminella gängens makt," *Forskning & Framsteg,* May 11, 2015.

26. Leo Cendrowicz, "Paris Attacks: Visiting Molenbeek, the Police No-Go Zone that Was Home to Two of the Gunmen," *The Independent,* November 15, 2015.

27. Andrew Higgins, "Terrorism Response Puts Belgium in a Harsh Light," *New York Times,* November 24, 2015.

28. Benjamin Weinthal, "German Jewish Leaders: We Are No Longer Safe Here," *Jerusalem Post,* January 19, 2016.

29. Steven Erlanger, "Gunman Believed to Be behind 2 Copenhagen Attacks Is Fatally Shot, Police Say," *New York Times,* February 14, 2015.

30. Andrew Higgins and Melissa Eddy, "Anger of Suspect in Danish Killings Is Seen as Only Loosely Tied to Islam," *New York Times,* February 16, 2015.

31. Latest figures from 2013, compiled by the Organization for Security and Cooperation in Europe, Office of Democratic Institutions and Human Rights, http://hatecrime.osce.org/france.

32. Michael Walzer, "Islamism and the Left," *Dissent*, Winter 2015.

33. Maajid Nawaz, *Radical: My Journey out of Islamic Extremism* (London: WH Allen, 2012), 210.

34. David Horovitz, "Does a Gritty Ex-Cop's Move to Israel Symbolize the End for France's Jews?" *Times of Israel*, October 28, 2015.

35. Brenner, "The Troubling Question in the French Jewish Community."

36. Natasha Lehrer, "The Threat to France's Jews," *The Guardian*, January 15, 2015.

37. Ben Judah, "Islam and the French Republic: From the Banlieues to Le Pen Land," *Standpoint*, July 8, 2016.

38. "EXCLUSIF: Ces collégiens qui placent la religion avant l'école: l'étude qui accuse," *Le Nouvel Observateur*, February 3, 2016.

39. Michel Gurfunkiel, "No Surrender this Time, " *American Interest Online*, December 5, 2015.

40. Olivier Roy, "What Is the Driving Force behind Jihadist Terrorism? A Scientific Perspective on the Causes/Circumstances of Joining the Scene," paper presented at "International Terrorism: How Can Prevention and Repression Keep Pace?" German Federal Criminal Police Office. Mainz, Germany, November 18–19, 2015.

41. Jason Burke and Julian Borger, "French Intelligence under Scrutiny in Wake of Paris Attacks," *The Guardian*, November 14, 2015.

42. *Islamophobia: A Challenge for Us All* (London: Runnymede Trust, Commission on British Muslims and Islamophobia, 1997).

43. Ziauddin Sardar, "The Next Holocaust," *New Statesman*, December 5, 2005.

44. *France 2013: The New Divisions* (Paris: IPSOS Survey for Le Monde, la Fondation Jean Jaurès and Cevipof, January 2013).

45. Suzanne Daley and Maïa de la Baume, "French Far Right Gets Helping Hand with Russian Loan," *New York Times*, December 1, 2014.

46. Ivo Oliveira, "National Front Seeks Russian Cash for Election Fight," *Politico Europe*, February 19, 2016.

47. Dominique Reynié, *L'Antisémitisme dans l'opinion publique française* (Paris: Fondation pour l'innovation politique, November 2014).

48. Judah, "Islam and the French Republic."

49. Paul Johnson, "The Anti-Semitic Disease," *Commentary*, June 2005.

Chapter 6. Brexit

1. Emily Cadman, "Carney Prepares for 'Economic Post-Traumatic Stress,'" *Financial Times*, June 30, 2016.

2. "'Brexit' Will Cost 6% of GDP," *Economist Intelligence Unit*, June 22, 2016.

3. Nazia Parveen and Harriet Sherwood, "Police Log Fivefold Rise in Race-Hate Complaints since Brexit Result," *The Guardian,* June 30, 2016.

4. Matthew Holehouse, "David Cameron 'Deeply Concerned' about Nigel Farage's Call to Scrap Race Relations Laws," *Daily Telegraph,* March 12, 2015.

5. Matthew Holehouse, "Nigel Farage Blames Immigration after Missing UKIP Reception," *Daily Telegraph,* December 7, 2014.

6. Ros Taylor, "Cameron Refuses to Apologize to UKIP," *The Guardian,* April 4, 2006.

7. Leveson Inquiry, testimony of Alastair Campbell, November 30, 2011.

8. Dennis Macshane, *Brexit: How Britain Will Leave Europe* (London: I. B. Tauris, 2015), 205.

9. "Boris Johnson MP," *Desert Island Discs,* BBC, November 4, 2005.

10. James Kirchick, "They Backed Boris," *Weekly Standard,* May 19, 2008.

11. Boris Johnson, "I Cannot Stress too Much that Britain Is Part of Europe—and Always Will Be," *Daily Telegraph,* June 26, 2016.

12. Boris Johnson, "UK and America Can Be Better Friends than Ever Mr. Obama . . . if We LEAVE the EU," *The Sun,* April 22, 2016.

13. Tim Ross, "Boris Johnson: The EU Wants a Superstate, Just as Hitler Did," *Sunday Telegraph,* May 15, 2016.

14. Nigel Farage, remarks at "Patriotic Voices from Europe" event, Heritage Foundation, Washington, DC, July 15, 2015.

15. *Eurobarometer Report #55* (Brussels: European Commission, 2011), 48, table 3.3b.

16. Kate McCann, "Nigel Farage: 350 Million Pledge to Fund the NHS Was a 'Mistake,'" *Daily Telegraph,* June 24, 2016.

17. Alastair Campbell, "Alastair Campbell Talks to Nigel Farage," *British GQ,* May 1, 2014.

18. Louisa Loveluck, "US Warships Accompany BRITISH-FLAGGED VESSELS through Strait of Hormuz," *Daily Telegraph,* May 4, 2015.

19. Radoslaw Sikorski, "The Blenheim Palace Speech (on the UK and Europe)," September 21, 2012.

20. Review of the Balance of Competences, Foreign & Commonwealth Office, Government of the United Kingdom, December 18, 2014, https://www.gov.uk /guidance/review-of-the-balance-of-competences.

21. Dominic Webb, Matthew Keep, and Marcus Wilton, "In Brief: UK-EU Economic Relations," House of Commons Library Briefing Paper, no. 06091. June 3, 2015.

22. Michael Rake, "Europe Boosts Britain's Strength on the World Stage," *Financial Times,* October 22, 2015.

23. Mark Carney, "The European Union, Monetary and Financial Stability, and the Bank of England," Cairncross Lecture, St. Peter's College, Oxford, October 21, 2015.

24. "How Much Legislation Comes from Europe?" House of Commons Library, Research Paper 10/62, October 13, 2010.

25. *EU Referendum 'How Did You Vote' Poll,* Lord Ashcroft Polls, 2016, http://lord ashcroftpolls.com/wp-content/uploads/2016/06/How-the-UK-voted-Full-tables -1.pdf.

26. *They're Thinking What We're Thinking: Understanding the UKIP Temptation,* Lord Ashcroft Polls, December 2012, http://lordashcroftpolls.com/wp-content/uploads/2012/12/THEYRE-THINKING-WHAT-WERE-THINKING.pdf.

27. Charles Grant, "Why Britain Voted to Leave (if it does . . .)," *Center for European Reform Bulletin,* June/July 2016.

28. Christian Dustmann and Tommasso Frattini, "The Fiscal Effects of Immigration to the UK," *Economic Journal* 124, no. 580 (November 4, 2014): F593–F643.

29. Nicholas Watt and Patrick Wintour, "How Immigration Came to Haunt Labor: The Inside Story," *The Guardian,* March 24, 2015.

30. "Gordon Brown 'Bigoted Woman' Comment Caught on Tape," BBC News, April 28, 2010.

31. James Bloodworth, "Brexit: New Labour Should Have Listened to 'Racist' Immigration Concerns Years Ago," *IBTimes,* June 24, 2016, www.ibtimes.co.uk/brexit-new-labour-should-have-listened-racist-immigration-concerns-years-ago-1567237.

32. "Jack Straw Regrets Opening Door to Eastern Europe Migrants," BBC, November 13, 2013.

33. Robert Ford and Matthew Goodwin, "UKIP Has Divided the Left, Not the Right, and Cut Labour off from Its 'Old' Support," *The Guardian,* May 16, 2014.

34. John Cruddas et al., *Labor's Future: Why Labor Lost in 2015 and How It Can Win Again* (London: One Nation Register, 2016).

35. Jon Stone, "Jeremy Corbyn Says There Could Be Benefits to Opening Diplomatic Back-Channels with ISIS," *The Independent,* January 17, 2016.

36. Hélène Mullholland and Allegra Stratton, "John McDonnell Jokes that He Would Have Liked to Have Assassinated Margaret Thatcher," *The Guardian,* June 7, 2010.

37. Kate McCann, "John McDonnell Signed Letter Calling for MI5 and Armed Police to Be Disbanded," *Daily Telegraph,* November 19, 2015.

38. Abdulaziz Almashi et al., "Stop the War Faces a Coalition of Critics," *The Guardian,* December 9, 2015. "Stand against the interference, Aggression of the US and Its Allies on the Korean Peninsula," motion passed at 2015 Stop the War Coalition annual general meeting, September 19, 2015, http://stopwar.org.uk/index.php/resources/reports/438-stop-the-war-coalition-agm-2015-resolutions.

39. Tony Blair, Council on Foreign Relations, December 4, 2015.

40. See https://twitter.com/jeremycorbyn/status/309065744954580992?lang=en.

41. Jon Stone, "Jeremy Corbyn 'Still Prepared to Call for Tony Blair War Crimes Investigation,'" *The Independent,* May 23, 2016.

42. Mike Harris, "This Is Either the Beginning of Labour or Its End," *Little Atoms,* August 18, 2015.

43. Asa Bennett, "Immigration Is Labor's Next Big Row Waiting to Happen," *Daily Telegraph,* February 4, 2016.

44. YouGov/Times of London poll, https://d25d2506sfb94s.cloudfront.net/cumulus_uploads/document/j84ytv1far/TimesResults_160524_EURef&Parties_W.pdf.

45. *EU Referendum 'How Did You Vote' Poll.*

46. Ian Johnston, "Brexit: Jeremy Corbyn May Have Voted to Leave, Claims Chris Bryant," *The Independent,* June 27, 2016.

47. Laura Kuensberg, "Corbyn Office 'Sabotaged' EU Remain Campaign—Sources," BBC, June 26, 2016.

48. Peter Dominiczak et al., "Jeremy Corbyn Branded 'Disloyal' after Refusing to Sing National Anthem on Day of Shambles for Labor Leader," *Daily Telegraph,* September 15, 2015.

49. Ben Riley-Smith, "Momentum Founder Admits Being 'Disturbed' by Members' Behavior and Warns against 'Personal Attacks,'" *Daily Telegraph,* December 17, 2015.

50. "Labor Leadership: Female MPs Urge Corbyn to Tackle Abuse," BBC, July 22, 2016.

51. Stefan Wagstyl, "Support for Mainstream German Parties Dips below 50%," *Financial Times,* May 31, 2016.

52. Emily Hruban, "Austrian Elections: When the Peoples' Parties Lose the People," *Bertelsmann Foundation Brief,* May 17, 2016, www.bfna.org/publication/bbrief -austrian-elections-when-the-peoples-parties-lose-the-people.

53. Josef Weidenholzer, "Die SPÖ, das Politbüro," *Die Zeit,* May 5, 2016.

54. Hasnain Kazim, "Austria a Step Ahead in Europe's Race to the Right," *Der Spiegel,* May 18, 2016.

55. Steve Erlanger, "Political Winner in Britain: Far Right, at Labor's Expense," *New York Times,* June 30, 2016.

56. Henri Aster, "French National Front: Far Right or Hard Left?" BBC, May 16, 2014.

57. Tom Whitehead, "Britain Has Become 'Semi-Pacifist' under Cameron, Says Re-tired General as He Warns of War with Russia," *Daily Telegraph,* May 18, 2016.

58. Richard Norton-Taylor, "UK Defence Policy Heading for Chaos," *The Guardian,* Defence and Security blog, March 26, 2015, www.theguardian.com/news/defence -and-security-blog/2015/mar/26/uk-defence-policy-heading-for-chaos.

59. Nigel Essenhigh, "Our Defence Cuts Leave Us Looking Feeble in the Eyes of the World," *Sunday Telegraph,* June 13, 2015.

60. Fraser Nelson, "George Osborne's Epic Kowtow to China," *The Spectator,* September 26, 2015.

61. Geoff Dyer and George Parker, "US Attacks UK's 'Constant Accommodation' with China," *Financial Times,* March 12, 2015.

62. Fintan O'Toole, "The English Have Placed a Bomb under the Irish Peace Process," *The Guardian,* June 24, 2016.

Chapter 7. Greece

Epigraph 1: Takis S. Pappas, *Populism and Crisis Politics in Greece* (New York: Palgrave, 2014).

Epigraph 2: Athens-Macedonian News Agency, September 19, 2010.

1. Nikos Kotzias, *Greece: Debt Colony; European Empire and German Primacy* (Athens: Patakis, 2013).

2. Paul Tugwell and Eleni Chrepa, "Tspiras Forges Anti-Austerity Coalition in Challenge to EU," *Kathimerini,* January 26, 2015.

3. Ersi Athanassiou, "Fiscal Policy and the Recession: The Case of Greece," *Intereconomics,* November/December 2009.

4. IMF Factsheet, September 30, 2014, https://www.imf.org/external/np/exr/facts/labor.htm.

5. OECD, *Greece at a Glance: Policies for a Sustainable Recovery* (Paris: OECD, 2010).

6. Martin Ehl, "Not Exactly Friends of Greece," *Transitions Online* (June 30, 2015), http://www.tol.org/client/article/24856-not-exactly-friends-of-greece.html.

7. "European Luminaries Reflect on Euro: 'Seventeen Countries Were Far too Many,'" *Spiegel International,* September 11, 2012.

8. Pantelis Sklias, personal interview, Washington, DC, July 17, 2015.

9. *TIME,* July 20, 2015.

10. Costas Azariadis, Yannis M. Ioannides, and Christopher A. Pissarides, "Development Is the Only Solution: Seventeen Proposals for a New Development Strategy," http://greekeconomistsforreform.com/wp-content/uploads/A-I-P-DEVELOPMENTw.-abs-10-06-10.pdf.

11. Fouad Ajami, "Beware of Greeks Bearing Debt," *Newsweek,* December 12, 2011.

12. Stathis N. Kalvyas, "Polarization in Greek Politics: PASOK's First Four Years, 1981–1985," *Journal of the Hellenic Diaspora* 23, no. 1.

13. Ibid.

14. Hubert Spiegel, "Kompromiss? Das ist hier unbekannt," *Frankfurter Allgemeine Zeitung,* July 10, 2015.

15. Takis S. Pappas, *Populism and Crisis Politics in Greece* (New York: Palgrave, 2014).

16. A. Bergh and C. Bjørnskov, "Historical Trust Levels Predict the Current Size of the Welfare State," *Kyklos* 64 (2011): 1–19.

17. Holman W. Jenkins, "Extend and Pretend for Migrants," *Wall Street Journal,* September 16, 2015.

18. Nikolaos T. Artavanis, Adair Morse, and Margarita Tsoutsoura, "Tax Evasion across Industries: Soft Credit Evidence from Greece," *Chicago Booth Research Paper* no. 12–25, Farma-Miller Working Paper, March 21, 2015.

19. Mancur Olson, *The Rise and Decline of Nations* (New Haven: Yale University Press, 1982), 69.

20. Kalvyas, "Polarization in Greek Politics."

21. Robert McDonald, "Greece Struggles to Rescue Economy," *Toronto Star,* August 21, 1991.

22. Anders Aslund, "Revisiting the Latvian and Greek Financial Crises: The Benefits of Front-Loading Fiscal Adjustments," *CASE Network Studies & Analyses,* no. 477, 2015.

23. Celestine Bohlen, "France's Largest Labor Union May Have Overplayed Its Hand," *New York Times,* June 13, 2016.

24. Virginia Harrison, "Debt Restructuring: What Can Greece Hope For?" CNN Money, July 15, 2015, http://money.cnn.com/2015/07/15/news/economy/greece -debt-restructure/index.html?category=home-international.

25. Task Force for Greece, *1st Quarterly Report* (Brussels: European Commission, November 17, 2011).

26. International Monetary Fund, *Greece: Ex Post Evaluation of Exceptional Access under the 2010 Stand-By Arrangement* (Washington, DC: International Monetary Fund, 2013).

27. Pappas, *Populism and Crisis Politics in Greece.*

28. Takis Michas, "Athens Rekindles Its Russian Romance," *Wall Street Journal,* January 29, 2015.

29. Andy Dabilis, "Tsipras Says Samaras Should Back Cyprus," *Greek Reporter,* March 21, 2013, http://greece.greekreporter.com/2013/03/21/tsipras-says-samaras -should-back-cyprus.

30. Noah Barkin and Andreas Rinke, "Germans in Shock as New Greek Leader Starts with a Bang," *Reuters,* January 28, 2015.

31. Dina Kyriakidou, "Special Report: The Man Who Cost Greece Billions," *Reuters,* July 20, 2015.

32. Interview, Athens, June 21, 2015.

33. Nektaria Stamouli and Stelios Bouras, "Greeks Investigate Statistics Chief over Deficit Figure," *Wall Street Journal,* March 22, 2015.

34. Kerin Hope, "Greek Statistician Andreas Georgiou Hits Back at Criminal Charges," *Financial Times,* August 14, 2016.

35. Yanis Varoufakis, "How I Became an Erratic Marxist," *The Guardian,* February 18, 2015.

36. Bruno Waterfield, "Greece's Defence Minister Threatens to Send Migrants including Jihadists to Western Europe," *Daily Telegraph,* March 9, 2015.

37. "Education Minister to Ditch Excellence as Main Principle," *Kathimerini,* February 10, 2015.

38. "Greek PM Tsipras Calls Referendum on Bailout on July 5," *Reuters,* June 16, 2015.

39. John Sfankianakis, "The Costs of Protecting Greece's Public Sector," *New York Times,* October 10, 2012.

40. Aslund, "Revisiting the Latvian and Greek Financial Crises."

41. Ibid.

42. Ilmārs Rimšēvičs, "Fostering Growth in the Current Economic Environment," Eurofi High Level Seminar, Riga, April 22, 2015.

43. Paul Krugman, "Latvia Is the New Argentina (Slightly Wonkish)," *New York Times,* December 23, 2008.

44. Anders Aslund, "Myths of Austerity," *Berlin Policy Journal,* June 2, 2015.

45. Aslund, "Revisiting the Latvian and Greek Financial Crises."

46. Organization for Economic Cooperation and Development, "Level of GDP per Capita and Productivity," http://stats.oecd.org/Index.aspx?DataSetCode=PDB _LV.

47. Richard Corbett, "The Plight of Greece: Beware Facile Comparisons," January 27, 2015, http://www.richardcorbett.org.uk/syriza-plight-greece-beware-facile-comparisons.

48. Matina Stevis, "The Politicians Who Warned Greece—but Were Ignored," *Wall Street Journal*, July 11, 2015.

49. Alexis Tsipras, "Europe at Crossroads," *Le Monde*, May 31, 2015.

50. Guy Faulconbridge, "'Europe Is Dying,' EU Opponents Say, as Greek 'No' Brings Delight," *Reuters*, July 5, 2015.

51. Peter Spiegel, "Greece: Donald Tusk Warns of Political Contagion," *Financial Times*, July 16, 2015.

Chapter 8. Ukraine

1. "Mystery at Manas," Subcommittee on National Security and Foreign Affairs, Committee on Government Oversight and Reform, U.S. House of Representatives, December 2010.

2. Adrian Blomfield, "Kyrgyzstan Agrees to Allow US Troops to Stay in Country," *Daily Telegraph*, June 23, 2009.

3. Philip P. Pan, "Russia Is Said to Have Fueled Unrest in Kyrgyzstan," *Washington Post*, April 12, 2010.

4. World Bank, Personal remittances received (% of GDP), http://data.worldbank.org/indicator/BX.TRF.PWKR.DT.GD.ZS.

5. Pan, "Russia Is Said to Have Fueled Unrest in Kyrgyzstan."

6. Steven Lee Myers, "In Putin's Syria Intervention, Fear of a Weak Government Hand," *New York Times*, October 4, 2015.

7. David M. Herszenhorn and Ellen Barry, "Putin Contends Clinton Incited Unrest over Vote," *New York Times*, December 8, 2011.

8. "Putin to Al-Ahram Daily: Discussion to Exclude US Dollar in Bilateral Trade with Egypt," *Ahram Online*, February 9, 2015, http://english.ahram.org.eg/NewsContent/1/64/122569/Egypt/Politics-/Putin-to-AlAhram-daily-Discussions-to-exclude-US-d.aspx.

9. Neil MacFarquhar, "A Powerful Russian Weapon: The Spread of False Stories," *New York Times*, August 28, 2016.

10. Concerned that unrest in Kyrgyzstan would hinder progress on the reset, Washington downplayed any suggestion that the Kremlin might have played a role in fomenting unrest in Kyrgyzstan. "This is not some sponsored-by-the-Russians coup," Michael McFaul, then National Security Council Director for Russian and Eurasian Affairs, said after Bakiyev's ouster. "There's just no evidence of that." Alan Cullison and Kadyr Toktogulov, "Kyrgyz Rebels Assert Authority," *Wall Street Journal*, April 9, 2010.

11. Carl Bildt, remarks at Heinrich Böll Stiftung Seminar, Berlin, June 25, 2015.

12. "Putin Reveals Secrets of Russia's Crimea Takeover Plot," BBC, March 9, 2105.

13. Ilya Yashin, remarks at Heinrich Böll Stiftung Seminar, Berlin, June 25, 2015.

14. See https://ukraine24news.wordpress.com/2014/04/25/russian-language-writer
    -from-donetsk-professor-of-history-of-donetsk-national-university-elena
    -styazhkina-in-moscow-said-that-the-russian-language-is-not-in-need-of
    -protection-and-ukraine-cannot-be.

15. Robert Coalson, "Top Russian General Lays Bare Putin's Plan for Ukraine,"
    Huffington Post, November 2, 2014.

16. J. Darczewska, "The Anatomy of Russian Information Warfare: The Crimean
    Operation, a Case Study," *Point of View* no. 42, Center for Eastern Studies, May 22,
    2014.

17. MacFarquhar, "A Powerful Russian Weapon."

18. Ben Ninmo, *Anatomy of an Info-War: How Russia's Propaganda Machine Works,
    and How to Counter It* (Bratislava: Central European Policy Institute, May 15, 2015).

19. Timothy Snyder, "Ukraine: From Propaganda to Reality," presentation at 25th
    Anniversary Chicago Humanities Festival—Journeys, November 9, 2014.

20. Anton Troianovski, "West to Woo Europe's Russian Speakers through Television,"
    Wall Street Journal, June 14, 2015.

21. Carl Schreck, "Russian TV Deserters Divulge Details on Kremlin's Ukraine
    'Propaganda,'" Radio Free Europe/Radio Liberty, August 7, 2015.

22. Ibid.

23. Adrian Chen, "The Agency," *New York Times,* June 2, 2015.

24. Mike Eckel, "Saakashvili: Ukraine Is 'First Geopolitical Revolution of the 21st
    Century,'" *Christian Science Monitor,* January 30, 2014.

25. Carl Bildt, "Staying the Course in Europe's East," *Project Syndicate,* May 20, 2015.

26. "Putin to Al-Ahram Daily."

27. Christopher Walker, "Authoritarian Regimes Are Changing How the World De-
    fines Democracy," *Washington Post,* June 13, 2014.

28. "Putin Creates New National Guard in Russia 'to Fight Terrorism,'" BBC News,
    April 6, 2016.

29. Alexander Cooley, "Countering Democratic Norms," *Journal of Democracy* 26,
    no. 3 (July 2015).

30. Benjamin Haddad, "How Putin Won French Conservatives," *Daily Beast,* Au-
    gust 18, 2015.

Conclusion

1. Carl Gershman, "Are Czechs Giving up on Moral Responsibility?" *Washington
   Post,* November 16, 2014.

2. Andrew Sullivan, "Union Due," *The New Republic,* May 21, 2001.

INDEX